Liberal Democracy 3.0

Theory, Culture & Society

Theory, Culture & Society caters for the resurgence of interest in culture within contemporary social science and the humanities. Building on the heritage of classical social theory, the book series examines ways in which this tradition has been reshaped by a new generation of theorists. It also publishes theoretically informed analyses of everyday life, popular culture, and new intellectual movements.

EDITOR: Mike Featherstone, *Nottingham Trent University*

THE TCS CENTRE
The *Theory, Culture & Society* book series, the journals *Theory, Culture & Society* and *Body & Society*, and related conference, seminar and postgraduate programmes operate from the TCS Centre at Nottingham Trent University. For further details of the TCS Centre's activities please contact:

Centre Administrator
The TCS Centre, Room 175
Faculty of Humanities
Nottingham Trent University
Clifton Lane, Nottingham, NG11 8NS, UK
e-mail: tcs@ntu.ac.uk
web: http://tcs.ntu.ac.uk

Recent volumes include:

The Tourist Gaze
John Urry

Critique of Information
Scott Lash

French Social Theory
Mike Gane

Veblen on Culture and Society
Stjepan Mestrovic

Liberal Democracy 3.0

Civil Society in an Age of Experts

Stephen P. Turner

SAGE Publications
London • Thousand Oaks • New Delhi

First published 2003

SAGE Publications Ltd
6 Bonhill Street
London EC2A 4PU

SAGE Publications Inc
2455 Teller Road
Thousand Oaks, California 91320

SAGE Publications India Pvt Ltd
B-42 Panchsheel Enclave
Post Box 4109
New Delhi 110 017

British Library Cataloguing in Publication data

A catalogue record for this book is available from the British Library

ISBN 0 7619 5468 6
ISBN 0 7619 5469 4 (pbk)

Library of Congress Control Number 2002115622

Printed and bound in Great Britain by Athenaeum Press, Gateshead

Contents

For Douglas Carrera Turner

. . .in the general interest, domination should be proportionate to enlightenment.
(Henri Comte de Saint-Simon [1803]1952: 8)

The decision of the question whether a man do reason rightly, belongs to the city.
(Thomas Hobbes [1651]1839: 268-9)

The Republic has no need of scientists.
(attributed to the Presiding Judge in the trial of Antoine Laurent Lavoisier, in response to the chemist's request for a delay in his execution to enable him to complete some scientific work)

Foreword

This book may be read in a number of ways, and by a number of audiences, so it is perhaps my task as author to identify, or confess to, a few of the ways it was *intended* to be read, and in the course of this to explain its relation to a number of other texts that are important to it, but either unmentioned or undiscussed.

The series in which this book appears, *Theory, Culture & Society*, together with my role in relation to the journal and its concerns, suggests one way of reading it: as a text that is in a broad sense a 'Weberian' or Weberian-Schmittian account of the problem of experts and its bearing on Liberal Democracy. The mode of explanation and the conclusions parallel, in some respects, the historical accounts that Weber gives of the origins of modern bureaucracy in the slow rise of the royal staff in its struggle with the feudal aristocracy, and, in his *Agrarian Sociology of Ancient Civilizations* (1976), the slow transformation of slaves and small-holders into serf-like dependents. In Liberal Democracy 3.0, the slow transformation is from a politics of sovereign citizens to a politics of diffused experts, in which electoral struggle is gradually supplanted by what I call 'commissions,' that is to say expert bodies. The '3.0' in the title refers to a periodization of Liberalism that is elaborated in Chapter 5, from the initial forms of Liberalism in which the franchise was restricted, to the late nineteenth century form, of government by discussion with full franchise, to the form that I argue is now emerging: a form in which 'discussion' is limited to those topics not delegated to experts. The argument, in this reading, can be seen to contrast to that of Foucault and Habermas, for reasons that will be discussed in the text itself. Habermas, like much of the Left today, has taken up the idea of civil society as an ideal. One of the followers of Habermas wrote a paper on the theme of nostalgia as critique. One point of this book is to ask whether a critique based on the ideal of civil society is an exercise in nostalgia.

The book may also be read as a text in political theory. It updates and extends arguments made by the great nineteenth century liberals, from Tocqueville and John Stuart Mill to Albert Venn Dicey, who lived long enough to see and understand what was happening as the older liberalism began to turn into the mode of governance we are familiar with today, which he identified with the 'collectivist' current of opinion that emerged, by his reckoning, in the period after the American Civil War. Dicey associated this socialist current with the idea of rule by experts, a political idea with an interesting subsequent history on the Left, which eventuates in one or another model of 'the democratic control of science.' To this largely familiar story, something is added: a consideration of the thinking of James Bryant Conant. Conant grasped that 'democratic control' was a dangerous illusion, and argued instead, so I will claim, for a different strategy, which I call 'Liberalizing Expertise,' by which I mean controlling experts indirectly and also by forcing the opinions of experts into the light provided by contentious discussion outside of the body of experts.

The text also has some philosophy, and even a few philosophical distinctions and theses, though these are purposely kept to the side, for the most part. A more detailed discussion of the issue of the corporate character of scientific authority can be found in my 'Scientists as Agents' (2002a). Another set of issues involves the status of rational considerations and their relation to disciplined communities: science is a paradigm case of the organization of discourse around a scheme of common skills and exacting training. 'Political' rationality is not organized in this way. But even science depends on 'political' discussion about itself. The claims I make here involve a defense, of sorts, of the primacy of non-disciplined rationality. It has affinities with a more general anti-Kantian line of argument I have developed elsewhere, particularly in *Brains/Practices/Relativism: Social Theory after Cognitive Science* (2002b).

The book is also a text in science studies, and its relation to that body of thought is sufficiently complex that a more complex explanation is owed. A better subtitle might have been 'A Political Prolegomena to Science Studies,' for that is what it attempts, in part, to provide: the tools for understanding the political significance of science studies. I considered, and indeed in an earlier draft attempted to formulate, the argument of the book as a critique of a series of various science studies authors, ranging from Ulrich Beck to Sheila Jasanoff and Brian Wynne, whose writings on science and politics have seemed to me interesting enough to be worthy of criticism. I decided that detailed critique was inappropriate. There was some point to a dialectical analysis of the inner contradictions of the attempt to be anti-essentialist (or 'social constructionist') about science and at the same time to provide some sort of external God's eye view 'critique' with 'policy' implications which bedevils 'science studies' attempts to be normative. But in the end I decided that this severely textual approach demanded too much and produced too little. It demanded too much from the reader, who would need to be provided with a great deal that was not in the text, notably the common ground of political theory and legal philosophy necessary to see the point of the analysis, and would produce little in the way of positive argument. But trying to do this reminded me of the difficulties that those of us with an interest in science and politics have had in establishing enough of a common problematic to start a meaningful discussion. I hope that the argument of this book, right or wrong, is sufficiently panoramic and rooted in the larger tradition of political and social theory to do so, and that someone rises to the bait.

My point about these writers, if I was to elaborate it, would be that they are insufficiently political – not in the sense that they are insufficiently critical, for they each in their own way make gestures toward critique, or in the case of Beck formulate an elaborate critical 'theory' of the problem of science and politics – but in the sense that each appears, in the words of *Casablanca*, to be 'shocked, shocked,' to discover that questions like 'what is science' are indeed 'political.' Evelleen Richards, whose studies of science controversies I greatly admire, concludes one of these studies, a study of the controversy over the therapeutic value of Vitamin C as a cancer treatment, with the following: 'therapeutic evaluation is inherently [!] a social and political process, and . . . the idea of neutral appraisal is a myth.' (1988: 685). This, it seems to me, is naive, and naive not about science, but about politics. The point of this book, in a phrase, is this: to be apolitical is a political strategy, and 'myth' is a political term. But understanding what sort of political questions these are requires more than slogans.

The implications of the argument for Beck are that he has stumbled upon the right problem, but addresses it with the wrong intellectual tools, leading him to what is essentially a retrograde conclusion – an attempt to reinscribe the nineteenth century problem of 'interests' onto the problem of experts, and then to solve this problem politically by insisting that everyone is an expert, which is a novel form of the nineteenth century solution of extending the franchise. To make this solution plausible, he must imagine that science can become a reflexive activity and thus in effect to equalize itself, and that citizens want, or should want, a form of decision-making based on discussions in which non-experts engage with 'experts' on equal terms, and in which considerations of competence are excluded as 'monopolization.' In my view, one of the implications of science studies is that science assures 'consensus' by the careful control (or 'social construction') of what is counted as science, what is counted as competent (for example in the form of the problem of who possesses the relevant tacit knowledge). Announcing 'demonopolization' is thus an empty gesture. 'Monopolization' is part of the point of the activity of scientists; so is a kind of self-discipline about what counts as science that excludes the kind of reflexivity Beck calls for. Not surprisingly, there has been a large chasm between science studies and the kind of concern reflected in Beck.

Saying this raises a more general question about the political meaning of science studies, at least science studies in the constructionist tradition, and its relation to 'critique.' Many scholars of science studies are sufficiently embattled in their struggles against the political myths of science to think of themselves as engaged in a project of critique related to the Left, and in some writers, like Steve Fuller, there is a systematic attempt to carry this idea out (2000). In my view, the naive form of this self-concept is a piece of self-misunderstanding. The social constructionist account of science is symmetrical with the Oakeshottian critique of Liberal theory. Like Oakeshott, it says that the theories of the nature of the activities, politics for Oakeshott, science for writers like Harry Collins, are false – 'abridgements,' in Oakeshott's language – that misrepresent the activity. The 'activity' in each case is shown to be practical, irreducible to explicit rational principles, dependent on the tacit, and has the form, as Oakeshott says, of a tradition: 'It is neither fixed nor finished; it has no changeless centre to which understanding can anchor itself; there is no sovereign purpose to be perceived or invariable direction to be detected; there is no model to be copied, no ideal to be realized, or rule to be followed . . .' (Oakeshott 1962: 128). But in neither Oakeshott's nor Collins' case is this a critique of the activity. It is rather a critique of crippling, or selfserving, misunderstandings of the activity.

Yet this critique does align with a 'political' understanding of the role of science in society: it aligns with Conant's. I might note that *The Golem* (Collins and Pinch 1993) is the kind of text that Conant would have commended, for it is a text about science that does not pretend that a little knowledge of scientific fact can make a good 'citizen scientist'. For Conant and for Collins and Pinch, the understanding we need of science as citizens is of what sorts of activity are the basis of the expert claims that are presented to us as citizens. To understand this rather cryptic comment, however, one needs a big picture of the political problem of expertise, something which Collins does not provide, but this book does.

I would like to acknowledge the support of various institutions: The National Science Foundation Ethics and Values Studies program funded the basic research out of which this project flowed; a second NSF grant (SBR-9810900) enabled me to examine thousands of actual expressions of 'political' thinking by scientists, which is in part the basis for the arguments in this book; SCASSS, the Swedish Center for Advanced Studies in the Social Sciences, where I was able to do some of the work on the book as a Fellow in 1998; and, finally, the University of Manchester, which enabled me, while an Honorary Simon Visiting Professor, to immerse myself in the papers of Bernard Lovell, but more importantly, to browse in the personal library of Lord Simon himself, which contained the writings of the Webbs, the British Left of the thirties and forties, and much more, about housing, municipal administration, and sewers, especially in Moscow. This was a lost letter from a world where the idea of benevolent rule by experts was not only alive, but revolutionary, and the object of passionate devotion.

1

Introduction: Thinking Politically about Experts

If we imagine a historian in the distant future faced with the task of explaining, in a few lines, the significance of the twentieth century, and specifically the task of identifying what remarkable and consequential transformations occurred within it, two particular changes would stand out. One is the development of science and technology. It would be noted that, for the first time in technical history, science and technology became closely linked. The difference from preceding centuries is stark. Earlier developments in technology were, for the most part, the works of craftsmen. Technologists, in even the most technically advanced industries, had little use for the scientifically trained. However, by the end of the twentieth century, academic science was rapidly becoming indistinguishable from commercial enterprise, particularly in the most advanced research areas in biomedicine.

The status accorded science grew as a result of warfare, notably during the Second World War, where advances in fields such as rocketry, atomic science and radar depended on modern science; and in the case of the atomic bomb, the technology depended on theoretical science of the most esoteric and advanced kind.

Penicillin not only transformed medical practice, it bound it more closely to science. In 1940, druggists (chemists) still compounded their own products, as had been the practice for centuries. By the end of the century, expensive and exotic science-based drugs were in daily use and their availability was a major political issue. The notion of international justice itself seemed to demand the universal availability of science-based pharmaceuticals as a basic human right, overriding international law and patent treaties.

The second significant transformation is in the realm of politics. The century began as an age of empires. European empires, with the exception of the French, were run by parliamentary democracies with limited monarchies. But these were still to a large extent controlled by a persistent 'old regime' of aristocrats, and of a civil service that came from similar social strata (Mayer 1981). The World War that began in 1914 was set off by the assassination of an Imperial Crown Prince. By the end of the century, crown princes and empires, along with the rest of the old regime, had ceased to have much more than ceremonial significance. After a century that began with radical constitutional experimentation – notably Bolshevism, Fascism, and Nazism – liberal democracies had, nominally and to a great extent in practice, become the world's standard constitutional form. The exceptions at the end of the twentieth century were for the most part small and backward states such as Afghanistan, or relics of Communism that were essentially personal dictatorships with a party apparatus, such as Cuba and North Korea, and various one party regimes including China and a series of Muslim states, as well as various impoverished African kleptocracies and military regimes. One-party states even mimicked features of liberal democracies, called themselves 'Republic' or 'Democratic', and adopted the liberal language of rights, so often employed by international bodies. Yet as late as 1940, the Imperial system was still largely intact, and matters could not have looked less promising for liberal democracy. Liberalism had few friends on the European continent and fewer still in the rest of the world, at least outside the English-speaking world. The Communist and Fascist regimes were dramatically vigorous and aggressive. The Colonial 'dependencies' of Europe were clamoring for independence, under attack from within by national liberation movements led by modernizing intellectuals who were predominantly anti-liberal or indifferent to liberalism (Kautsky 1971). The Hitler-Stalin Pact seemed to seal this future, making liberalism appear an Anglo-American peculiarity. Liberal Democracy, to many people (including many scientists), had shown itself in the 1930s to be unworkable and feeble in the face of economic crises and depressions. The Weimar Republic ended, succeeded by Hitler, who proclaimed a new order. The fortunes of war reversed the fortunes of liberalism, but there was nothing about liberalism as a political form that assured the outcome of the war.

Our imagined historian would see that the obvious questions to ask would be these: what are the *connections* between these two developments, and what were the consequences for science and liberalism of having their dramatic turns of fortune occur more or less simultaneously? To answer these questions she might first attempt to study the writings of influential political thinkers of twentieth century liberalism and democracy, especially in the period after the Second World War, to see what they had to say about the connections and about science and science-related technology. What would she find?

The Silence of Political Theory

Our historian would be astonished by the *absence* of any discussion of science. If she turned to such influential texts as the writings of the Frankfurt School she would find almost nothing that attempted to make sense of the connection; what she would find attempted to force science into familiar Marxist categories. The Frankfurt School began in the nineteen twenties and thirties with a despairing rejection of the cultural fatuities of 'Bourgeois Liberalism' and the falsity of its slogans. The century ended with the writings of Jürgen Habermas, who turned the slogans into a normative model of the full realization of 'civil society,' a kind of maximized liberalism against which ordinary or actual liberalism could be critically measured. Technology appears, but subject to nineteenth century Marxist thinking, as the augmentation of human powers. Science itself presents a category problem for Marxism : if it is not material technique it must be consciousness, and if it is consciousness it must be either true or false. As such, in the writings of Herbert Marcuse, science appears as false, as another manifestation of a 'bourgeois ideology' (1968: 223). This account was later rejected by Habermas in 'Technology and science as ideology'(1970), who put science back into the category of technology. The argument was revived by Ulrich Beck, who viewed science and technology as dangerous producers of a risk society. His proposed cure was internal reform, for science itself to *come* to true consciousness, which he envisaged as radicalization in the form of a reflexive coming to self-awareness by scientists with respect to the meaning and social role of science (Beck 1992, 1995). One must mark the response of Critical Theory to these changes as an intellectual failure, not least because they have only a remote connection to actual science.

If one instead turns to the key documents of American liberalism, something equally astonishing can be found: the greatest single work of liberal political philosophy of the late twentieth century, John Rawls's *A Theory of Justice* (1971), is utterly devoid of any mention of science. When Rawls (and indeed Rawls's many followers and admirers) provides practical reflection on the implications of this admittedly purely theoretical work, the silence continues. In *Political Liberalism* Rawls comments that the rules of evidence are different in a scientific society from those of democratic politics, and that scientific reason is therefore not 'public reason,' it does not occur to him to follow up this thought by considering what might happen where they conflict, or to ask what would be left of the notion of public reason in a political world which relied on scientific reason in the settling of its most central problems (1996: 221). Even the influential American critics of Rawls, such as Robert Nozick and the communitarians, find it possible to write passionately and seriously about contemporary politics as though science contained absolutely nothing of relevance to political life. The topic is no more visible in a thinker such as Michael Sandel (1996), who wrote in an apparently comprehensive substantive way about American politics, than in Rawls himself.

Earlier American philosophers, notably John Dewey, did have something to say about the relationship between democracy and science, relating the experimentalism of science to the experimentalism of democracy (1922), conceiving 'education' broadly as preparation for both citizenship and scientific advance. Charles Peirce described the authority of the consensus of the scientific community in terms that recall the authority of democratic consensus (Peirce 1901). But by the end of the twentieth century, political philosophers rarely mentioned such things.

In defense of these thinkers, it might be argued that the relevance of science and science related technology to politics is in fact close to nil. From a political point of view, science has a role in various obscure bureaucracies, the military, and in such arcane fields as health and environmental policy. But its role in these actual political settings is almost entirely instrumental – a role that is more or less akin to the role played by a calculating machine or the accounting programs on the computer in the same agency. It must be conceded that governments have a need for technical knowledge just as

3

government buildings have a need for plumbing. But no-one imagines that political theory has failed or is somehow inadequate for failing to recognize the significance of plumbing.

A common view is that big questions of political life are, as Harold Lasswell famously put it, about 'who gets what, when, and how' (1936). The normative issues of politics are thus fundamentally questions about justice or equitable distribution. The problems that concern practical politics, problems of race, gender, exclusion, and so forth, are problems that arise because of the existence of competing conceptions of equity or of competing conceptions of the common good or of the human good that must be struggled for and reconciled through political means and through the exercise of a state's coercive power. Science has only the most marginal relation to this domain of problems. Science may have had some role in increasing the goods to be struggled for. But its relation to these questions of politics is no greater and fundamentally no different than the relation of these questions to plumbing. Indeed, it is commonly asserted that the gooseneck drainpipe did more to improve sanitation and consequently to lower mortality than all of the scientific discoveries of the nineteenth century combined. So perhaps plumbing deserves to be taken very seriously as an adjunct to the rise of liberalism, perhaps even a condition, but one that is properly regarded as irrelevant to the content of political theory. But not science.

This line of defense, however attractive, is simply wrong. In Chapter 5 I will argue that the familiar 'interests' conception of politics that made sense of nineteenth century liberalism is now outdated; one only needs to open a morning newspaper, such as the *New York Times*, the *Wall Street Journal* or the *Financial Times* to see how it is outdated. One will be faced with a large number of stories involving problems of the following kinds:

- Are European Union (EU) standards for food imports from non-EU countries actually health standards with a basis in scientific fact, or reasonable judgements about risk, or are they covert devices to suppress competition and trade?
- Is there such a thing as global warming?
- What is the quality of the evidence for the cancer producing dangers of cell phones?
- For new regimes of educational practice?
- Can a drug company's claims about the effectiveness of their treatments be believed?
- Should tobacco be regulated as a drug?
- Does mammography reduce mortality, and if not should it be subsidized?

These are political issues that arise over assertions by experts. Any reader of the daily press will be able to identify dozens of similar examples – examples that occur not only every day, but dozens of times a day. What we might call 'the new politics of expertise' is a politics in which expertise itself is at stake and in which the establishment of expertise, the judging of expertise, the assertion of bias, and the problems and conflicts of interests, are central. This new politics is intelligible as politics, but not as interest politics of the traditional kind. Making sense of it as politics requires that we think again, and more seriously, about some of the basic problems of liberalism and democracy.

The argument presented here is that specialized technical discourse – not only science but other kinds of expert knowledge– presents a fundamental *political* problem for liberal democracy. By 'liberal democracy' I mean something very general and very minimal: 'government by discussion', in which the discussion is largely intelligible and effectively subject to the political influence of the population generally, for example, through more or less effectively functioning representative forms. In the face of expertise, something has to give: either the idea of government by generally intelligible discussion, or the idea that there is a genuine knowledge that is known to a few, but not generally intelligible. This is a fundamental problem that is not reducible to interests. Writers such as Foucault, Beck, and Bourdieu can be seen in the face of a deep change in the nature of politics as employing an essentially backward-looking strategy of attempting to extend 'interest' theory by transforming these issues into matters of interests.

The 'problems' presented by technical discourse to liberal democracy are problems that have precedents in the history of liberal democracy. Although for the most part they have not figured centrally in political theory, it is nevertheless important in that they are similar in kind, and in a sense the lineal descendants of, the fundamental political conditions of Western politics, a politics that emerged out of a conflict over beliefs in God. The topic is fundamental, and not merely a concern of science studies, because it concerns the conditions for the possibility of political discussion. The topic is fundamental in another sense: the new problem of isolating the undiscussable from politics cannot be collapsed into the formulae of past politics. The character of this novelty will be explored in Chapter 6 and in the conclusion. In what follows in this chapter and in Chapter 2, the problem of expertise will be located in the 'problems of liberalism' literature, which provides a starting point for discussion that is familiar and easily understood.

The Underside of Liberalism

Writers such as Rawls are determined to locate liberalism on universal principles, and there is a long tradition of universalism in liberalism. There is an equally strong tradition of seeing liberal democracy as conditional on circumstances outside of liberal theory, and on conditions that must be secured by the state to protect liberal democracy from its enemies. These conditions are not understood to be the by-products of liberal democracy; they may even under certain circumstances conflict with the basic principles of liberalism. Threats from anti-liberal minorities or hostile outsiders, or consequences of decisions made by liberal democracies that have the effect of undermining the contingent conditions of liberal democracy, expose the fragility of liberal democracy and the risks to its self-perpetuation. Yet the basic ideas of liberalism, such as the rule of law and tolerance, may undermine the ability of liberalism to defend itself. These 'problems of liberalism', rather than the creedal statements of liberalism, provide a better framework for a serious discussion of expertise and science. As such it is useful to see what rubrics exist in this domain, in order to see what in the tradition of liberalism can be called on to deal with these issues, and to identify the analogies between these 'problems' and problems that arise with science and expertise.

The 'problems of liberalism' that today excite the most discussion within liberal political theory arise over multiculturalism and the creedal character of liberalism: if liberalism is tolerant of divergences of opinion, how does it deal with opinions that abhor tolerance? To what extent can liberal regimes tolerate enemies within, such as parties that reject the liberal rules of the game, the conventions of discussion that make persuasion possible? When liberal regimes are faced with external enemies of these conventions, for example the fatwa against Salman Rushdie, are 'tolerance' and the limitation of responses to discussion appropriate? Or is liberalism a fighting creed, which needs to affirm its creedal character and dispense with its universalist pretensions? In practice, conventions, in the case of Rushdie the conventions of international diplomacy, keep these issues in check. But conventions do not always work, and when they fail, as the conventions of diplomacy did in the face of Nazism and Communism, and have since in the face of Islamic fundamentalism, the theoretical muddles had practical consequences.

Consider the idea that the problems that expert knowledge poses for liberalism are most closely akin to the problem posed by secrecy. In his classic formulation, *The Torment of Secrecy*, Edward Shils demonstrated how perplexing and ultimately insoluble was the problem posed by the fact that liberal democracies, which were premised on open discussion, were nevertheless also forced to defend themselves and, in the course of doing so, to keep secrets (1956). The detailed measures governing secrecy cannot themselves be subject to public discussion, without making them ineffective. But if people in authority use the legal powers given to them to classify as 'secrets' things that ought properly to be part of genuine 'government by discussion,' public discourse quickly becomes a sham, for all that is discussed is that which governmental secret-keepers permit to be discussed.

The parallels with expertise are clear: experts are needed by liberal democracy, but only experts understand what they are talking about and what is a matter of expert knowledge; to allow them to decide what belongs in the expert domain means that experts might place topics that should be subject to public discussion in the domain of 'expert knowledge.' Secrecy is not only a good model of the problem of expert knowledge: in many cases the expert knowledge in question is itself based on secret information, circulated primarily in a community that may itself be secret and made up of persons with access to secret information. Nuclear weapons information and a good deal of political policy information about foreign policy take this form. Nevertheless there are some important differences between these cases and the problem of expert knowledge generally. To fully understand the difference requires us to have a greater understanding of liberalism and its relation to democratic theory, but before turning to this let me indicate where in this complex domain this difference and its significance lies.

For the most part, if we are ordinary citizens, we are ignorant of the secret world, though we are aware it exists and may even be fascinated by its fictional representation in spy thrillers and in the titillating experience of historical events taking on new appearances because of government releases of information previously made secret. Nevertheless, secrecy is for the most part accepted as part of the package of realities that come with the fact of governing. State secrets are not revealed when new governments take office. They are kept even with the most radical changes of government. The exceptions to this rule, such as the action of the post-Versailles government of Germany, stand out in history. The public accepts both the necessity of secrets and the fact that the domain or the boundaries of the domain of secrets is itself defined in secret, beyond public discussion and therefore immune to intelligent democratic reform. Secrecy and its boundaries are thus, from the point of view of the voters or citizens, a conventional matter, and we trust that secret keepers are bound in their conduct by conventions such as of avoiding direct involvement in domestic political affairs. When questions are raised about the violation of these conventions, there is discussion, usually oblique, over whether and what they are, and whether the conventions have been honored or have been violated only in insignificant and harmless ways. The problem of secrecy, one might say, is insoluble in theory, but soluble in practice, as a matter of the conventions on which liberal democracy depends.

One way of encapsulating the argument of this book would be to formulate it as a negative thesis: that expert knowledge generally and in science in particular cannot be governed by similar conventions or a similar accepted understanding, and that this condition may represent an ineradicable and troubling problem for all future liberal democratic regimes: one that alters the character of liberal democracy. To understand this argument requires a broader analysis of the role of conventions – a terribly inadequate word – in liberalism. We can begin with the relationship between liberalism and democracy, a relationship which is best understood in the light of issues about conventions, because it is usually in connection with conventions that the liberal and democratic elements of the phrase 'liberal democracy' conflict. These terms are used in such a variety of ways that it would take an extended discussion to provide a defense of the specific uses to be made here, but the basic point can be presented more or less as a matter of definition.

Democracy is, in Lincoln's famous phrase, government *of*, *by*, and *for* the people, but the three elements of the concept may be realized in quite diverse ways, and the emphasis may fall heavier on one or two of the elements. Communist regimes labeled themselves democratic because they were egalitarian and therefore at least in this sense 'for' the 'people.' They were also, and often ostentatiously, 'by' the 'people' in the sense that many of the regimes made extraordinary efforts to recruit bureaucrats and leaders from the working class and to exclude the children of the former bourgeoisie and the professional classes from positions of power. This was simultaneously a means of legitimation and a method of assuring the solidarity of the bureaucracy and its responsiveness to party rule. What Communist regimes were *not* was 'liberal.' They were illiberal not only in the sense of disrespecting liberal property rights and restricting liberal economic rights, but also characteristically in the sense that the state and the party undermined the basic liberal idea of 'government by discussion' government in which the free exchange of ideas indirectly produced public opinion – by controlling the means of production of public opinion.

In classical liberal democracy, public opinion was the basis of political action. But opinion operated through the medium of representative government that itself operated according to a large number of conventions. The conventions ranged from legal definitions not embodied in the law, such as the conventions underlying the meaning of the terms of legal and political art in the American constitution, to conventions of decorum, such as rules of personal honor in parliamentary debate. Legal conventions in the American constitution, including the meaning of such terms as 'impeachment', were carried over essentially unmodified from the pre-revolutionary legal order, as they needed to be in order to give the Constitution and the documents of the Constitution, such as the Declaration of Independence, any determinate legal meaning.

Parliamentary rules are also conventions, adopted by parliamentary bodies to bind them and give a specific form to discussions that lead to formal decisions and expressions of will by parliamentary bodies. But more interesting are the conventions that cannot be easily formulated into rules, and that are not in the category of 'largely arcane and seldom problematic.'

A standard name for the public conventions of citizenship – the conditions for 'government by discussion' – is civility. Without civility, that is to say without a great many unstated or vaguely articulated but still binding and operative limitations on such things as what is a permissible political argument, discussion is impossible and therefore government by discussion is impossible. Discussion would seldom result in consensus if, in the course of settling some issue it is allowable for one person to attack another person for their personal habits, their appearance, their sexual predilections, their parentage, and so forth. All representative bodies have various limitations, sometimes explicitly stated though typically unstated, defining what is civil and admissible. The purpose of these conventions of civility is to make civil life possible. And civil life is not possible if there are no boundaries. The boundaries do, of course, change: what was public once may now be private, and what was once private, may now be considered public. These changes can occur as new groups are admitted into the full world of citizenship in the public domain, and concessions are made to either the sensitivities of the newly admitted group or to the need to address issues that formerly were thought to be best left undiscussed.

Liberalism, as government by discussion, arguably is historically bound by its origins to one particular exclusion, one particular way of handling that exclusion, and one kind of convention. The exclusion is religion and it has been handled through a specific means: neutrality. The conventions this requires are of recognizing religions as religions, or the religious as religious. Liberalism in its modern form arose at the time of, and out of, the wars of religion that wracked Europe in the seventeenth century. One issue in these wars was the relationship between religion and the state and particularly the question of state policy in relation to religious minorities or persons whose religion was different from, and offensive to, the religion of the rulers. Indeed, these wars demonstrated that religious controversy and religious diversity were disruptive to the state, threatened social peace, and in many cases led to civil warfare.

Yet religious differences were of a kind that 'discussion' did little to resolve, and if anything inflamed. Thus a variety of political solutions to the problem of religion were invented by rulers and by governments, which had the effect of eliminating the problem of religion. The main response was for the state to disengage from actively supporting religion or enforcing religious practice. This self-removal from the religious took two basic forms. One was for the state to constitutionally tie it's own hands: to refuse to be involved in religious questions and to firmly move them to the private sphere. Americans are most familiar with this solution, enshrined in the First Amendment to the Constitution, in the form of a rule binding Congress to not make any laws that serve to establish religion. The principle was ignored at the time of the 'founding' by several states that had preferences for certain religions. The amendment applied to Congress, not the states. Only when judicial change produced a constitutional doctrine called 'incorporation' were the governments of states and thus subordinate state bodies held to be bound by the same rule. The first time this was applied to religion was in the 1940 case *Cantwell v Connecticut*.

Even in the United States, where state neutrality toward religion is considered to be a founding and absolutely basic idea, religion has always been a contentious issue. What is a religion? Is, for example, Scientology a business, a cult that brainwashes people with a business intent and therefore a form of fraud, or a religion? This question is repeatedly before the courts, and in recent years has appeared as a matter of controversy between the United States and Germany, which has refused to classify Scientology as a religion. What counts as religious is equally problematic for courts when deciding how to interpret the application of the First Amendment. Is a license plate urging adoption in preference to abortion 'religious'? Are particular practices of decorating graves 'religious' and thus protected? Must public prayer at 'state' events, such as high school football games, be proscribed, in order to avoid 'establishing religions'? The line is not easily drawn. Nevertheless, the principle of neutrality is a part of constitutional doctrine, even if its application is inherently controversial and problematic (Sullivan 1994).

In Europe, the problem of neutrality was solved in a variety of different ways. One was to create an established church with a degree of conventionally accepted autonomy, with formal control exercised by the monarch, together with tolerance of religious beliefs outside the limits of the established church. The state thus controlled and limited the place of religion and religious controversy was kept out of politics. In the standard versions of this arrangement, there were no religious parties, and religion was not an appropriate subject for parliamentary attacks or disputes, precisely because the state's relation to religion was limited. It is this neutralizing or withdrawal from discussion that is the characteristic strategy of political liberalism with respect to problematic beliefs, and this characteristic strategy can be applied to topics other than religion. But the use of the strategy places it in a peculiar relationship with democracy, and threaten the notion of discussion itself.

In one very straightforward sense there can be no democracy, no government genuinely *by* the people, *without* political discussion. If the people acclaim and consent out of ignorance or on the basis of what they are allowed by the government to hear, or are prevented from receiving conflicting information, then democratic consent is essentially an illusion. The conditions and therefore the content of what is consented to is the product of manipulation. The manipulation is not different from the kind of fraud that salesmen might commit by giving false or partial information and preventing his victim from getting conflicting information.

There are also a great many subtle problems relating to the form of discussion and the admissible topics that potentially undermine and distort discussion. Consider the distortion that occurs in conducting political campaigns on the basis of polling information and advertising techniques.[1] If the substance of the 'discussion' takes place in the form of an exchange of ads, 'discussion' may effectively be limited to the small range of symbolic, emotional issues that can be manipulated by advertising campaigns. The usual transparency of the connection of a speaker to his interests is also lost. Furthermore, if such campaigns must be bankrolled by persons or parties such as business groups or unions that have a strong financial interest in the outcome of an election, and who do not wish the actual decisions that interest them to be subject to genuine public discussion, but simply acted on favorably by the candidate they support, they may have a strong interest in suppressing or confusing discussion, and use the ads to do so. Conventions and the older notion of civility typically fail in these cases, because the conventions are manipulated to suppress discussion rather than enable it.

Expertise and the Left

The Left has had, historically, a somewhat ambivalent attitude toward expertise. In one form, exemplified by Saint-Simon and concurred with by an important part of the Marxist tradition, is the idea that politics, being simply the continuation of the class struggle by other means, will disappear when the class struggle concludes through the triumph of the proletariat and the abolition of property and therefore of class interests and class itself. In the absence of class struggle, a politics which consists in governance or authority will be displaced by what Engels, paraphrasing Saint-Simon, called the administration of things (Engels [1894]1947: 307): a neutral and expert activity that is implemented on behalf of the people and does not require discussion, scrutiny, or 'politics.' Essentially the same idea figured in the thinking of the Communist movements of Western scientists in the 1930s and 1940s, who saw nothing wrong with the idea of government by experts. The New Left, in contrast, stressed 'participation', especially in the course of its own struggle against the rigid exclusionary conventions of liberal democracy, and sought to realize an ideal of popular government that it believed these conventions traduced.

The ideal of participatory democracy was embodied, in its most extreme form, by French and Chinese revolutionary tribunals that summarily punished miscreants and hoarders by bringing them to revolutionary justice. Revolutionary tribunals displaced the ordinary courts. The replacement is instructive. The courts are the original governmental form of the use of a category of expertise. The courts represent a delegation of authority to specialists or experts, judges, whose job is of operating within a set of conventionally imposed restrictions (involving the elimination of conflicts of interest, among other things) to produce technical 'justice', according to rules of law on which the judges are better qualified than ordinary people to determine. This delegation is basic to developed forms of government, and perhaps to the notion of legal order itself. In the context of liberal democracy, it represents a means of rendering technical or neutral decisions on matters of truth that might in principle be made by parliamentary bodies or popular tribunals, but in practice are best reserved to courts.

If we assume that participatory democracy is a form of rule in which every political action is the direct result of discussion by people who are not assembled according to any particular and limiting fixed form, whose sovereignty is boundless and for whom there are no restrictive neutralizing conventions, such as restrictions on political action with respect to, for instance, religious belief, it is obvious why this model conflicts with expertise. If the only weight that expert knowledge has is the weight that it gains by the power of persuasion, one would have to be an optimist to imagine that expertise would be recognized, properly understood and assented to: the ignorant will choose ignorantly. Dire predictions have been made in the writings of those who think that democracy is no longer relevant to a world that requires expert knowledge on the part of political authorities. The most famous example, ironically, given what will be discussed in Chapter 5, involved socialism itself and the fear that an electorate composed of those who are not economically expert will act in a way that conflicts with their own interests under the influence of demagogues or the peddlers of economic nostrums (cf. Schumpeter [1942]1950).

The idea of government by experts is subject to very similar kinds of difficulties. *Recognizing* expertise is a problem, whether it is dealt with by a sovereign and genuinely wise leader such as a platonic philosopher king or by the ordinary bureaucrat attempting simply to employ the expertise of others in making a prosaic bureaucratic determination in order to apply a regulation, because it is a problem that cannot be solved by power. It is intrinsic to the notion of expertise that the expert knows something that the consumer of expert knowledge does not and cannot know. When bureaucrats are faced with problems involving expert knowledge they are faced with problems of who and what is expert, and of attaining a minimal level of mutual comprehension necessary either to engage in meaningful discussion or to simply make competent bureaucratic decisions. Nor are these 'academic' problems: the most spectacular error in recognizing expertise of the twentieth century was the Stalinist acceptance of the theories of T. D. Lysenko, whose new biology rejected 'the chromosome theory' as 'reactionary, idealist, metaphysical, and barren' (Medvedev, 1971: 21).

In the case of liberal democracy, the means is discussion. One assumption of meaningful discussion is some degree of mutual comprehension. But in the case of expert knowledge, there is very often no such comprehension and no corresponding ability to judge what is being said and who is saying it, and consequently no possibility of genuine 'discussion.' So expertise poses a problem that goes to the heart of liberalism. But it also goes to the heart of every 'participatory' alternative to liberalism, and particularly to the normative ideas of 'civil society' and democratic deliberation.

Polanyi, Conant, and the Scientists' Defense of Liberalism

It would be misleading to give the impression that no one, or no one of significance, had made an effort to think through the problems that this simultaneous rise of science and liberal democracy have presented. Part of my project here is to recapture the significance of those who have dealt seriously with them. One response has been to think of the problem in terms of competent citizens. As it happens, there is a body of work in American political theory that has taken seriously this topic of expertise and science, and its approach is revealing. Robert Dahl and his students have viewed the problems of normative political theory in terms of empirical political studies, and, unlike the political philosophers, have dealt extensively with the problem of citizen competence in the face of issues involving science and technology (for example, Dahl 1993; Wildavsky 1995). As we will see in Chapter 5, the problem of citizen competence has a long history in liberalism, a history closely bound up with the long-running nineteenth century debate over the extension of the franchise. The problem obviously is of policy relevance, especially educational policy, and particularly the problem of the role of science education in general education. Failure to assure the 'competence' of citizens could lead to bad decisions, perhaps to liberal democracy being not only sub-optimal, but dangerous to itself and its citizens. In this literature the problem is defined *not* as one of expert knowledge, but of its audience – citizens, policy makers, etc. who must be informed, educated, and transformed to face the changed conditions.

The background to this literature is a large and confusing body of attempts to find affinities between science and democracy through the idea of an Enlightened Public. Some such thinkers have been influential in liberal theory. The similarities between democratic and scientific deliberation, (as a model and point of comparison) have recently attracted some of the best young minds on the Left. Much of the background to this reflection, for example in the work of John Dewey, has been concerned with the claim that there is some sort of special affinity between democracy and science, and the problem has been to see where this affinity might lie.

Enlightenment thinkers characteristically saw the affinity in terms of the contrast between science and the old regime. Consequently the particularism of the old regime, and the irrationality of a system in which individuals acquired special rights and authority by birth, was contrasted to science, in which authority was natural and meritocratic. The idealized notion that recognition of the authority of great scientists by other scientists was natural and unforced and also uncontroversial was later seized upon by Saint-Simon as a model for political authority. Alternatively, the view was taken that the universalistic character of the claims of science were matched by the universalistic character of the claims of democratic liberalism, that 'the laws of nature and nature's God', in the words of Jefferson in the Declaration of Independence, were the basis of both. This idea of a universal rational grounding of liberalism of course unraveled. Yet it has proven remarkably persistent in changed forms. The first French revolutionary regime, which was the most enthusiastic and unambiguous proponent of this universalistic notion of a regime rooted in the rights of man, was also catastrophic in its consequences and brief in its duration. Yet functioning regimes, with strong areas of public discourse that in turn produced public opinion, did develop, and by the end of the nineteenth century public opinion was recognized as the dominant factor in modern politics.

A key theorist of the affinity between liberalism and science in the mid-twentieth century, Michael Polanyi, seized on the 'traditional' character of proven and successful liberal republics and contrasted them with political orders based on doctrines (1946, 1951). This was an important argument in the face of Communism, which was self-professedly revolutionary, ideological, *and* scientific. What Polanyi sought to avoid was the claim that liberalism itself was merely another ideology, rationally equivalent (because it was based on unprovable assumptions about human nature) to other ideologies or doctrines based on other assumptions.

Many thinkers had argued that science is itself constructed on assumptions, and this implied that science was itself a kind of ideology. Such widely read philosophical texts as E. A. Burtt's *The Metaphysical Foundations of Modern Physical Science* (1927), and in Europe the writings of the neo-Kantians pointed in the same direction. Much of Logical Positivism needs to be read as an inner struggle with this way of thinking about science (Friedman 1999). Polanyi responded by characterizing science itself in an anti-rationalist way, as strongly *traditional*, comparing it to the learned professions of the law and to the church, each of which was governed by strong but changing conventions and tacit understandings. He also argued that genuine liberal regimes were strongly traditional, in a quite different way from how the Enlightenment had understood 'tradition.'

To put his argument in the terms used earlier, Polanyi stressed the conventional, 'civility' conditions of liberalism, the tacit commonalities and constraints that preserve the possibility of consensus, which he believed to operate in a parallel way in science. In reasoning in this way Polanyi placed himself in a long line of thinkers who had also embraced liberalism in practice but rejected its supposed universalistic 'foundations' and opted for the continuation of liberalism as a practice rather than as a dogma. The affinity between science and politics and liberal politics thus lies in the common feature of their traditionalism. Because traditionalism was understood in contrast to ideology, but also as necessarily rooted in faith or commitment, both science and actually functioning liberal political traditions were genuine competitors to ideological faith of the totalitarian kind, and neither merely neutral or creedal.

Polanyi argued that science needed to be left alone by the state in order to flourish: that its autonomy as a tradition and its self-governance needed to be respected, and that it not be misunderstood as technology, as an instrument that could be subject to bureaucratic control or 'planning.' This argument has led to a series of efforts to make sense of the problem of the governance of science. The problem arises because the state has goals that science can serve more or less successfully if it is regulated or funded according to different policies, and because scientists may in the course of research harm others. Discussions of democratic control of science have focused on these matters.

It should perhaps be noted with respect to this book that the place of expertise in liberal democracy is a different though not unrelated issue. The governance of science is an arena in which expert opinion plays a large role. It is the reflexive moment in expert opinion in which experts construct, under the conditions of bounded decision-making, uncertainty, and conflict of interest, sufficient consensus to sustain collective action, ensuring the continuation of science itself. The governance of science is thus a microcosm of politics. But it is nevertheless a minor matter in comparison to the vast range of topics subject to state policy about which experts make claims. More important is the difference between the argument that science should be self-governed because only scientists have the requisite expertise in scientific matters, and the argument that only experts are capable of governing where expertise is required and of *determining* the areas in which expertise is required.

Polyani's American counterpart, James Bryant Conant, was more directly concerned with this broader range of issues, especially the problems of the role of expertise in state decision-making, and he had a very sure grasp, based on personal experience, of the difficulties faced by both sides. His own proposals for reforming the processes by which scientific and technical advice was given are valuable as a starting point for an understanding of the problem of institutional design posed by experts for liberal democracy. The key problem, he remarked when commenting on military procurement decisions, was that 'political forces almost automatically generate compromise decisions at every level. Those who must make policy cannot bring the wisest judgment to bear on scientific or engineering matters unless protected from pressures generated by outside experts or interested parties' (1951: 337). The alternative, he suggested, is

> the rapid development of a tradition of quasi-judicial review throughout this whole area. When a question comes up to be settled, even if three or four echelons below the top, one or more referees might hear the arguments pro and con. If there are no contrary arguments, some technical expert should be appointed to speak on behalf of the taxpayer *against* the proposed research or development. Then adequate briefs of the two or more sides should be prepared (*not* a compromise committee report). With opposing briefs, arguments, and cross-questioning, many facets of the problem, many prejudices of the witnesses will be brought out into the open. The referees could then report their findings to those who have the responsibility for decisions and the latter would be in a position to give unequivocal answers based on adequate documentation. Such decisions when they reached a higher echelon would be unlikely to be reversed without adequate reason; the briefs and counterbriefs would be there to show that all the relevant arguments had been explored. (1951: 337–38)

This was a quintessentially liberal solution to the problem of expertise: all the arguments would be explored. Experts and other stakeholders should be prevented from presenting a consensus as a *fait accompli* for the representatives of the people to accept and ratify. It was not enough that the experts wanted to close the dispute, and there was no sense in which experts should be freed from the demands of 'government by discussion'. To the contrary, for the fulfillment of the demands of government by discussion, an *extra* set of checks and balances was required. The public, or in this case their stand-ins, the responsible policy-makers, should not be presented with conclusions which they were compelled to naively accept. Indeed, they should not accept the advice of experts until at least they could see their advice attacked by other experts.

Although Conant's proposals were never institutionalized, new forms of public discussion did emerge. A recent discussion by a prominent climate scientist, Stephen Schneider, characterizes present discussion as 'dueling experts . . . where congressional hearings or courtroom juries hear two opposing sides deliver politically selected extremes instead of the current scientific consensus on a given technological problem' (1997: about 2). His alternative to this 'politicized' kind of discussion, which he deplores, is one we have already encountered – the idea of the competent citizen, here characterized as a citizen-scientist, a citizen sufficiently educated in science to ask basic questions of experts. The deeper political meaning of this argument will be explored in Chapter 5. Here it will suffice to note that Conant did not neglect this aspect of the problem: he devoted much of his practical work to the reform of high school education to produce better (and more science-sensitive) citizens, and as President of Harvard did much to reform the teaching of science to non-scientists in pursuit of the goal of making them into better decision-makers when faced with scientific and technological problems (Fuller 2000). But as we shall see in Chapter 5, his approach was radically different from the long tradition of the promotion of a 'public understanding of science,' a tradition which he opposed.

Conant's model of a forum in which experts debate is a useful one because it demonstrates at least one way that expert knowledge can be compelled to shape itself into a form suitable for liberalism. Of relevance here is the fact that Conant recognized that some such compulsion was necessary, that expert knowledge was not unproblematic for liberalism, and that experts and expert opinion neither could be nor should be accepted at face value by the participants in government by discussion. None of his famous contemporaries, including Polanyi, Robert Merton, John Dewey, and for that matter Conant's own student Thomas Kuhn, understood that there was a problem of this sort, or rather understood it politically, from the viewpoint of the liberal citizen rather than of the scientist.

The Larger Issues

Science and expertise are not the same, and the solutions to the problem of science and liberal democracy do not readily carry over to other forms of expertise. Science, as we shall see later, is an activity in which neutrality and self-limitation play a special, explicit, and deeply integrated role. Things change at the periphery of science, especially in fields bound up with state power, such as psychiatry (which is involved in the commitment of the insane to treatment), or policy fields funded by state bureaucracies and part of a community of expertise including bureaucrats. The rules of the game are less clear. Bureaucratic forms enforce conformity: to disagree will often mean to lose one's position or career. And there are more subtle issues. Is the expertise that goes into the 'administration of things,' to use the Saint-Simonian phrase, *ever* genuinely neutral or instrumental? If it is not, but represents itself as such, its relation to liberal democracy is problematic – liberalism itself may be seen, as Foucault saw it, to rest on an illusion that conceals its political character and significance.

An even more subtle issue is this: does the very substance of liberal democracy change with the phenomenon of expertise, such that all of the traditional meanings of terms in the liberal lexicon, of popular sovereignty, discussion, and perhaps even the idea of sovereignty itself, come to have an increasingly ceremonial significance, as did the 'Royal' authority of the constitutional monarchies of the nineteenth century, but without completely disappearing? Could it be that the rule of experts will arise, not as the product of a Leninist revolutionary cataclysm followed by the gradual withering away of the state, but by a withering of the content of liberal politics and a slow transformation of the way in which governmental institutions function?

These are questions that cannot be directly answered, but they do provide a framework for inquiry and a motivation for inquiring. They also point to a method. Actually existing political institutions characteristically embody tensions between principles, principles that cannot be realized simultaneously. The form of the institutions and the ways in which they work reflect the fact that the tensions are not resolvable. Democratic parliamentary representation, for example, is a product of the principles of popular sovereignty together with, among other things, the principle of expedience and efficiency, principles either of which might lead to the acceptance of dictatorial rule if fully acceded to. But it also embodies other compromises and tensions, for example between the ideal-types of civil association (or mutual loyalties), and enterprise association, (the goal-orientated state), as Michael Oakeshott argued (1975). This feature of political institutions enables the interpreter to work inward from the outside, or the ideal, or from the key conflicting principles, to an understanding of actual courses of events, and to see the larger significance of the piecemeal changes that institutions undergo. What bearing does this have on expertise? The tension between knowledge and power is among the most fundamental tensions of politics. Plato resolved it in *The Republic* by making philosophers kings. That this ancient problem should be among the defining political issues in societies in which knowledge is central should be no surprise. The method I shall follow in this book is not unlike that of Oakeshott himself: the meaning of institutions and practices in the present will be seen in terms of an underlying and irresolvable conflict.

Note

1   That these methods had fatally undermined liberal democracy was one of Habermas's theses in The Structural Transformation of the Public Sphere (1991).

2

The Last Inequality

... he who participates in rational principle enough to apprehend, but not to have, such a principle, is a slave by nature. (Aristotle, The Politics, 1254b:20)

In the previous chapter it was remarked that liberalism and expertise were simultaneous, though accidental, historical developments, and that although mainstream political theory took little notice of the arrival of expertise, scientists *had* puzzled, albeit with mixed results, on the relation between politics and science. The scientists' discussions pointed to a variety of issues, but, with the exception of Conant, little of this discussion had much bearing on what was characterized as 'the new politics of expertise': the massive phenomenon of the political discussion of problems that arise in the public assessment of expert claims.

In this chapter the question of what is special about the phenomenon of the new politics of expertise will be considered from the point of view of liberal democratic theory – of the challenge that expert knowledge poses. The first step will be to more clearly identify the problem in relation to *theory*. The second step will be to better identify what kinds of experts and what zones of expert claims are problematic. For example, the existence of physicists with specialized scientific knowledge does not pose the same political problem as the existence of a bureaucratic culture with shared beliefs and preferences. But the two may often be grouped under the same heading and treated as though a 'solution' or reform that makes sense for one, such as greater democratic accountability in the form of citizens' advisory panels, or greater reflexivity and self criticism, makes sense for the other. Similarly, there is a difference between experts speaking within the limits of a technical consensus and experts seeking consensus on (or seeking to create and impose a consensus on) policy subjects with some technical content, such as global warming or economic policy, that are not simple applications of 'what all genuine experts in a domain know,' but instead are the collective opinions of experts on subjects that are not reducible to specialist knowledge. Nor are there simple truths, such that we can say 'all attempts by experts to impose a policy consensus are bad' or 'all bureaucratic discretionary control is good.' Similarly, denouncing 'expert power,' is an empty gesture, unless we mean something other by 'expert power' than the mere possession of expertise: even the self-described 'anarchist' protesters against globalization rely on expert opinions about the global situation to justify their animus and give their cause a point.

Two Problems: Inequality and Neutrality

The relation between experts and the public is the source of at least two distinct theoretical problems for established modes of social and political thought. It is also a problem for the normative 'enlightenment' goal of enhancing the life of the public, of extending the reach of 'public discourse,' and improving present public discourse by opening previously settled topics to new voices and new perspectives.

The first problem arises from social theory and concerns democracy and equality. In the literature concerned with the political threat to democracy posed by the existence of expert knowledge, expertise is treated as a kind of possession that privileges its possessors with powers that 'the people' cannot successfully control, acquire or share in. Expertise is a kind of violation of the conditions of rough equality presupposed by democratic accountability. Some activities, such as genetic engineering, are apparently out of reach of democratic control, even when these activities, because of their dangerous character, ought perhaps to be subject to public scrutiny and regulation, precisely because of imbalances in knowledge. As such we are faced with the dilemma of capitulation to 'rule by experts' or democratic rule that is 'populist'; that valorizes the wisdom of the people even when 'the people' are ignorant and operate on the basis of fear and rumor.

This leads to the second problem, which arises from normative political theory. Posing knowledge difference as a problem of equality leads in a direction that is even more troubling. If there are genuine knowledge differences, the solution, admittedly with practical limitations, is egalitarianization through difference-obliterating education. But if the differences are differences in viewpoint, rather than knowledge, then, as Paul Feyerabend insists, a program of extensive public 'science education' is merely a form of state propaganda for the faction of 'experts', and thus a violation of the basic neutrality necessary to secure the opportunity for genuine discussion (1978: 73–6). If the liberal state is supposed to be neutral with respect to opinions, that is to say it neither promotes nor gives special regard to any particular beliefs, world views, sectarian positions, and so on, what about expert opinions? Do they enjoy a special status that these things lack? If not, why should the state give them special consideration, for example through the subsidization of science or by treating expert opinions about environmental damage differently from the way it treats the opinions of landowners or polluters?

If expert opinion, or some category of expert opinion, requires a special political status, what status should that be? The special status granted to religious opinion leads to its exclusion from the domain of state action. Religion should either not be subject to state action, or should be granted a protected status of limited autonomy, as was the case of the established church in England, in exchange for the church's renunciation of politics. This has often been proposed as a model for the state's relation to science (Price 1965). However, it is a peculiar analogy, because the state not only protects and subsidizes science, it also attends to the opinions of science. It grants science a kind of authority, and reaffirms this authority by basing regulations on the findings of science or on scientific consensus, and by promoting these findings.

The issue of state neutrality may seem to be a rather arcane problem, but it has conflicting manifestations, especially when 'sectarian' beliefs conflict with expert opinion and the non-sectarian character of expert opinion is called into question. For example, in the USA conflict has arisen in connection with the teaching of creationism. These easily ridiculed cases are not easily resolved. For questions such as 'is "creation science" "science"'?—there are, in principle, no very convincing answers and no 'principles' on which to rely that cannot themselves be attacked as ideological.

The problem of neutrality arises from the Left as well as the Right. Similarly, scientific research on the genetic background of criminals has been denounced as 'racist' and government agencies have been intimidated into withdrawing support. Studies of race and intelligence similarly have been attacked as inherently racist, which is to say 'non-neutral.' A letter-writer to *Newsweek* wrote that 'theories of intelligence, the test to measure it and the societal structures in which its predictions come true are all developed and controlled by well-off white males for their own benefit' (Jaffe 1994: 26). This idea is commonplace, even a matter of consensus in some academic fields, while it is treated as absurd in others. The idea that science itself, with its mania for quantification, prediction and control is merely an intellectual manifestation of racism and sexism – that is to say, is non-neutral – is widespread. A more general problem for liberalism is this: if the liberal state is supposed to be ideologically neutral, how is it to decide what is and is not ideology as distinct from knowledge?

This seems like a small and not very central question, at home only on the politically correct campus or in the fundamentalist churches and alien everywhere else. I shall argue, however, that these cases are the tip of a large and very important iceberg. The iceberg contains forms of this set of questions that have a direct bearing on the nature of liberal democracy and on the whole notion of public discourse, public life, and the ideal of the public. By reconsidering some of these ideas in a deeper fashion, liberalism itself can be seen in a novel way, and the whole notion of the public realm can be seen quite differently and less sentimentally.

The Two Issues Together

If each is taken on its own terms, these two problems can be discussed in a mundane political way: the solution to the problem of experts uncontrolled by democracy is to devise democratic controls (such as the citizens' councils on technology that have been set up in Denmark and elsewhere). The solution to a public incapable of keeping up with the demands of the modern world is to educate it better, a traditional aim of scientists, economists, and others, for whom 'public understanding' is central. The problem for liberalism doesn't require a complicated solution: we can continue to do what we do now, which is to say devise ad hoc solutions as problems present themselves. For example, we may just declare science to be non–sectarian and deal with oddities like 'creation science' by judicial fiat, or decline to fund science, such as stem cell research, or to permit technology, such as genetically modified food, that has controversial implications or arouses the antagonism of 'public interest' or 'religious' groups. However, taken together, the two problems raise more difficult questions. The basic question can be formulated simply: if experts are the source of the public's knowledge, and this knowledge is not essentially superior to unaided public opinion, then the 'public' is not merely less competent than the experts, but is more or less under the cultural or intellectual control of the experts. This means that liberalism is a sham concealing an anti-democratic reality.

This idea, inspired by Foucault, is perhaps the dominant idea in present 'cultural studies', informing its historiography: the ordinary consumer of culture is taken to be the product of mysterious forces that constrain them into thinking in racist, sexist, and 'classist' ways. These constraints are, so to speak, imbibed along with cultural products. In Donna Haraway's famous (but disputed) example, a person exposed to an 'expert' representation of human evolution at a natural history museum in which the more advanced people have features that resemble modern Europeans, for example, becomes a racist and a sexist (Haraway 1984–85; Schudson 1997). It is now widely accepted that this 'framing' or cultural effect of expertise is the true realm of 'politics'. Furthermore, politics as traditionally understood is subordinate to – because it is conducted within the frame 'defined by' – cultural givens that originated in part in the opinions of 'experts'. These opinions, formulated in the past, have since become hegemonic. It is this general form of argument that will be examined in this chapter, from the perspective of liberal political theory, for it is liberal political theory that it poses a challenge to.

The Centrality of Persuasion to Liberal Politics

As suggested, liberalism might be characterized as the product of the lessons learned from the wars of religion of early modern Europe[1]. Liberal politics developed as the consequence of the adoption of a certain kind of convention: matters of religion were to be determined outside the political domain. The domain of the political was reduced, de facto, to the domain of opinions about which people could 'agree to disagree', to tolerate, and, further, agree to accept the results of parliamentary debate and voting in the face of disagreement. It was also implicitly understood that some matters, such as matters of fact, were not subject to 'debate', but were the common possession of, and could be appealed to by, all sides in public discussions.

Carl Schmitt made the point that parliamentary democracy depended on the possibility of 'persuading one's opponents through argument of the truth or justice of something, or allowing oneself to be persuaded of something as true or just' ([1926]1985: 5). Without some such appeal – if opinions were not amenable to change through discussion and persuasion was simply a form of the negotiation of compromises between pre-established interests – parliamentary institutions would be meaningless shells. What Schmitt saw in Weimar era parliamentary politics was that this assumption of parliamentarism no longer held. However, the parties of Weimar politics were more than mere interest parties. They were 'totalizing' parties that construed the world ideologically, ordered the life experiences and social life of their members, and rejected the world-views and arguments of other parties.

Schmitt believed that the former historical domain of parliamentary discussion, in which genuine argument was possible, had simply vanished. The world of totalitarianism, of the rule of totalizing parties, had begun. He doesn't say that the idea of liberal representation was wrong in principle. But there is currently an argument that comes to this conclusion. Stanley Fish claimed that liberalism is 'informed by a faith [a word deliberately chosen] in reason as a faculty that operates independently of any particular world view' (1994:134). Fish denies that this can be anything more than a faith, a creed, and concludes that this means that liberalism doesn't exist. This is an argument, in effect, for undoing the central achievement of the modern state and unlearning the lessons of the wars of religion. But it is a curiously compelling argument nonetheless, especially if it is conjoined with the idea that the major products of the modern liberal state have been racial and gender inequity and injustice.

Expert knowledge is susceptible to a variant of this argument: expert knowledge masquerades as neutral fact, accessible to all sides of a debate; but it is merely another ideology. Jürgen Habermas makes this charge implicitly when he speaks of 'expert cultures.' Many other critics of past experts, influenced by Foucault, have substantiated this claim in great detail. Their point, typically, is that 'expert' claims or presentations of reality by experts have produced discursive structures – ideologies – that were unwittingly accepted by ordinary people and politicians as fact, but were actually expressions of patriarchy, racism, and the like. Present day 'expertise' raises the same problems: the difference is that we lack the historical distance to see the deeper non-neutral meaning of the claims of experts.

If it is true that expert knowledge is 'ideology' taken as fact, the idea of liberal parliamentary discussion is, intellectually at least, a sham. The factual claims that determine the direction of parliamentary discussion are exposed as ideological. The true ideological basis of liberalism is not the sacred texts of dead revolutionary leaders, the creedal statements, but rather what is *agreed to be fact*. Moreover, what is agreed to be fact is, some of the time, the product not of open debate but of the authority of experts. Actual discussions in parliament and before the electorate are thus conducted within the narrow limits imposed by what is agreed to be fact, and therefore, indirectly, by expert opinion. To accept the authority of science or of experts is thus to accept tutelage: authoritative ideological pronouncements. As such, liberal regimes are no less ideological than other regimes; instead, the basis of liberal regimes in ideological authority is concealed under a layer of doc-trinal self-deception about what a fact is.

These two problems, the problem of the character of expert knowledge, which undermines liberalism, and the problem of the inaccessibility of expert knowledge to democratic control, thus combine in a striking way. We are left with a picture of modern democratic regimes as shams, with a pub-lic whose culture and life world is controlled or 'steered' by experts whose actions are beyond public comprehension and therefore beyond intelligent public discussion, but whose 'expert' knowledge is nothing but ideology, made more powerful by virtue of the fact that its character is concealed. This concealment is the central legacy of liberalism.

Habermas gives a version of the social theoretical argument that suggests why the usual solutions to these two problems, of neutrality and democra-cy, fail. The argument depends on a characterization of the viewpoint of ordinary people, which he calls the internal perspective of the life-world. This perspective, he claims, is governed by three fictions: that actors are autonomous beings, that culture is independent of external restraints, and that communication is transparent, by which he means that everyone can, in principle, understand everyone else ([1981] 1984:149–50). In fact he argues that the life-world is the product, at least in part, of external controls, which he calls 'steering mechanisms', operated by experts whose thinking is not comprehensible within the traditions that are part of, and help to con-stitute, the life-world. There is an unbridgeable cultural gap, in short, between the world of illusions under which the ordinary member of the public operates and the worlds of 'expert cultures' ([1981]1984: 397). The fictions of the life-world themselves prevent its denizens from grasping the manner in which it is controlled.

Robert Merton expresses a related point in a different way, with the notion that professionals and scientists possess 'cognitive authority'. Presumably Habermas has many of the same people in mind when he refers to 'expert cultures', but there is an important difference in the way the two conceive of the problem. Habermas's experts don't seem to exert their influence by persuasion, but rather by manipulating conditions of social existence, which Habermas calls 'colonizing the life-world'. Merton's model, the relation of authority, is more mundane. The example he gives is the physician who gives us unwelcome expert medical advice. Merton notes that this authority is experienced as a kind of alien power against which people sometimes rebel: the coexistence of acceptance and rebellion he calls 'ambivalence' (Merton 1976: 26).

Authority is, in its most common form, a political concept, signifying the problem posed by expertise for the theory of democracy. Experts are not democratically accountable, but they nevertheless exercise authority-like powers over questions of what is true. Habermas's picture is different: the experts he is concerned with are not professionals that we deal with face to face, but policy-makers hidden behind a wall of bureaucracy. Whether this difference is significant is a question that I will leave open for the moment.

But it highlights some difficulties with the expertise concept itself that need to be more fully explored.

Expertise is a more complicated affair than my original formulations supposed. Cognitive authority seems to be open to the Foucaultian options of resistance and submission, but not to the usual compromises of democratic politics. It is not an object that can be distributed for egalitarian ends, nor can it be simply granted, so that everyone can be an expert, as distinct from being treated as an 'expert,' for example for the sake of service on a committee evaluating risks. Certainly, legal fictions of equality can be extended to such political creations as citizens' oversight committees. But cognitive authority is likely to elude them, for reasons pinpointed by Habermas: the limitations of the perspective of the life-world preclude communicative equality between expert and non-expert. Yet Habermas's formulation also seems to be incomplete. Some experts, at least, *are* judged from within the life-world. There is a lively and contentious discourse about the expertise of experts. However, it is flawed by the very problems of inequality and neutrality discussed above.

Construed in either a Mertonian or Habermasian way, expertise is trouble for liberalism. If experts possess Mertonian cognitive authority, they pose a problem for neutrality: can the state preserve its neutrality in the face of the authoritative claims of experts? Or must it treat them, based on an act of faith or trust, as inherently non-sectarian or neutral? Experts in bureaucracies pose a somewhat different but no less troubling problem. If we consider the German contribution to liberalism as being the idea that official discretionary powers ought to be limited as much as possible – the ideal of a 'state of laws, not of men' – it is evident that 'experts' have an apparently irreducible role precisely in those places in the state apparatus where discretionary power exists. Indeed, expertise and discretionary power are notions that are made for one another: if there is irreducible discretionary power, a 'liberal' solution to the dangers of this power is to limit its exercise to experts. But if expertise is not neutral, this is simply to hide the power of expertise under the veil of administration.

Cognitive Authority and Audiences: Three Relations

'Authority' is a peculiar concept to use in conjunction with 'knowledge': in political contexts one thinks of authority in *contrast* to truth, as for example Carl Schmitt does when he paraphrases Hobbes as saying that authority, not truth, makes law. By authority Schmitt means effective power to make and enforce decisions. Cognitive authority is, in these terms, an oxymoron. If one has knowledge, one need not have authority. But the term makes sense as an analogue to 'moral authority'. And there is of course an earlier, and perhaps more fundamental, notion of *auctoritas* as authorship. In all of these cases is the notion that 'authority' has at first hand something that others – subjects or listeners – get at second hand by way of authority. This is also part of the notion of expertise: the basis on which experts believe in the facts or validity of knowledge – claims of other experts of the same type is different from the basis on which non-experts believe in the experts. For example, the facts of nuclear physics, are 'facts' in a real sense – facts that can be used effectively — only by those who are technically trained in such a way as to recognize the facts as facts. The non-expert is not trained to make much sense of them. Accepting the pre-digested views of physicists, on their authority, is pretty much all that even the most sophisticated untrained reader can do. The point may be made very simply in the terms given by Schmitt: it is the character of expertise that only other experts may be persuaded by argument of the truth of the claims of the expert; the rest of us must accept them as true on different grounds.

The literature on the phenomenon of the cognitive authority of science (cf. Gieryn 1994; Gieryn and Figert 1986) focuses on the mechanisms of social control that scientists employ to preserve and protect their cognitive authority. The cognitive authority of scientists in relation to the public is, so to speak, corporate. Scientists possess their authority when they speak as representatives of science. And the public judgment of science is of science as a corporate phenomenon, of scientists speaking as scientists. Therefore these social control mechanisms are crucial to the cognitive authority of science, as they are to the professions, the source of Merton's original examples. But what these literatures have ignored is the question that arises in connection with the political concept of authority, the problems regarding the origin of authority. How did cognitive authorities establish their authority in the first place? And how do they sustain it?

If we consider physicists as the paradigm case of cognitive authorities, the answer to this question is relatively straightforward, and it is not surprising that the issue is seldom discussed as being problematic. We all know or have testimony that comes from users or recipients about the efficacy of the products of physics, such as nuclear weapons, which we accept. We are told that these results derive from the principles of physics, from the 'knowledge' that physicists certify one another as possessing. Consequently we have grounds for accepting the claim of physicists to cognitive authority, and in this sense our 'faith' in physics is not dependent on faith alone. Of relevance is the fact that these are not wholly the grounds that physicists themselves use in assessing one another's cognitive claims.

If we take the model that is suggested by this discussion of cognitive authority in science we have something like this. Expertise is a kind of possession, certified or uncertified, of knowledge that is testified to be efficacious and in which this testimony is widely accepted by the relevant audience. But if this were all there was to expertise, it is difficult to see why anyone would regard claims to expertise or the exercise of expert authority to be a threat to *democracy*. Authority conceived of as resting in some sense on widely accepted, at least within the relevant audience, testimony to the efficacy of the knowledge that experts correctly claim to possess is *itself* a kind of democratic authority, for this acceptance is a kind of democratic legitimation.

One might go on to suggest that these authority claims are themselves subject to the same kind of defects as those of democratic political authority generally. Public opinion may be wrong, and mistakenly accept authority. One might cite the relation between theological authorities and audiences of believers as an example of the way spurious or at least mysterious assertions of special knowledge can come to be regarded as authoritative, and in which highly problematic esoteric knowledge is granted the same or similar deference as scientific knowledge. In the case of theological knowledge we do see something that was not so clear in the case of the cognitive authority of science, namely that the audiences for authority claims may be very specific, and may not correspond with the public as a whole, much less the universal knower. And claims made to, and accepted by, delimited audiences may themselves be in error and subsequently rejected by these same audiences or by their successors.

Thinking about the audiences of the expert – the audiences for whom the expert is legitimate and whose acceptance legitimates her claims to expertise – illuminates a puzzle in the discourse of the problem of expertise and democracy. Merton and Habermas were not really talking about the same kinds of experts. For Merton, the paradigm case was the physician, whose expert advice, say, to cut down on cholesterol, we receive with ambivalence (1976: 24–5). For Habermas, the 'experts' who steer society from a point beyond the cultural horizon of the life-world, and do so in terms of their own expert cultures ([1985]1987: 397) are themselves a group that exercise power through bureaucracy. This is a distinct situation that is discussed shortly as the fifth type. It is important at this juncture to distinguish this kind of quasi-bureaucratic authority from physics. If the account of the cognitive authority of science given is more or less true, the authority of physics is itself more or less democratically acknowledged. Physics, in short, not only claimed authority, embodied in the corporate community of physicists, but its corporate authority has achieved a particular kind of legitimation, of universal acceptance.

If we begin with this as a kind of ideal-type or paradigm case of a particular kind of legitimate cognitive authority, we can produce a list of other types in which the character of legitimacy is different. In this list we can include experts of the type discussed by Habermas, who seem not to possess the democratic legitimation of physicists. The easy distinctions may be made in terms of audience and legitimators. As I have suggested, the theologian is an expert with cognitive authority. Like the physicist, the authority of the theologian is legitimated by acceptance by an audience; the audience is simply a restricted one. So the cognitive authority of the theologian extends only to the specific audience of the sect. We may call these 'restricted audience' experts.

If the first two types of expert are experts for pre-established audiences such as the community of physicists, or a community of sectarian believers, the third type is the expert who creates her own following. This type shades off into the category of persons who are paid for the successful performance

of services. Such experts may seek political power by mobilizing a following for political ends. Literary crusades may, for example, turn into political
movements, seeking the acceptance of a wider audience. There are many
fascinating historical instances of the transformation of intellectual into
political movements: feminism, the creation of a Greek political party out
of a sociological society, the 'technocracy' of the twenties, the Green Party,
and so forth. But generally 'expertise' is not the flag under which electoral
politics is conducted. The secondary type of legitimacy that celebrity scientists have, for example, is ordinarily too weak to compete with the legitimacy of interest group politicians, unless it becomes a form of interest group
politics. Indeed, the separation of the claims of experts from those of interest groups is central to the notion of expertise, and to the idea that expert
knowledge is a threat to democracy. In any case, self-transformations of
experts to representatives of interest groups eliminates them as 'threats' to
democracy: the 'experts' become simply spokespersons for causes.

None of these types corresponds very closely to the idea of expertise that
appears in Habermas, and indeed if the 'experts' were limited to these three
types, it is difficult to see what the issue might be. The massage therapist is
paid for knowledge, or for his exercise of it, but payment depends on the
judgements of the beneficiaries of that knowledge to the effect that the
therapy worked. The testimony of the beneficiaries allows a claim of
expertise to be established for a wider audience. But some people don't
benefit from massage therapy, and don't find the promises of massage therapy to be fulfilled. So massage therapists have, so to speak, a created audience, a set of followers for whom they are expert because they have proven
themselves to this audience by their actions. 'Experts' who are considered
experts because they have published best-selling books that do something
for their audiences, such as the sexologist Dr. Ruth Westheimer, are experts
in this sense as well: they have followings that they themselves created, but
which are not general. They have *auctoritas* in the original sense.

Experts of these three kinds – those whose cognitive authority is generally accepted, those whose cognitive authority is accepted by a sect, and
those whose cognitive authority is accepted by some group of self-selected
followers – each have a place in the scheme of liberal democracy. The
expertise of the physicist is taken to be itself neutral; the state is neutral
toward the other two, but in different ways. Experts can enter politics – Dr.
Ruth might, for example, run for the Senate, or promote some political
cause, such as sex education in elementary schools – but in doing so they
become 'political.' The religious sectarian can also enter politics, but not as
a religious authority. Religious authority is excluded due to the neutrality
of the liberal state: the domain of politics is delimited, by agreement, to preclude the state, as the First Amendment of the United States Constitution
puts it, from establishing a religion, and therefore of doing the things that
specifically religious authority pertains to. But literally 'establishing' religion
and at the same time restricting it, for example as occurred in Britain, can
serve the same purpose of both separating religion from politics and assur-

ing that the boundaries of the domain of the political are decided politically rather than by religious experts. Religious regimes, such as Iran, operate on the premise that the domain of religious authority is decided by religious experts.

There may be conflicts of a transitory kind between the authority of physicists and political authority – Canute may attempt to command the tides against the advice of his physicists. Conflicts of a less transitory kind, between expert economists and people who respectable economists consider to be economically inexpert political ideologues, such as concerned Joseph Schumpeter ([1942]1950: 252–68), might constitute a threat. This is because the economist's expertise is systematically relevant to policy, and the physicist's is so only transitorily. But if the economists deserve legitimacy as experts with the general public it presumably is because, like Canute, the politicians who ignored their advice would fail to achieve their goals.

The incomplete legitimacy of economists highlights some interesting issues. Claims to cognitive authority are not always accepted. Establishing cognitive authority to a general audience is not easy: major achievements, like nuclear weaponry, antibiotics, new chemicals, and new technology are the coin of the realm, and these are rare coins. Policy directives rarely have the clarity of these achievements, and policy failures are rarely as clear as Canute's. Economists do agree among themselves, to a great extent, on what constitutes basic competence and competent analysis. There is a community of opinion, and some people who aren't members of the community – the 'public' of economics – accept the community's claims to expertise. But the discipline's claims to corporate authority, that is to say claims that would enable any economist to speak 'for' economics on elementary issues, such as the benefits *ceteris paribus* of free trade, in the way that even a high school teacher can speak 'for' physics, is limited. The not infrequent sight of ads signed by several hundred economists is a kind of living demonstration of the difference between the claims by physicists and economists to speak representatively. In economics, agreement on the basics – long since assured within 'the community of professionals' – still has to be demonstrated by the ancient ritual of signing a petition. Even these near unanimous claims are not always accepted as being the truth: sectarians, textile interests, unions, or a skeptical public may contest them.[2]

There is a more important issue, to which we will repeatedly return. Around every core of 'expert' knowledge is a penumbra, a domain in which core competence is helpful but not definitive, in which competent experts may disagree, and disagree because the questions in this domain are not decidable in terms of the core issues that define competence. This is perhaps the most important of all the issues to be discussed under the heading 'the new politics of expertise'. Experts routinely give opinions, individually and even collectively, on issues such as global warming, economic policy, or health care, which are penumbral in the sense that having technical knowledge is helpful in understanding the policy issues, and often essential. But the issues cannot be adequately formulated within the limits of what the members of the relevant communities themselves, in judging one another's claims, define as knowledge. And the boundaries and the subtleties of the relevant distinctions are often inaccessible to the policy audiences for these experts, and sometimes contested within the community.

Atomic scientists provide an example of this issue. In the wake of the Manhattan project, many scientists believed that because of their specialized knowledge of the physics of weapons, physicists ought to control weapons policy, and many spoke as experts on policy matters. Much of this talk was based on a belief that Russian and Western scientists could, by negotiating with one another, find a means of controlling nuclear weapons. In fact, they misunderstood the political character of the Soviet regime, the role of Soviet scientists, and the significance of what they were told by their scientific contacts. We may reasonably suppose that the same goes for scientists who today make pronouncements beyond their specializations. But deciding when to believe scientists or experts, deciding when they are speaking beyond the limits of their knowledge, and deciding what the limits of their genuine expertise are, are not easy matters, since deciding presupposes understanding, understanding that the democratic public does not possess.

In the case of the atomic scientists, there was a movement, an attempt to speak collectively, and even an abortive Lysistrata strategy. Yet there was not enough unanimity to pass policy preferences off as science, to deprive non-compliant governments of scientists, to halt weapons research, or to persuade governments that their policy preferences were in fact produced by their expertise in physics as distinct from their personal political ideologies. This was a grasp for political power based on claims of expertise that failed, though it produced powerful effects on science and international affairs that are still built into institutional forms, and are the original source of organizations that still have influence. Later cases were less straightforward. To understand these cases it is easiest to employ a strategy of ideal-types together with some elaborated examples. In discussing the next two kinds of expertise considerations of social science and social reform will take precedence over natural science. These cases are not distractions from the problem, but are a way of identifying the features of the problem of distinguishing 'expertise' by understanding the forms and guises of expertise.

The Fourth Type: The Expert with a Cause

Consider the 'expert' who is subsidized to speak and claim expertise in the hope that the views he advances will convince a wider public and thus compel them into some sort of political action or choice. This is a type – the fourth on our list – that came to prominence at the end of the nineteenth century in the United States, and developed concurrently with the development of foundations. The fifth type, to be discussed below, is a variant of the fourth, and differs in its target audience. Where the audience for the fourth type is the public, the audience for the fifth is professionals, typically bureaucrats who have discretionary power. In some contexts the fifth type has been an historical development of the fourth. Where the effort to create and subsidize recognized public 'experts' failed, typically because their expertise was not as widely accepted or effective as the funders hoped, an effort was made to professionalize target occupations and to define professionalism in terms of acceptance of the cognitive authority of a particular group of experts. Some of the most consequential of these efforts have involved the temporary subsidization of experts to instigate the system. The Rockefeller philanthropies played a large role in this process. In other cases, academic disciplines or factions have asserted expertise over issues in domains formerly thought to be political, or public, or the province of all practitioners.

Both types are best understood as ideal types, which is to say that most actual cases have a hybrid character. The examples I will discuss here have historical precedents of various kinds, from which some were lineal descendants through the inspirations of the cases I will consider here. In some fields there is no clear distinction between the two types. In many cases, such as the situation of psychotherapists, who are sellers of services, and not infrequently also publicists for viewpoints, and persons with bureaucratic discretionary powers or legal standing as experts, the line blurs. The key difference between the types is in the kind of audience they have, but the 'professional' audience for many fields, psychotherapy for example, is not very different from the public with respect to their actual sources of information and wisdom.

The early history of social work in the United States provides a rich example of an attempt to establish a claim of expertise, which is further distinguished by the self awareness of its leaders of the politics of claiming expert status. When the Russell Sage fortune was put to charitable purposes by Sage's widow, her advisors, themselves wealthy community activists, created an organization that attempted to persuade the public to adopt various reforms. The reforms ranged from the creation of playgrounds to the creation of policies for tenement housing and regional plans. Some of the participants were veterans of 'commissions' such as the New York Tenement Commission. Others were products of the Charity Organization Societies, still others came from social movements, such as the playground movement (cf. Sealander 1997: 197–203). Among the informal advisors to the early leaders of the Sage Foundation were women with long records in charitable efforts, beginning their charitable career in one case by wrapping bandages for soldiers injured in the Civil War. Here the lineal inspirations were particularly clear: the lesson of the Civil War was that a great cause of reform originating outside of politics, namely abolitionism, could succeed. This realization imposed on the post Civil War generation the obligation to continue the struggle and extend it to new domains. The Russell Sage Foundation depended on volunteers, but went beyond volunteerism and subsidized 'departments' with people employed as experts in these various domains. Some of them, such as Mary Richmond, had a great deal of experience, had written books, and were well known. Others were not well known, but learned on the job and played the role of advisor to volunteer groups of various kinds, such as women attempting to promote the construction of playgrounds in their community, who needed advice on what to ask for, and were given 'standards' and organizational advice.

The Russell Sage Foundation had a particular model of how to exert influence, a model that other foundations were to follow. Like other wealthy persons, Mrs. Sage was deluged with individual pleas for help. The foundation was designed to replace this kind of 'retail' philanthropy, with 'wholesale' reform, also leveraged, so that others, notably municipal governments, would commit their own resources to the cause. Playgrounds, for example, were not to be directly financed by the Foundation, or even partly subsidized, as Carnegie had financed libraries (Lagemann 1989). At most, demonstration projects would be directly financed. The means of exerting influence was thus through the creation of public demands. This required means of reaching the public and at the same time persuading the public of the validity of the demands.

The Foundation thought it had hit on the ideal device for doing this: the 'Social Survey'. Much could be said about the whole class of intermediary objects through which expertise is mediated, and this will be taken up again in connection with 'boundary organizations' in Chapter 4. The model used here is of the nineteenth century geologists who carried out surveys and produced maps that became valued objects for their patrons and audiences. They also served as a means of turning expertise into a depersonalized object. Literally hundreds of social surveys – of sanitation, education, housing, race relations, child welfare, crime, juvenile crime, and so on – were done in the period between the turn of the century and the depression. Many of these surveys were little more than reports on such things as the furnaces that heated the schools and how the grounds were kept, requiring no novel professional expertise. The comprehensive community survey was a different matter: it required the co-ordination of the existing professionals, administrators, and charitable workers of a community, and co-ordination was conceived as a novel practitioner-expert role. These new experts were 'social workers' and the task was 'social work'. The foundation had one great success with community surveying – the Pittsburgh survey – and a few minor successes. What the Pittsburgh survey did was examine all of the aspects of community life that were of special concern to the nineteenth century reform movements, and 'publicize' them. For example, to influence the building of better sewers and a better water system, they included in their public exhibit to the community (one of their primary means of publicizing the results of the survey) a frieze around the top of the hall that illustrated pictorially the number of deaths annually from typhus in Pittsburgh. Some of this effort worked; change did occur, though in this case the reformers, who gained the office of mayor, were soon turned out (cf. Greenwald and Anderson, 1996).

In the full flush of this success, the leading intellectual figure behind what he called 'The Survey Idea', Paul Kellogg, wrote extensively on the meaning of such surveys, and on the difficulty of persuading others of the expertise of 'social workers'. The foremost need was to persuade people to pay for expert knowledge. As Kellogg complained:

> while many of the more obvious social conditions can be brought to light by laymen, the reach of social surveying depends on those qualities that we associate with the expert in every profession; knowledge of the why of sanitary technique, for example, and of the how by which other cities have wrought out this reform and that. And townsmen who would think nothing of paying the county engineer a sizable fee to run a line for a fence boundary must be educated up to the point where they will see the economy of investing in trained service in social and civic upbuilding. (1912: 13)

Kellogg himself said that the task of persuasion would have been easier if there were an event like the Titanic disaster, which had dramatized the need for lifeboats and confirmed the warnings of naval engineers. The survey and its publicity were designed to serve the same purpose as a disaster:

> To visualize needs which are not so spectacular but are no less real . . . to bring them into human terms, and to put the operations of the government, of social institutions, and of industrial establishments to the test of individual lives, to bring the knowledge and inventions of scientists and experts home to the common imagination, and to gain for their proposals the dynamic backing of a convinced democracy. (1912: 17)

Ultimately, few communities were 'educated' up to the point of accepting the generic kind of reform expertise that Kellogg and his peers claimed to possess. But to an astonishing extent, the strategy worked, especially in such politically uncontested areas as playgrounds and juvenile justice. Major reforms that stand to this day were enacted on the basis of supposed expert knowledge based on little more than the highly developed opinions of the organized reformers themselves.[3]

If this is an ideal-type, there are many organizations, like the Sierra Club, which operate in a very similar way. Such organizations support 'experts' on policy matters, whose expertise is at best part of the penumbral regions of scientific expertise. These 'experts' are not unlike those subsidized by the Russell Sage Foundation in its early years. Their role is both to persuade the public of their expertise and of the proposals they support. What distinguishes the fourth type from the expert who is supported by the experts' target audience, for example through book sales, is the triad of support, audience, and legitimation their role involves. Experts of the fourth kind, whose audience is the public, do not support themselves by persuading the public to pay for their books, services or advice, as Dr. Ruth does, but by persuading potential subsidizers of the importance of getting their message out to the public and accepted as legitimately expert. The passing of the collection plate at an abolitionist meeting, or its modern variant, the mass mailings of Amnesty International or Greenpeace seeking 'members' or funds, amounts to the same thing: the money is collected from those who want the message to be heard by others. This pattern holds for scientists' groups as well, though the emphasis on fund raising in these cases, for example the Federation of American Scientists, an organization involved in 'public education' with respect to nuclear power production, is characteristically muted, and the scientific credentials of the experts emphasized.

The Fifth Type

The fifth type of expert is distinguished by a crucial difference in this triad: the fact that the primary audience is not the public, but individuals with discretionary power, usually in bureaucracies. The legitimacy of the cognitive authority exercised by these individuals is not a matter, ordinarily at least, of direct public discussion, because they deal with issues, such as administration, that are not discussed in newspapers until after they become institutional fact, and indeed are rarely understood by reporters, and may be subject to administrative secrecy of some kind. A paradigm case of this fifth kind of expertise is public administration, which contains the three distinctive elements of the type (1) a distinctive audience of 'professionals'; (2) experts whose legitimacy is a matter of acceptance by these professionals but who are not accepted as experts by the public and ordinarily are not even known to the public, and; (3) experts whose 'professional' audience is itself recognized as possessing, at most, only partial expertise by the public.

Public administration was a major target of American reformers of the early part of the century— corrupt and incompetent city officials, given jobs as part of a system of patronage appointments, were major obstacles to the correction of the conditions the reformers objected to. But political reformers – reform Mayors, for example – came and went, and the underlying problem of ineptitude and corruption remained. The movement for the professionalization of public administration, sponsored in large part by the Rockefellers (who also invested heavily in the professionalization of social work) changed this.

The Rockefeller strategy was rooted in the successful experience of Abraham Flexner in the reform of medical education and in the Rockefeller efforts in creating a medical profession in China (Fosdick 1952). It targeted *practitioners* and sought to turn them into an audience for expertise. One of the pillars of the reform of medical education was to make it 'scientific', and this meant creating a distinction between medicine as a craft skill or an eclectic collection of remedies, and medicine taught and validated by medical scientists, culminating in the eventual elimination of the former. One of the major goals of the reform of medical education was the removal of part-time clinical faculty: this was made a condition of grants for improvement (Brown 1979: xv).

The professionalizing strategy employed by the Rockefeller philanthropists in this and other domains ignored, for the most part, the 'general public', except to educate them in the differences between professional and non-professional workers. This education was supplemented by legal requirements and schemes of certification designed to drive non-professionals from occupations that had previously been weakly professionalized. The strategy, when in the 1930s it was applied to public administration, was well-tested and mature. The Rockefeller philanthropies already had a well-established relationship with the social sciences, particularly through such individuals as Robert Merriam and such organizations as the Social Science Research Council, as well as long-standing relationships with certain major universities. Some such universities were 'major' largely as a consequence of Rockefeller largesse. One, the University of Chicago, was effectively a Rockefeller creation. During the 1930s Rockefeller funding was being redirected away from 'pure' social research; professionalizing the social sciences was a Rockefeller project of the 1920s, and social science institutions, many of which were in dire financial straits, were dependent on Rockefeller funds. The Rockefeller philanthropists induced, through the use of their financial muscle, several key universities, such as the University of North Carolina, to establish training programs in public administration (Johnson and Johnson 1980: 111–12).

In the space of a few years, a number of schools of public administration and a professional organization of public administrators came into existence, and the creation of a class of specially trained public administrators followed. The training, by experts, of municipal workers who had traditionally been 'amateurs' appointed as political favors led to the creation of a distinction between trained and untrained administrators and between political and professional administrators. The expertise of the teachers of public administrators was not appreciably different from the expertise that already existed as a result of a previous reformist effort done in the name of efficiency and structured in the Russell Sage fashion: the municipal research bureaus that were established in major American cities, which addressed the public with the results of its studies of local government. The institutional structures were novel: they took the form not of training schools but of university departments that eventually produced professional academic public administrators. These then became the experts and their audience became the professional public administrators. The organizations they worked for became, in the phrase I will use in Chapter Five, 'expertized.'

The striking feature of this development is that it solves the problem of the audience of the expert by creating an audience and assuring indirectly that this audience is in a position to compete successfully with amateurs. A similar kind of development took place during and after the war regarding foreign policy, area studies, and similar domains related to the postwar American imperium. Such organizations as the Russian Research Center at Harvard, for example, were the product of this strategy, and involved some of the same players – previous recipients of Rockefeller funds. Later the newly created Ford Foundation played a significant role in the creation of foreign policy experts. In this case the primary consumer of professional employees was, often indirectly, the federal government. The training of

Foreign Service officers, military officers, and the like was a major task of these experts. Indeed, Harvard investment in regional studies began with contracts during World War II for the training of occupation army officers (cf. Buxton and Turner 1992).

It is with this step that the problem of democracy and expertise becomes salient. The experts whose expertise is employed are so in the sense that they have an audience that recognizes their expertise by virtue of being trained by these experts. The audience, in a sense, is the creation of the experts, but their power is the power of the state. With respect to audience, this expert more closely resembles the theologian whose expertise is recognized by the sect he successfully persuades of his theological expertise. In the case of theologians, however, liberal governments withdrew or were based on the withdrawal of public recognition of expertise to such sectarian 'experts.' In the case of the kinds of experts I have been discussing here, there is a discrepancy between the sectarian character of their audience and their role in relation to political authority. Since a great deal of political authority in modern democratic regimes resides in discretionary actions of bureaucrats, the control of the bureaucracy by a sect can amount to the denial of the original premises of liberal regimes. The Habermasian formula of expert cultures has some bearing here as well, for these are 'expert cultures' that actually exert state power. But there is also a kind of democratic control or democratic legitimacy, however indirectly it operates.

In the case of physics, with which we began, there was a kind of generalized approbation and acceptance on the grounds of indirect evidence of the physicist's claim to expertise and the claim to exercise powers of self-regulation and certification that should be honored by the public at large. In the case of professional bureaucrats and administrators there is perhaps something analogous. In the course of creating an audience for public administrators and area studies experts there was indeed a moment in which the offer of 'professionally trained' workers could have been resisted, and the amateurism of the past been allowed to persist. Similarly, there might have been, in the United States, a strong civil service core that exercised some generalized quasi-representative functions for the nation, as arguably is the case in, for example, France and Britain. However, the pattern was this: professional administrators displaced 'amateurs' and this occurred with democratic consent.

Legitimation by the public is not the same as agreement in opinions with the public. There has often been a large disparity between the views of experts (and the kinds of facts upon which these views were claimed to be based) and the views of politicians (and the kinds of facts and results on which their acceptance or validation by the general public is based).[4] In the case of foreign policy, opinions based on secret information gain a certain prestige and a foreign policy analyst who can't access information that the public does not have is diminished in his credibility in the eyes of the target audience of the expert, namely government officials who themselves operate on the basis of information that the general public does not possess. The implications of this discrepancy are obvious. Conflicts between democratic and expert opinion are inevitable, not so much because the expert invariably possesses relevant secret information (though that may often be the case with respect to foreign policy and in practice there are, typically, bureaucratic secrets or features of bureaucratics procedure that are known to experts but not to the public), but is a consequence of the fact that the processes by which knowledge is validated by audiences are separate. Equally, the processes of validation of theological expertise by sects are distinct from the processes by which public validation is achieved. This is perhaps a good model of the problem of assessing the expert claims of scientists as well: the basis of their claims is, in effect, secret, since it is largely inaccessible or incomprehensible to their public audiences, who also cannot assess whether it is actually relevant to the claims they make to the public. What public audiences can do in each case is to legitimate, or accept the claims to expertise. Legitimation is a 'solution' to the conflict. But in the case of bureaucratic expertise the legitimation is very indirect.

The Impossible Instrumentalization of Bureaucracy

The difficulties that have concerned theorists of democracy about the role of expert knowledge must be, I have suggested, understood as arising not from the character of expert knowledge itself and its inaccessibility to the public but from the sectarian character of the kinds of expert knowledge that bear on bureaucratic decision making.[5] There is, in the case of science, an important check on claims of expert knowledge that is lacking in the case of experts of the kind who threaten or compete with democratic decision processes: scientists need to legitimate themselves to the public at large, and to other scientists. The expert who *is* a threat is the expert who exerts influence through the back door of training and validating the competence of professionals and whose advice is regarded as authoritative by other bureaucrats but not by the public at large. The authority of the expert whose expertise is not validated by public achievements bears authority that comes into conflict with democratic processes. Of course, there is, in a sense, a check: governments that fail to deliver on promises may earn the contempt of their citizenry. If we know that the juvenile justice system is failing, this is not the same as knowing who in the system is to blame, what part of the system is to blame, or which of its various 'professions' with claims to expertise ought not be regarded as expert. The 'public' may be dissatisfied, and find outlets for its dissatisfaction, but the very fact that the bureaucrats themselves are not directly elected and do not appeal to the general public for legitimation means that there is no direct relationship of accountability.

There is another problem with bureaucratic expertise that derives from the structure of bureaucratic careers. Classic bureaucracies create internalized expertise – expertise about the rules and the procedures of the bureaucracy. Frequently there are systems of career advancement, through examinations, that link advancement to knowledge of these rules. Similarly for the selection of entry-level positions: the classic Chinese bureaucracies operated on systems of examination; British bureaucracies employed possessors of Oxford degrees and public school educations, each representing distinctive selection mechanisms. Selection mechanisms and mechanisms of advancement served important purposes in producing uniformity, internal communication and agreement, and so forth. But these very processes conflicted with the demands of technical knowledge, and often with the need for particular skills or talents, needs that were often brought to the surface in time of war. The arrival of telephone technology posed a major problem for the British civil service. Nothing that was learned in gaining a first in Greats at Oxford was of much use in decisions about siting telephone lines. But the civil servants who were formally responsible for the decisions outranked the technically trained persons who were employed to deal with such questions. And technical training was not a good basis for career advancement in a system that prized generalists.

Influenced by Foucault, a large academic industry has developed that is concerned with the creation of a 'political' understanding of state uses of expert power, notably in psychiatry and in relation to crime, trading on the commonplace fact that past uses of expert knowledge by the state, especially those that become the ideology of large bureaucracies, go out of fashion, usually long before the bureaucracy changes its practices. The lesson, typically, is that expertise is not 'neutral' but 'interested' and serves hidden purposes, including purposes of suppression and control under the appearance of neutrality and bureaucratic rationality. I will simply note in passing that this line of interpretation is not *too* political, but rather not sufficiently political. To be shocked that the boundaries of what is considered 'neutral' historically vary, that opinions about this change, and that political strategies are used to fix official definitions and practices, and that political decisions are made, is at best the beginning of wisdom.

The more interesting problem is historical. How did it come to be that there could be bureaucracies that operated in terms of theories or expertise that could conflict with either the ordinary understanding of citizens or with that of other experts? Obviously they did not emerge with Merriam, the brains behind public adminstration as a field, and the Rockefellers. There was a long history. Merriam was trained in the Columbia faculty of Social Science, founded by John Burgess with the express intention of creating experts for a 'professional' American civil service on the European model. The original effort faltered. Columbia found the American bureaucracies to be unreceptive to its 'expert' graduates who, like Merriam, became professors in the newly established social sciences. Burgess drew his inspiration from the models of the French and German bureaucracies, each of which had its own traditions of theory and training. In his study of a group of thinkers he called the Cameralists, Albion Small traced these back to 1555. Their main concern, as he put it, 'was to show how the welfare of the state might be served' (1909: viii). The body of theory they created,

Staatswissenschaft, supplied the bureaucratic wisdom of the civil servants of the German states. The diversity and weakness of these states meant that here, as in legal training, craft skills obtained locally were not enough. Theory, which had to imported, assumed a greater significance than it did in large states, such as Britain, in which rich internal bureaucratic and legal traditions could be established by precedent and usage.

This was professionalization without the Rockefellers, that is to say, without a plan, funding, and self-conscious political decisions on the part of rulers to 'accept' expertise. Hobbes and Machiavelli were reflexive practitioners of the art of politics who also believed it could be made into a science. Their employers presumably did not have any interest in expertise in this sense: only when there was a body of knowledge that required some of the elements of the 'Rockefeller' type would it have been possible to impose it as a solution, that is to create administrative schools for bureaucrats in which this science was taught. But, if we take the Rockefeller form as an ideal-type we can see that *Staatswissenschaft* as a body of claimed expert knowledge raises precisely the same questions: was it neutral, as it purported to be – an instrument for securing the welfare of the state? Or was it, as later critics came to think, a body of thought deeply committed to a collectivist conception of society antithetical to human freedom? The answer is simply that pure instrumentality in the realm of administration is an impossibility. The ideal of depoliticization derived from Saint-Simon, the replacement of the rule of man over man by the administration of things, is utopian. But the strategy of presenting oneself or one's expertise as purely instrumental can be an effective one, a point that will be returned to in Chapters 3 and 4.

The final two types are interchangeable, and not infrequently combine with the problem of the boundaries of expertise and the problem of the penumbral regions of expertise. Where these types combine with the penumbral regions problem, there is trouble, in a specific sense, for the basic liberal principle of neutrality. Richard Posner gives the example of United States constitutional law scholars, a group that both speaks to a general audience, and also serves, or seeks to serve, as experts for the judges who apply the constitution and the lawyers who argue cases on constitutional grounds (2001: 198–220). Constitutional law scholars play a role in assessing the qualifications of judges in the public domain, and their opinions are widely reported and often consequential. Are they politically neutral? And in what sense does it matter? After all, the opinions they give are opinions about the law, which presumably is a technical matter. Yet, in examining their behavior during the legal controversy over the Bush-Gore election of 2000, Posner points out that as 'public intellectuals' commenting, not (as Noam Chomsky does) on matters other than their professional expertise, but on the areas in which they *were* supposed to be professionally expert, they routinely presented a highly partisan interpretation of the relevant law.

Posner argues that the politicization of expert opinion, in this particular case, reflects in part the politicization of the subject matter itself, by which he means the political character of the case law decisions on which the experts are technically 'expert'. Many of the crucial cases of present day constitutional law arise from the details of the administration of reformist programs enacted into law or federal procedure, such as the affirmative action program, rather than, for example, cases involving the responsibilities of 'fictional' legal persons or corporations, a theme of earlier constitutional law. But it also reflects what he calls 'the leftward drift' of academic constitutional law, by which he means the fact that the 'discussion' of academic constitutional law includes few conservative scholars (2001: 209). These would be grounds for questioning the neutrality of particular scholars in the face of questions that are open to alternative plausible answers and the neutrality of a 'consensus' on such questions produced by academic discussion of such questions. Further, these are judgments that ordinary people can make, and the non-expert press can find columnists to articulate.

The more subtle forms of non-neutrality, however, require some inside knowledge of constitutional interpretation to detect and assess: the happenstance of political diversity within the 'expert' community would allow the biases to be exposed by insiders, and divergent expert opinions to be presented to the public. In the case of this particular dispute even the few conservative scholars in the field were absent from the public discussion, a point seized on by the critics of the court's decision. But, Posner notes, this was because most of the conservatives were critical of judicial activism on the grounds of their own academic 'original intention' theories of constitutional interpretation, and consequently were unlikely to defend a decision that required an 'activist' rationale. So the check provided by political diversity among experts – a check that may not exist at all in some fields – failed in this case.

Posner of course is making his own expert judgement here-one which is open to expert contestation. His own view is that the case of Gore v Bush was a matter of formal law: it required formal legal construction of express provisions, which, under the circumstances of shortness of time, required a pragmatic decision about application. He rejects the notion that there was any legal basis for ignoring the express provisions of the 'manner directed' clause of Article II of the constitution, which gave relevant powers solely to the state legislators. This meant that state constitutions did not override these powers (the basis of the Florida Supreme Court decision that was vacated). Simiarly, the express provision of the United States legal code designating November 7, 2000 as election day precluded re-voting. Posner is, in this case, a critic of the Supreme Court with respect to the grounds it gave for its decision, namely the equal protection clause, but not of the results of the decision itself, which would have been essentially the same under either argument. Thus he provided an 'alternative justification'. If his legal opinion is correct, the academic discipline of constitutional law is defective: unable, because of the biases of its academic discourse, to correct its errors. Moreover, Posner suggests, constitutional scholars routinely made claims that amounted to a political act 'masquerading as a statement of professional expertise' (2001: 212). In the face of such claims, of course, the non-expert *is* vulnerable: rules of statutory construction are constitutive of legal expertise, not matters of public opinion. And it is here where the theoretical problems with which the chapter began take on a place at the center of poltical life, rather than at the periphery.

Neutrality in Theory and Practice

The discussion so far has distinguished five kinds of experts: experts who are members of groups whose expertise is generally acknowledged, such as physicists; experts whose personal expertise is tested and accepted by individuals, such as the authors of self-help books; members of groups whose expertise is accepted only by particular groups, like theologians whose authority is accepted only by their sect; experts whose audience is the public but who derive their support from subsidies from parties interested in the acceptance of their opinions as authoritative; and experts whose audience is bureaucrats with discretionary power, such as experts in public administration whose views are accepted as authoritative by public administrators.

The first two do not present any real problem for either democracy or liberalism: physicists are experts on physics by general consent, and their authority is legitimated by rational beliefs in the efficacy of the knowledge they possess. But there is an important qualification to be added: it is not always clear where the limit of their expertise lies, especially to non-physicists. The expertise of self-help authors is private, and the state need not involve itself in the relation between sellers of advice and buyers. Theologians and public administrators present a different problem. Neutrality is the proper liberal state's stance toward theologians, because the audience that grants them legitimacy is sectarian. The state ought not to subsidize them or to give one sect preferential treatment over another. The fourth and fifth type present more serious problems. Both typically are indirectly subsidized by the state, in that foundations derive some of their money from tax expenditures. Had the Rockefeller fortune been taxed as an estate, there would either have been no foundation, or if there were it would have been smaller.

What does this list of expert types establish? It makes no claims to completeness as a taxonomy of expertise. But it does contain all of the types of experts that figure in the problem as traditionally conceived. Habermas's shadowy expert cultures are not there, but something similar is: bureaucrats with discretionary powers, schooled in intellectual traditions that are a kind of culture. No bureaucracy is completely free of the need for legitimacy, even if the legitimacy in question is that of the state itself, and the expertise of the bureaucrats is granted legitimacy indirectly. And if we reconsider the traditional problems – and the Fish/Foucault 'cultural studies' form of the problem as well – in the light of the list, some of the difficulties vanish or are greatly modified, and some features of the problem of neutrality stand out more sharply.

The term ideology is a good place to start, for it figures in Fish's attack on liberalism. Fish, we have seen, regards liberalism as a sham because it rests on a bogus notion of reason, on the assumption that there is such a thing as neutral 'reason', reason that is outside of the battle between world-views (1994: 135). As such Fish thinks of liberalism as founded on an ideology it takes for granted, ideology is not neutral, so, paradoxically, liberalism can't exist, because the idea of liberalism as neutrality represents a kind of self-contradiction. It can exist only by hiding the untruth of its foundations.

There is bite to this criticism, deriving from the naturalism of natural right thinking out of which liberalism historically grew. The liberalism of the American founding tended to regard the truths relevant to politics as immutable and self-evident, accordingly regarding them as neutral facts in a way that we no longer can. But the fact that expertise goes through a process of legitimation, that legitimacy may be withdrawn, and that the cognitive authority of experts may collapse, suggests something quite different than the idea that liberalism is a kind of self-contradiction, and something much more interesting.

The liberal principle of neutrality is not an assertion about the nature of beliefs, but a core rule that establishes a means of organizing the discussion of political matters, that is to say the discussion of political decisions. It is no surprise that in order for there to be genuine discussion some things would be temporarily taken as fact, or, alternatively, some things would be left to the experts. We can give these cognitive objects a name: 'fact-surrogates'. A fact-surrogate is something taken as a fact for the purposes of political discussion. It may be a fact – a truth – but it need not be. It need only be accepted as true, with this proviso: it is somehow legitimated, that is to say given general acceptance, which may derive from an acceptance of the legitimacy of experts who produce these surrogate facts. 'Politicizing' everything, taking nothing as fact and making everything into the subject of political dispute, would lose the advantages of the intellectual division of labor, and make political discussion impossible. *Some* facts need to be taken for granted in order for there to be genuine political discussion, and some of the work of establishing the facts is, properly, delegated to experts. Indeed, to imagine a world in which such delegation did not routinely occur would be to imagine a simpler society, a society of Jeffersonian yeomen whose de facto equality of knowledge is enforced by circumstance, or a utopia of omni-competent citizens. To preserve the possibility of political discussion that past societies established, it is essential to delegate to experts and grant them cognitive authority. But granting them cognitive authority is not the same as granting them some sort of absolute and unquestionable power over us. We, the non-experts, decide whether claims to cognitive authority, which in political terms is a request to have one's conclusions treated as neutral fact, are to be honored. And we have, historically, changed our minds about who is 'expert.' But we have nevertheless accepted expert claims, fact-surrogates, as a basis for political discussion.

Or so it seems. Thinkers like Foucault and Habermas present a more serious challenge than Fish does when they attack the power of the public to judge whether or not something is expert knowledge, because this undermines the notion of reasonable delegation and thus of democratic or liberal legitimacy itself. For Habermas, the communication on which the legitimacy of uncontested as well as contested viewpoints is based may be 'distorted' and its results therefore bogus. Foucault is even more direct. The beliefs that we share or widely accept as true are all essentially the product of non-consensual manipulation, or rather a kind of hegemonic intellectual influence. The acceptance of the beliefs does not require conscious manipulators. But the process of the production of acceptance prevents the ordinary citizen from, to put it in somewhat different language, giving 'informed consent' to the arrangements under which he or she is compelled to live. These fact-surrogates are prison bars, and our 'acceptance' of them is not 'reasonable' because the very notion of reason as it applies to expert claims is tainted with submission.

For Foucault, the condition of religious believer, the voluntary acceptance of the authoritative character of that which cannot be understood, is realized in an involuntary way by the citizen: the religious believer voluntarily accepts mystical authority; the ordinary citizen is mystified into the acceptance of uncontested givens through which he or she is deprived of the volitional and cognitive powers necessary for citizenship. Foucault holds out no hope that there can be any escape from this kind of 'control' and provides no exemptions from its effects, except perhaps to intellectuals who can recognize and protest against their fate, but who are politically irrelevant because they can provide no alternative to this fate. In Foucault, the experts and the public disappear simultaneously into the thrall of forms of discourse which is constitutive of their mental world. In Habermas, in contrast, there is an exemption for experts, of a sort. The people who do the steering are not trapped within the limitations of the life-world that they steer. This is not to say that they are not limited, however, by the effects of distorted communication. But their limitations are different from the limitations of those they administer over. Their control cannot be truly legitimate because the consent that they depend upon is not genuinely 'informed'. Those who assent are governed by myths, myths of neutrality, that preclude their being truly informed or informable.

This argument depends on a dubious premise: the claim that there is a duality between ordinary people trapped in their life-world – or more precisely life-worlds – and experts who inhabit different life-worlds but rule over the life-world of the many. However, experts are not a caste and do not share a single life-world. With respect to areas beyond their specialist knowledge, they are members of the many. There is a danger, as suggested above, of a clique of experts acquiring de facto control over some domain of discretionary decision making done on behalf of the state. Ultimately, it is the fact that the public has no effective way of checking the competence of these discretionary decisions that is the source of the problem. The phenomenon of bureaucratic 'expert cultures' is simply a by-product of an arrangement of bureaucratic discretion, selection, training, and so forth that creates 'cultures'. But the problem of assessing competence includes the stubborn problem of determining whether experts are over-reaching.

We can address the problem of bureaucratic discretion in a less abstract manner, and restate it in terms of the notion of 'democratic deficit'. Bureaucratic agents are, by definition, accountable to democratic discussion only indirectly – very indirectly indeed in the case of the bureaucracies of the European Union, which brought the term into prominence. Expertized bureaucracies, Type 5, are doubly in deficit. Not only are the links to democratic control indirect, there is also a fundamental problem about over-reaching, that is to say of claiming expertise beyond what is warranted. In the case of many of the experts found in the inner parts of bureaucracies, there are few occasions where they are called to account by competent discussion partners. Type 4 experts must be 'democratically' recognized as expert, but like type 5 experts, their influence depends on a claim of neutrality. The claim is typically misleading: their claims to expertise are promoted and financed by persons who are not neutral, and the ulterior conditions that make the activities of these experts possible are typically concealed.[6]

Although most of the examples I have given here derive from social science, it should be evident that the same kinds of problems arise for 'scientific' cases. Morone and Woodhouse, in their study of nuclear power expertise (1989), show what happens when a body of expertise and expert claims – fact-surrogates upon which public policy decisions about energy production were based – was produced by a scientific community bound up with the policy. 'Public understanding of science' became public acceptance of the claims, and huge 'educational' efforts were made that served the purpose of legitimating the experts and the policy. Careers in reactor science depended on the consensus. Critics were dismissed as 'not real scientists', or not experts, because they were outsiders to a complex system of mutual dependence that was partly financial.[7] 'Competence' and agreeing with the consensus have a mutually reinforcing relationship in this, as in many other settings. Regulators, academics, industry experts and engineers, 'public education' groups, settled on a consensus, which the public accepted. The safety of nuclear plants was an important fact-surrogate, accepted as a basis for political discussion.

The Three Mile Island accident delegitimated this consensus. Before the event itself, there was nothing that the ordinary citizen, deferring to the respectable expert opinions of the competent participants in the consensus, could have used as a factual basis for rejecting the consensus, or at least nothing that would have counted as competent.

The nuclear physicists who supported claims about nuclear safety made no 'scientific error' strictly speaking. What later came to seem to the public as an error, the falsity of the picture of nuclear safety they presented as a fact-surrogate, was in the penumbral region, the zone of claims that require a 'scientific' basis and scientific background to fully understand but that cannot be established scientifically. This problem combined with another – the discretionary power of government experts who were themselves party to the consensus. And with this we come to the place at which 'expertise' *is* a problem for liberal democracy. The 'experts' in the social survey movement never had that much influence. But they had their own Three Mile Island, in the form of Prohibition, which they supported and defended to the bitter end on the basis of their special 'social work' expertise – a bit of overreaching that effectively ended that conception of 'social work'.

Why is this a 'problem'? To the extent that we recognize expertise as real, we acknowledge an inequality. To fail to recognize expertise is to accept a fiction, and to base politics on a fiction. The inequality cannot be eliminated except in fiction. The effects of expertise in these cases are political in the most familiar of senses. They involve the exercise of state power. Here the inequality has tangible consequences for the 'discussions' that are the basis of liberalism. We have reached the last inequality, and perhaps the most difficult 'problem of liberalism'.

Notes

1 A simple discussion of this idea in relation to religion is found in Turner (1996), which considers some of the unusual conditions which historically have constrained American religious groups in politics.

2 The claims about the nature of intelligence to which the letter-writer to Newsweek objected, curiously, produced a similar kind of collective letter signed by a large number of prominent psychologists, designed to correct what they saw to be the alarming disparity between what was presented by journalists and commentators as the accepted findings of psychological research on intelligence and what psychologists in fact accepted, namely that there were persistent differences in scores. Here the issues were different: the accepted facts were simply not known to the journalists, who seemed to assume that the facts fit with their prejudices.

3 It would require an Encyclopedia to catalog these efforts, and indeed there is one, which went through several editions, edited by W.D.P. Bliss (1908). It is a parlor game to expose the errors of past experts, but one 'survey' prediction is worth giving as an example. Among the 'causes' producing experts was the movement for 'comfort stations'. To adapt to the projection that after World War I, the airplane would become a widely used conveyance, it was suggested by one survey that a system of comfort stations be established with large enough fields to allow planes to land, for the convenience of aviators with full bladders.

4 This is a major theme of the literature that inaugurated 'professional' diplomacy and foreign policy analysis. Hans Morgenthau, for example, stressed the idea that it was often a necessity for the leader to act against the democratic consensus with respect to foreign policy (1946).

5 Elsewhere, I have discussed some other aspects of the problem of expert knowledge in relation to power. In 'Forms of Patronage' (1990) I discussed the problem faced both by scientists and governmental patrons in deciding whether to patronize scientists, and I suggested that there was a generic problem that arose from the fact that politicians and bureaucrats were not trained in a way that enabled them to judge the promises made to them by scientists. It is questionable whether scientists are able to adequately judge such promises, as they do, for example, in peer review decisions on grant applications, but it is not questionable that politicians and civil servants who are not themselves scientists are in a position to make these decisions. I pointed out in that paper that the knowledge possessed by scientific experts was so specialized and fragmented that there was no general threat of scientists or experts as a group supplanting democracy. In a paper called 'Truth and Decision' (1989), I discussed the issue of

the limitations of specialist knowledge in the face of ill structured decisions of the sort that policy makers and politicians actually face. I noted that typically experts with different backgrounds framed issues in ways that conflicted and that consequently there was no univocal expert opinion in such decisions. This speaks to the notion that 'expert culture' is some sort of unified whole: clearly it is not.

6 One simple example provides a paradigmatic example of the type. Gunnar Myrdal's *An American Dilemma: The Negro Problem and Modern Democracy* (1944) was a classic of social science expertise. It was made possible by lavish funding by the Carnegie Corporation, which conceived the project and paid the researchers whose specialist reports were given to Myrdal to write the text. The promotion of the book was subsidized by the Carnegie Corporation. All this was concealed. Myrdal was chosen because he was not an American, and therefore could not be immediately dismissed as non-neutral, as either a northerner or a southerner. The aims of the funders were not neutral, but they were well-hidden.

7 I do not mean to suggest that the financial or career aspects of these relationships are essential. Kellogg, for example, was a committed advocate who needed no financial incentive (Chambers 1971). Neither do the participants in the Federation of American Scientists. But the machinery of publicity usually requires money, and the money trail usually points to interests, which may be ideological or material, in the promotion of some expert consensus. In the nuclear power case, the industry's motives are clear, as is the trail of funding. Similarly for the survey movement. In other cases it is less clear.

3

Is Rational Discourse With Experts Possible?

> . . .let us go down, and there confound their language, that they may not understand one another's speech. (Genesis 11:7)

Imagine a convention that guarantees that experts speak only the truth, and in a way that virtually everyone can understand. Of course this is utopian. The situation of Aristotle's 'slaves by nature' presumably is no utopia. Nevertheless, if we were perfect 'natural slaves', in Aristotle's sense, we could recognize expertise when we saw it without having to understand. But this is, in fact, beyond our capacities: we cannot make these discriminations *because* we cannot understand, or understand sufficiently, the experts whose claims we must discriminate between. In the face of expertise, we are *less* than slaves – unable even to correctly apprehend the expertise of others. The demands of liberal democractic citizenship are higher. To be fully functional citizens in a liberal democracy we must be political reasoners more or less equal to other political reasoners. But we are not, with respect to the questions that concern experts. Paradoxically, experts are as trapped by this situation as citizens. Experts must produce, in Beck's phrase, 'cultural acceptance', but they cannot persuade their fellow citizens if their audiences are unable to understand. And they can be held responsible for advice that has been misunderstood, or which they have given honestly in response to inappropriate demands and misguided expectations. Moreover, those who are expert are often in competition with charlatans who are better able than the experts to sell their ideas and even to appear to be genuinely expert.

Despite all of this, in practice liberal democracy accommodates expert knowledge. Experts manage to persuade and to be understood. So, as serious as these conundrums are in theory, matters are not so grim in fact. Debate occurs, decisions are made, makeshift devices are invented to produce expert consensuses, citizens' consensuses, and consensuses of stakeholders, and the devices that produce consensus and the results of the process are criticized and revised. Consumers of expertise also learn from their experiences with experts. Yet the basic theoretical question remains: Is all this practical endeavor necessarily fraudulent because underlying it is the reality that experts and consumers are not really communicating or rationally persuading? Are they, in actuality, playing a kind of blind man's bluff, in which experts seek to get the confidence of their audiences, sometimes successfully and sometimes not? And if it is a game, does it conceal deeper operations of power?

Rational Persuasion: A Minimal Account

To begin to deal with the question of how expertise can possibly work, it is necessary to deal with theory, specifically the theories that lead us to believe it cannot work. We might conclude that the theories are right, that the presence of expert opinion does make liberal democratic discourse a complicated sham. Or we might discard the theories. The theories behind the various terms that figure in the usual formulations of the problem of communication between experts and non-experts are usually not explicit. Some basic usages pervade the existing literature, notably the term 'paradigm', and other metaphorical terms, such as 'viewpoint' and more recently (and now ubiquitously) 'social construction'. These terms are widely employed both in writings on the problem of failed discussions between experts and the public as well as in the context of explaining how some particular 'expert' idea comes to be taken to define the situation. 'Defining the situation' is itself a technical term of sorts, used by the sociologist W. I. Thomas (1923), in the practical context of talking about the aims of expert persuasion (which he characterized as *changing* the definition of the situation).

The terms in this loose family of concepts are used to refer to the *conditions* of 'rational persuasion': the things that must be shared for rational persuasion to occur, rather than the things *about which* rational persuasion might occur. To purport that science and common sense do not have the same 'paradigm' is to say that it is impossible for the occupants of the two paradigms to communicate because the things one says within one paradigm are incommensurable with the things one says in another. As such, people are not talking about the same things; to say they are different viewpoints is literally to say that what their adherents see is different. By definition a social construction is something artificial, or created partly through a social process, that is treated by some particular group of people as 'real,' as distinct from partly social.

It might be thought that the problem here is simply a matter of a malignant terminology, and that by using other terms one could make the problem vanish. But the terms have a hold on us because of an issue that seems not to be dependent on any particular term, or indeed on any sharply defined conception of the problem of rational discourse. It is the problem of irremediable disagreements that facts are seemingly unable to resolve.

Concepts like 'paradigm' came into vogue in connection with such disagreements for a good reason, namely the failure of the main rival to such terms, what might be called the 'information model.' The information model treats all factual assertions as bits of data, and all disagreements as resolvable on the basis of more information. The problem with this model is that it often does not work to add more information. Sometimes, when new facts are introduced, instead of resolving disagreements, the new facts become subject to divergent interpretations, often of more or less the same kind as the divergence that the new information was supposed to resolve. Disagreements persist without being significantly altered by the 'information' because the viewpoints that enable the facts to be given divergent interpretations also persist. The sheer existence of such disagreements raises a question about the possibility of rational discussion. This chapter will be concerned with the question of whether it rational discussion is possible, and thus of whether there is a conception of rational discussion sufficient for liberal democracy that overcomes these problems.

By 'rational discussion' I mean something quite minimal: an exchange of opinion in which participants are willing to be persuaded of the truth or justice of something. The idea that such discussion is possible is basic to liberalism and the liberal theory of parliamentary democracy. The key to the definition is that one is open to being persuaded of the truth or justice of something *new*, something one does not believe going into the discussion. This is precisely what present models of the role of experts in discourse do not permit. The standard models imply that experts can persuade one another, and can persuade non-experts, while non-experts cannot persuade experts. The non-expert can at most supply information, which becomes meaningful for the expert only when translated into expert terms, which the non-expert cannot do, but the expert can. There is, in short, a 'discursive asymmetry' . Experts possess the grounds and means of mutual persuasion; non-experts do not. A non-expert can at best apprehend, as a consumer of expert opinion, that others posses expertise. As suggested in the last chapter, this kind of relation between people is in fundamental conflict with the basic principles of liberal democracy, which is why expertise is today as fundamental a problem for democratic theory as the existence of revolutionary opponents of liberalism was for liberal theory over the last two centuries, and the existence of religious opponents of the state was to liberalism in the two centuries before. The expert must speak in the language of the non-expert in order to be understood. But this is not the language they use to persuade one another, nor the one in which the grounds for their opinions can be expressed. So accepting the opinions of experts is not rational, or at least is different with respect to the grounds for acceptance.

The problem is of establishing rational persuasion through discussion, instead of acceptance occurring entirely on the basis of faith in the expert. In the first sections of the chapter I will show how the standard accounts of persuasion rule this out. In the final section I will give an account of how such persuasion is possible, and what this implies for our image of dependence on experts. In the intervening sections I will examine the kinds of problems that give rise to disputes involving expert opinion. Much of the discussion will be concerned with the ideas of objectivity, science, and neutrality, which have traditionally been central to the authority of experts. The remaining discussion will be concerned with the question of just what scientists and other experts do when they reason *as experts* about actual problems.

The 'Paradigm Plus Authority' Model

The term 'paradigm' and similar terms are best understood as means of explaining. They serve in explanations of the kinds of disagreements and discrepancies in conclusions that arise in connection with virtually every domain in which technical and nontechnical considerations bear on the solution of real world problems. The reason this kind of explanation of differences is so tempting is that it does appear to account for some basic problems of risk communication and policy discussion. The fundamental thing that the notion of paradigm seems to explain is the fact that different things are taken to be true in different domains or by people holding different points of view (cf. Turner 2002b: 74-107).

If we say that this is *because* the participants in these domains hold different paradigms, we have said *why* they hold these different opinions about what is true. We also explain why it is so difficult to rationally persuade the participants in one domain with the reasoning of the participants in other domains. The problem can be stated in other ways, but the basic point remains: the conclusions people draw and the things they believe to be true are connected with the modes of reasoning that are accepted within a particular domain, or for a particular group, and do not simply transfer or carry the same weight in other domains or other groups.

The problem with 'paradigm' or 'point of view' formulations is that they go too far. They explain disagreement by making some very typical processes of reasoning or forms of rational justification entirely unintelligible. For example, if someone else witnesses an event and describes it to me and I explain how I assessed this description, and what I believe as a result of my assessment, I am still in some sense within the domain of common sense. I use essentially the same vocabulary (and many of the same modes of assessing claims) when faced with advice from experts whose 'authority' I must assess and whose views I might accept or reject, and I freely incorporate the conclusions drawn from the domain of the expert into my own. I can, for example, explain why I think beta-blockers are useful in treating heart disease by reference to the experiences of my brother-in-law without being able to understand fully the reasoning of the scientists who understand the chemistry involved. I accept their claims as valid, and believe them, without grasping their 'paradigm'. Yet I am not simply expressing faith in physicians, for I am explaining and reasoning myself, however inadequately.

The paradigm picture is unhelpful in connection with these ubiquitous assessments because it does not allow for the incorporation of the results of 'other' forms of reasoning except as, so to speak, foreign bodies. It denies that people operating within different paradigms are genuinely talking about the 'same' things: their criteria of sameness differ for the things they are talking about, so they are actually not, despite appearances, talking about the same thing. Thus there is a kind of affinity between the use of the notion of 'authority' in relation to the claims of experts and the paradigm picture. Given the paradigm picture, the only way in which I could come to accept the conclusions of experts, it appears, would be through some act of incorporation of this foreign idea, an act which could not be justified in terms of my 'own' framework.

The reason the paradigm picture leads to these conclusions is that it implies that the products of expert knowledge are indeed foreign in a very radical sense, namely 'incommensurability', and leaves it unclear as to how these claims are usable for reasoning within a particular common sense framework. The paradigm picture, indeed, suggests that the medical researchers and physicians are only *apparently* talking about the same things as the patients. In the discussion so far I have assumed that at least some expert claims and conclusions can be stated or translated into the framework or domain of non-experts, and I have allowed for the possibility that some cannot. In a sense this conflicts with one of the most basic elements of the paradigm picture, which is that *no* translation is fully possible between paradigms. This is a major weakness of the model, for, as the philosopher Donald Davidson has famously pointed out, Thomas Kuhn is excellent at describing the views of the previous paradigm and the terminology of the present one – something the paradigm model seems to rule out as impossible (Davidson 1973-74).

For there to be a phenomenon of expertise at all, as opposed to merely mutually exclusive linguistic communities, some such translation has to be possible. Something, such as practical conclusions, must be able to be taken from the expert domain and placed, as a foreign but intelligible claim, within the non-expert domain. The usual way of accommodating this commonplace occurrence is to amend the paradigm model slightly by allowing for the possibility that experts can and do speak intelligibly in public domains. Scientists themselves, presumably, speak both the 'languages' of science and of common sense, and can translate from one to the other as bilinguals. But the results of translation, such as 'this table is composed mostly of empty space,' do not have common sense *credibility*, because the grounds for the claim cannot be expressed in common terms.

So translation is not enough. Something more is needed, and the usual solution is to characterize these utterances in terms of the notion of 'authority', making the problem one of expert *authority*. Indeed, there is an affinity between the notion of authority and the notion that scientists and common sense are operating in different paradigms. Authority is often portrayed thus: experts are prophet-like beings, who exercise 'authority' or 'cognitive authority' by making claims that no-one can challenge. The claims derive, so to speak, from another world – not a supernatural world, as in the case of prophets, but an expert world to which ordinary people have no access. This way of thinking about authority itself can be traced to Max Weber. It has exercised enormous influence, especially over sociologists and political scientists, on the larger problem of the authority of experts.

Weber, himself a lawyer, constructed a typology of authority in which the distinguishing feature of the three basic forms of what he termed legitimate authority was the type of ultimate justificatory belief in political or legal authority. The three legitimating beliefs were: 1) belief in the validity of written rules, rationally interpreted, which designates a person acting in a particular capacity as authoritative; 2) belief in the validity of unwritten rules or traditions that designate, usually more vaguely, particular persons in particular roles as authorities; and 3) charismatic authority, which derives from the belief in the specialness of the person exercising authority. For Weber, each type of authority in some sense rests, ultimately, on an act of faith. In the case of traditional and rational authority the faith is indirect, that is to say the rules are the thing that the believer accepts on faith. However, in the case of charismatic authority, it is the fact of the specialness of the person exercising the authority that is the issue that requires faith, and it is direct faith in the leader and her or his special standing that justifies the acceptance of their command.

To treat experts as authorities in this sense requires us, in an act of faith, to believe that they do indeed possess some special cognitive powers analogous to those of charismatic leaders speaking prophetically of religious truths. In the case of prophets, of course, the 'reasoning' is hidden because it is God's reasoning – the prophets simply pass on His commands. In the case of science, it is hidden because it is meaningful only to scientists, and, similarly, scientists report the results, not the grounds for them. The results are accepted as the sayings of the prophets are, as a matter of faith in the powers of the scientists or experts, not as a result of the reasoning that led to the results, which is not accessible, because it is not understandable.

Is there an alternative to the 'paradigm plus authority' model? Does the problem here result from an inadequate picture of the problem of communication? Is there an alternative to the paradigm picture (augmented in this way by the notion of the cognitive authority of experts)? Would an alternative picture of the problem, or a revised version of the paradigm picture, provide an improved understanding of the problem, and perhaps an even better understanding of the limited possibilities for changing the forms of political discussion involving expert knowledge, to make the discussions more rational or more democratic? I think the paradigm picture *is* wrong, but it contains some elements of truth. It trades on some features of expert communication that *are* unusual and need rethinking. The alternative, of saying 'the facts are available to everyone,' which is implicit in the 'information' model, is also wrong, unless it too is substantially altered.

The obvious strategy in the face of this polarization between accounts is to begin with one or the other to see whether the middle ground and the alternative can be accounted for, or subsumed within, one or another of the theories. However, this would be difficult to achieve precisely because a 'paradigm' cannot easily be reconciled with the kind of translation that citizens and decision makers routinely do in construing the results of science. A better approach might be to construct an account of the middle ground that includes problematic cases, whereby the less problematic cases of information and paradigm are viewed in relation to the middle ground.

That is essentially what I propose to do in what follows, though my aim will primarily be to make some basic distinctions between types of claims in the hope that these distinctions will clarify the relevant cases and more adequately define the relation between different types of claims.

Lying between these models are some facts that neither model accounts for very effectively. For instance, people do indeed form judgments about the competence of experts and the truth of expert opinions on topics such as global warming. These judgments and opinions, however else one may characterize them, are rarely acts of faith. People make reasonable assessments of credibility, interests, and the standing of people making claims, and they actively seek not a professional education but an understanding of the reasoning of scientists, including the evidential reasoning. Often their concern is to construct, in their own terms, a simulacrum of this reasoning. Put simply, people do not simply *accept conclusions*. They think critically about them, and have a substantial array of resources to bring to bear on their reasoning, including incorporating (at least some of) the reasoning of the scientist into their own reasoning.

Science, Objectivity and Neutrality Revisited

To make any progress on the problem of understanding what goes on in reasoning about expert claims requires that we get away from these very high-level abstractions about 'paradigms' and 'information' and deal with some of the concepts that figure in the middle domain of reasonable beliefs about what experts say. There are a number of intermediate concepts that figure in this middle domain, concepts that we use in the course of differentiating between experts and assessing expert claims, and one place to start on an understanding of the probem is to analyze these concepts. Three concepts in particular play a large role in public discussions of expert claims: 'scientific truth', 'objectivity', and 'neutrality'. There are large literatures on each of these concepts, of course, and it would be presumptous to try to supplant these literatures or solve all of the problems that these concepts have produced. Yet to proceed we need a way to make sense of these concepts in relation to one another – to have a kind of topography of the ideas. And to produce this, it will be useful to simply stipulate some definitional starting points, just as one might stipulate topographic co-ordinates. As it happens, I think it will be possible to illuminate some of the issues that have concerned those writers who have objected to abstract notions of objectivity and denied the possiblity of neutrality. But some basic definitions are needed to begin.

The three basic concepts can be defined in this way: 'Scientific truths' are results accepted as scientifically true by the community of scientists or by all competent scientists speaking as scientists. 'Scientifically true' means not only agreed to, but agreed to be 'scientific', which is to say 'in accordance with methods and forms of reasoning that are scientific'. 'Objective' truths or results have been produced by an objective, impersonal, procedure: one that would produce the same results when performed by any competent person. The paradigmatic objective procedure is one in which the same (typically numerical) conclusions are produced by each competent user. 'Neutrality' refers to interests, material or ideological. Neutrality, in a political sense, is simply freedom from considerations of interest. A neutral person is one without relevant interests. A neutral result is one in which the consequences do not differ for people with different interests.

The literature on experts has typically treated *scientific* expertise as paradigmatic, and, as we shall see, this is at the root of a problem. The basic facts of science are scientific truths in the sense of the definition given above: they are agreed to be true by all competent scientists. They are based on experiments or observations that all persons with the relevant competences can perform. And to the extent that everyone who is competent agrees, interests are irrelevant. Critics of expertise have sometimes thought that they needed to reject this kind of reasoning, by showing that interests *are* relevant, or by collapsing some of these concepts into the concept of paradigm, for example by showing how 'objectivity' is relative to one's paradigm, or by making scientific truth 'that which is warranted within a scientist's paradigm,' or to argue that because all knowledge depends on paradigms, no one can be neutral, because paradigms themselves represent non-neutral choices.

Fascinating as some of these arguments are, they typically fail to be persuasive. Some scientific facts or problems seem to work just as the model says that they should – objective procedures are used to produce the facts, which are accepted by the scientific community, after which the problem of interest does not arise. But sometimes the model does not work as expected. To understand where it works and where it does not requires a different distinction, between well-formed and ill-formed problems (cf. Simon 1977; Turner, 1989). A well-structured problem is one in which there is a single best solution. An ill-structured problem is one in which there are multiple possible solutions, each of which is 'best' in a different sense or dimension of quality, and none of which is best in all the relevant senses. In the face of ill-structured problems, the three concepts – scientific truth, objectivity, and neutrality – behave differently than in the standard model. Interests may be connected to different ideas of what is 'best.' More than one scientific community (or expert community) may have something to contribute to the discussion, and each may employ different competencies in producing objective results. More than one scientific community (or expert community) may have something to contribute to the discussion of alternative solutions, and there may even be 'scientific truths' or other expert truths (such as legal truths) that are 'true' for one community and not another, or may be difficult to translate into the expert terms of the other community of experts.

So we have two kinds of situation: one that fits the model of scientific, objective, neutral expertise; another in which there is no one objective, neutral, and scientifically preferred solution or decision-determining fact. In the case of policy decisions of any degree of complexity, and even in the case of many interdisciplinary problems in which scientists are expected to decide on the facts relevant to the policy, ill-formedness is the *norm*. Problems of this sort typically involve different kinds of expertise, with different standards, and different controlling considerations. Nothing assures us that they can be made to neatly mesh, and indeed they often do not. The nature of the problem can be made evident by a famous example of an ill-structured problem, the grandfather of American environmental policy discussion, the problem of the arid lands in the west. As these lands were opened to settlement it became clear that they would not support the same kind of cultivation, with the same type and size of farms, as earlier settlements had. One suggestion was to close the land to homesteaders. Another was to irrigate. Another was to create new kinds of ownership that reflected the fact that water rights were what made land valuable in these regions, not merely rights to the use and sale of space. Another was to intervene to produce different micro-climates in which there was more rainfall. Each of these 'solutions' had powerful interests behind them, and each reflected divergent beliefs about the world and about the ability of people to intervene successfully in the environment. However, the beliefs also differed in part with the technical background of the proponents of the various points of view. Lawyers and politicians were reluctant to tamper with the 'right' to homestead and the rights in land that were enshrined in the legal tradition, and saw some solutions as impractical from their expert point of view. Government geologists disputed the belief that 'rain follows the plow' and the idea that artesian wells would suffice for irrigation in dry times. Farmers had the incontrovertible empirical experience of a long cycle of good farming and rejected expert opinions that the land could not support agriculture. Soil scientists proposed novel plowing methods. Engineers proposed dams. Each believed that they had special expertise. Each believed that their opponents who lacked their expert knowledge misunderstood the technical difficulties, costs, or consequences of various courses of action. Each also had different interests, background knowledge, experience, positional interests, professional values, hopes, personal desires, and so forth; and their time horizons also varied (cf. Goetzmann 1966; Turner 1987).

It is best to begin with neutrality. The problem of what to do about the arid lands amounts to a kind of problem space in which there are a variety of undisputed 'neutral' facts – facts with the same consequences for everyone regardless of their interests – that do not do very much to constrain the possible solutions. Or, to put it differently, to aid the application of a single solution that is satisfactory to all sides, or an 'adequate' solution that is acceptable according to the divergent criteria of satisfactoriness that each side holds. The definitions of 'the problem' themselves vary according to the different desiderata the solution needs to fulfill. And the 'intellectual' differences are connected in various ways to the interests, values, experiences, and so forth, of the stakeholders. Moreover, there is an issue which is generic. In politics, not to decide is often to decide. In science, consensus or acceptance is something that can be waited for. Science faces many ill-structured problems, but science can wait for some discovery or idea that makes the problems well-structured or soluble, soluble in terms of methods or modes of reasoning accepted by scientists as scientific. In politics, or policy, this is not feasible. Perhaps the characteristic or defining fact of politics that it is concerned with is the question of whether to use state power, and in what way, in the face of ill-structured problems. Politicians in liberal democracies attempt to solve problems by rational persuasion – just enough persuasion to secure a majority – and this gives liberal democracy its distinctive flavor. But as we have noted, liberal democracies have many devices for dealing with questions that cannot readily be 'solved' in this way. One is to define them as non-political and to refuse to discuss them: this was the response of the liberal state to religious questions. Another is to delegate them to neutral parties. The courts are the paradigmatic case of a neutral party. The court is 'positionally neutral' in relation to the parties to a dispute. Positional neutrality means that the person in the position of decision-maker has no stake in the issues at hand other than the minimal responsibility to arrive at a decision. Judges are positionally neutral. The salaries of judges are unaffected by their decisions. To jeopardize their neutrality by bribes is illegal. The jurisdiction and powers of judges are sharply circumscribed. The office, not the person, has the powers.

Other decisions are delegated as well, for related reasons. The political purpose behind granting decision-making authority to what is sometimes called a 'positionally neutral' party is as follows: in the face of high levels of complexity, insolubility, or underdetermination where a decision nevertheless needs to be made, the politically important thing is to arrive not merely at a solution, but at a solution that does not arbitrarily advantage one side over another. If this cannot be done by delegating the decision to one particular group, such as the Army Corps of Engineers, or the Geological Survey, or the Bureau of Land Management, the solution might be to grant it to a body or person who is neutral in the sense of having no interests that would affect, or be seen to affect, the decision.

In these cases of ill-structured decisions one can see why and how one would wish to secure neutrality. There are standard political means of producing positional neutrality. Judges are obliged to step aside if they know the parties to a court case or have an interest that would be affected by the outcome, and jurors are excluded for the same reasons. Plato's guardians were made positionally neutral by depriving them of property and parental ties. But there is a generic problem with expert neutrality. Experts are never quite positionally neutral: they have an interest in preserving the power that goes along with their status as experts.[1] The problem often is also an organizational one: organizations that speak collectively as an authority must make collective decisions about whether to say things that may affect their interests, and one of their interests may be to avoid political confrontations in which they will be attacked as non-neutral. The interest of the organization in satisfying the desire of the public for neutrality, and the consequent need, on the part of the expert institution, to produce the appearance of neutrality, sometimes produces strange anomalies. The evidence of risk of contracting HIV from ordinary heterosexual contact in the general United States' population has always been clear both to epidemiologists and to health care professionals with substantial experience with AIDS cases. The risk level is negligible, in contrast to the risk level in relation to certain 'homosexual' practices and IV drug use. But the fear of political pressure from AIDS activists, and the desire of AIDS activists to prevent AIDS from being treated merely as a disease of homosexuals and IV drug users, led the Center for Disease Control in the United States to endorse propaganda about AIDS and about the possibility of contracting AIDS from heterosexual contact that was highly misleading. What is striking about this case is not simply that a respected institution would lie, but that it would lie for the higher purpose of preserving the appearance of neutrality.

Neutrality in this sense can be distinguished from 'objectivity'. An 'objective' solution or fact would be a solution or fact arrived at according to procedures which would produce the same result regardless of who was following the procedures. The problem with objectivity-generating procedures and objective facts is that they are rarely sufficient to settle a question or make a decision unless one has decided in advance to let the results settle the question.[2] Flipping a coin is a paradigm of objective decision-making: the coin throwers need not be neutral, they must merely agree on the procedure. It makes no difference who flips the coin, or what their opinions are, though in the case of ill-structured problems, of course, parties to the dispute typically disagree about which objective procedure should be used to settle the issue, and how results produced by such procedures should be interpreted. The value of objective procedures is that once one has secured an agreement to decide particular issues according to the results of the procedure, the objective process can take over.[3]

Scientific facts are another category entirely. To be 'facts', they must be accepted as such by the scientific community or the competent peers of the scientist. In the case of ill-structured environmental problem situations, typically there are pieces of scientific fact that bear on the problem, but, as I have suggested in relation to neutral facts and objectivity, they are insufficient to constrain the solutions. Critics like Ulrich Beck are quite right to point to the self-imposed limitations of scientists, and to argue that ecological problems cannot be solved, or even plausibly addressed, within the framework of science. But the reason he gives for this, namely that the conservative standards of validity in science are biased against the establishment of 'genuine possibilities', namely that of ecological threats, is misguided. It is, so to speak, that the problems themselves are not structured in a way that science can 'solve' them. Risk analysis problems typically are ill-structured problems that the risk analyst attempts to restate in well-structured terms that objective calculations, based on (some sort of) data, can settle. But the choice of a definition of the problem, and its acceptance as a problem to which policy ought to be directed, is a political decision, not a scientific or 'objective' one.

Neutrality, and particularly problems of conflict of interest and institutional bias, is among the easiest topics to discuss in a liberal democracy. Indeed, problems of interest and conflict of interest are central to the very question of what the state is and what the state should do. Positional neutrality, in some respect, is one of the core features of the state and it is perhaps the feature that distinguishes it from a clientelistic gang. And part of 'politics' is monitoring and correcting conflicts of interest. So it is not all that surprising that liberal politics and political discussions of expertise often stay on this familiar ground. The problem of conflict of interest has the effect of converting issues of expertise into issues of neutrality, of converting questions about whether what the expert says is true into questions about who pays for the expert and what benefits the expert might be hoping to gain by making a particular claim. This is, despite the objections of experts (who of course claim to represent expert opinion rather than themselves), often a good practice. If experts are merely partisan, because they are 'blinkered' and can't see past their own prejudices, or because they are connected to the identity of a particular problematic institution, they are necessarily engaged in misrepresentation when they represent themselves to public discussion as genuinely neutral. In the face of ill-formed problems that require solutions, truth is not enough, because the things that are known to be scientifically true are insufficient to be decisive. Objectivity is not enough, for the same reasons, and because there will inevitably be disputes about the significance of the results obtained through 'objective' means. But neutrality may be possible. It is not 'enough' in the sense that it guarantees 'correct' decisions. But it is enough in the sense that it may enable a decision that is acceptable as the best possible under the circumstances.

The neutral, objective, or scientific facts may be insufficient to be much of a constraint on decisions. However, the desire to move a topic out of political discussion and into the hands of experts may nevertheless be strong, because doing so may facilitate rational persuasion, and lead to a decision that is accepted as legitimate. Indeed, this is the logical core of the political phenomenon that will be discussed in subsequent chapters. One of the central devices of liberal democracy is to delegate discussion and remove issues from particular institutions of discussion and give them to others. In nineteenth century America, for example, discussions of public health measures against cholera were transferred, by acts of state legislatures, from the hands of city councils and the boards of health they appointed, to other boards and commissions. In the twentieth century, monetary decisions – an important topic of political debate – were delegated to the Federal Reserve Bank. In both cases, there was relevant expert knowledge. In neither case were the problems well-structured. They were problems in which the science or expertise at hand were necessary to full understanding of the discussions, but which were not structured in such a way that the science was sufficient to identify the solutions.

In these cases we can notice an important fact: there may be a disparity between what experts can competently assert and what they are asked to assert. The desire to resolve problems by delegating them to experts may not match the capacities of the expert. The legal tradition has a complex set of means for dealing with situations of this sort – notions like the preponderance of evidence, which together with neutral procedures can produce decisions. But other domains of expert knowledge which lack these traditions are nevertheless called upon to provide objective, neutral, and as far as possible scientific guidance. The reasoning that is employed in these situations is the concern of the next section, on casuistics.

Delegating to neutral bodies is a useful political device in the face of conflicts of interest, and technical disputes are almost always to some extent matters of conflicts of interests. But positional neutrality and expertise are notions that do not always fit together very well. Even a judge who is positionally neutral is a member of a class, race, and gender, and thus, it can be claimed, not truly neutral.[4] For many technical problems there are no positionally neutral experts: Everyone has been paid by, or depends on, the industry whose interests are at stake (cf. Morone and Woodhouse 1989). Worse, as Beck suggests, perhaps the attitudes of scientists toward evidence prevent them from being truly neutral about 'possibilities'. The alternatives to neutral expert bodies are various. The Danish model, copied in various other contexts, is to use citizens as panelists (Sclove 1997). The Welsh Institute for Health and Social Care has established 'a national Citizens Jury to consider ethical issues surrounding human genetic engineering' (Hinde 1997: 17). These follow the familiar pattern of attempting to produce neutrality by eliminating persons who have an interest, which is the model of the jury.

Panels and juries pose a problem: what sort of reasoning is actually employed in the persuasion that occurs within them? The legal analogy is again revealing here. In Anglo-American courts the distinction is made between matters of law and matters of fact. Judges decide matters of law. Juries decide matters of fact. What arguments the jury is privy to are at the discretion of the judge. The judge decides what the jury is to hear, and what the jury is to consider. The judge may add to this by admonishing the jury to ignore something they may have heard, or by preventing the jury from hearing things that one party to the case regards as a relevant fact. Similarly, a physician discussing a patient's problems may simply prescribe a treatment without explaining (or giving the patient any) 'choices', or, alternatively, may describe certain options, give an opinion of the probability of outcomes, and then let the patient make the choice. The information given to the patient may be such that their own distinctive preferences or beliefs may lead them to prefer one course of treatment or action to another. So the choices are real and they may even be 'rational' in the sense discussed earlier in connection with politics, in that the beliefs and preferences of the patient may themselves be open to change through persuasion by the physician. But the physician provides the information, or by its nature the information is not fully accessible to a person without medical training. So there is a great asymmetry in this persuasion. The main point is this: large areas are *de facto* off limits to the patient or consumer of this expert advice.

The possible forms of dialogue, balanced or unbalanced, whatever these terms might mean in this context, are restricted. A patient giving a history or undergoing blood tests is simply providing data for the physician to make a medical judgment about. A bad physician would fail to take a good history or would do the wrong tests. But in the end the *physician* recognizes the disease as a particular kind of disease. To be sure, a patient involved in his or her own care may be able, with a rudimentary understanding of the disease, to identify possibly relevant symptoms that the physician had overlooked or failed to elicit, and in this way collaborate in his or her treatment. Collaboration may indeed be therapeutically beneficial even if it is based on the illusion of choice rather than reality. Then again, placebos are often therapeutically beneficial. The question this raises is whether citizen participation in technical decision-making is the political analogue to placebos, which create an illusion of 'equal footing', which has the political effect, on the legitimation of decisions, of genuine collaboration and equality. This of course is Habermas's question, which motivates critics like Beck.

Whether it is an illusion or not depends on the question of what sort of reasoning is actually operative in the case of the physician identifying a disease in discussions with the patient, or a scientist attempting to speak to a non-scientist about a policy problem, such as the setting of a standard, the enforcement of a regulation or its formulation, or the formulation of risks. Part of the answer to this question is that when the problems are ill-structured, no form of expertise is sufficient to determine the single optimal solution, simply because there are no single optimal solutions; rather there are solutions that satisfy different desiderata, such as the desiderata that define optionality in different professional domains.

But there is an additional problem. The physician or expert is *not* simply acting *within* a domain of expertise, applying technical considerations in a scientific or objective way *directly* to the decision in question. Instead the reasoning is casuistic (a term I will explain shortly). One can consider again the cases of the physician or the lawyer, knowledgeable about the ideal types of disease and crime and possessing an arcane technical capacity for reasoning and for assessing the evidence that is relevant to asserting that an action is of a particular legal type or a symptom a particular disease. If expertise is anything, it is expertise about these ideal uses. But actual cases ordinarily do not conform perfectly to ideal cases or standard categories. Many cases are similar to, but not perfectly like, a particular disease syndrome or legal form of action, or may resemble more than one type, and each type has different legal or medical implications. The problem of deciding which ideal applies in these cases can be resolved only by reasoning by analogy, by seeing how similar and in what respect one case is like another. This is casuistical reasoning: to identify intermediate cases so that a kind of similarity can be constructed, and one can say in some approximate way, given one's understanding of what similarities are important and what similarities are not, whether a case is of one type or another.

Brian Wynne's excellent paper on the errors of scientists answering questions about radioactivity in soils relates to this problem (1996). The issue Wynne described was a simple one. Scientists were asked when it would be safe for farmers to return sheep to particular fields that had been polluted with radioactivity. Based on their empirical experience with, and understanding of, the causal process in a particular kind of soil, they estimated that the effects would dissipate in three weeks. In fact they were wrong. The kinds of soil that the sheep were grazing on contained a great deal of clay, and the clay retained the radioactivity much longer than the scientists had predicted (1996: 63-4). Wynne uses this example to make the point that scientists are often ignorant of the truth about the things that they confidently make pronouncements on. From Wynne's point of view, the decision based on the scientists' advice was, in effect, a vast and involuntary human subject experiment in which scientists learned that their predictions did not match reality and were forced to revise their models. He does not explain how this particular kind of experiment could be avoided, other than by more complete scientific research prior to the making of expert pronouncements. His emphasis is on the arrogance of scientists and of their ignorance of the relevant conditions, foolhardiness in subjecting others to risk, and on the morality of scientific pronouncement.

All of Wynne's points may be valid. Nevertheless, one still must ask what sort of discourse the scientists were engaging in when they were making these erroneous pronouncements. Whether what they were doing was 'science' is a point to which I will return in a moment. What they clearly were doing was reasoning casuistically. They had one case, a laboratory case, that they understood; they extended this understanding to another case that looked to them, with their knowledge (albeit limited in ways they did not realize) of the causes and conditions under which radioactivity diminished, to be equivalent. The predictions turned out to be false. What went wrong with this reasoning? There is an important difference between analogical reasoning of the kind used in casuistry and causal reasoning (cf. Jonsen and Toulmin 1988). Analogies and casuistic reasoning both operate by comparison and by identifying similarities thought to be important and relevant. But causal processes are *not* 'similar in similar cases'. If 'A' will cause 'B' is true, 'cases similar to 'A' have outcomes similar to 'B" does not follow. In causal contexts a single difference may be enough to change the outcome, even if the difference is 'minor'. The conditions for causes to produce their results are, so to speak, absolute. Omitting one necessary condition changes the process into a different process entirely. So casuistic reasoning is, in terms of the strict logic of causal reasoning, inapplicable to causal contexts.

Yet in practice scientists and scientific practitioners know that much of the time they *can* generalize more or less safely from the cases they know and understand well to cases that are similar and which, again, they know and understand well. Indeed the method of analogy is enshrined in regulatory law in the case where chemicals or drugs are fed to animals in order to see whether these chemicals or drugs produce various effects, such as cancer, and projections are made regarding humans on the basis of this. As a matter of the logic of causal reasoning, this is unjustified. A large number of unknown differences exist between animals and humans, and between the processes that are observed in laboratory cases and the processes that operate in the real world on real people. In some cases, scientists discover that they understood less than they thought they did. But much of their knowledge relates not to the particulars of cases, but to general knowledge about disease processes. This warrants a general practical expectation that certain kinds of disease processes are similar in relevant ways, and that a well designed animal experiment containing the important relevant variables ought to produce results that are roughly similar to the results in human beings. Quantitative (and of course 'objective') as the procedures for performing these experiments and generalizing from them might be, the reasoning is still analogical and casuistic. If you get the conditions wrong, or do not understand exactly what the relevant conditions are, analogy is a bad basis for inference about causation. And if the disease is anomalous, as for example AIDS is, one's general practical expectations will be misleading. The analogy, so to speak, mimics prediction only in the circumstance that the similarities thought to be relevant are in fact causally relevant. But there are no guarantees that this is going to be the case unless one has complete causal knowledge, and in these cases no one has complete causal knowledge.

Soft Consensus

'Complete causal knowledge', it must be said, is not a scientific idea, nor is it a standard of scientific acceptability. Perhaps a few branches of physics aspire to and claim complete causal knowledge of their subject matter, but science itself, as my definition suggests, is a matter of results accepted by the scientific community as valid. Unfortunately for the purpose of drawing distinctions, this line is not as sharp in the eyes of consumers of expert opinion as it might be, and scientists themselves not infrequently blur it, or define it differently. Discussions of global warming, for example, are concerned with models, that is analogical constructions – as indeed much of physical science is – rather than fundamental laws or complete causal knowledge. Is the partial consensus obtained about the plausibility of the most widely employed models of atmospheric temperature processes 'scientific'? There are 'scientific' traditions, such as medicine, in which an intermediate or soft notion of consensus about what amounts to 'knowledge sufficient for good practice' prevails. It is this notion – a notion of what one should do, given the present state of scientific knowledge – that policy makers and politicians wish to appeal to as though it is equivalent to the question of what is scientifically true. One can see why doing so is so tempting as a political device: It takes contentious political issues out of the political domain, where they cannot easily be settled, and puts them into the category of 'facts' that are neutral. This neutralizing device is essentially a matter of a political decision, a political consensus to stipulate certain facts, and is no different in its effect than stipulating the validity of a particular religious creed: it moves the topic from the realm of subjects for political disagreement to another category.

Given this, it should be no surprise that there is a large gap between the following three matters: accepted scientific truth; consensus on the present state of knowledge and its practical implications; and what politicians would like to have stipulated as true (and therefore neutral) in order to proceed with public discussion. A simple example of the difficulties this creates is the current dispute over mammography for women. There is some 'science' here, involving the technology itself, and the science is black boxed into the technology and is not in dispute. What also is not in dispute is that a series of studies in several countries have shown no effect of mammography on mortality rates of breast cancer. These studies are procedurally 'objective'. The explanation is not known, but it is a reasonable conjecture that people who 'pass' tests of this sort gain a false sense of security and that, at the low breast cancer rate of younger women, this effect exceeds the benefits. There may be more complex reasons as well: all the effects are small, and all the rates are low, so it is difficult for the objective procedures to take the analysts beyond this point, at least 'objectively'. If one then applies standard cost-benefit ratios, objectively, the result is clear: money is better spent elsewhere. But the soft 'consensus' of medical scientists is to promote mammograms.

If we retrace our steps, we can see where the problem arises. The scientists who are asked their opinions and asked to produce a consensus, work within limits of discourse formed both by science and by objective procedures, but also in the light of other considerations – medical prudence, a desire to not discriminate against women, and other considerations that form part of a vague idea of responsible medical practice. The objective procedures are not strictly scientific. The scientists are being asked to go beyond science, to combine their general scientific knowledge with objective procedures. They are required to reason from necessarily limited evidence (about the past and about samples)about a policy question that is broad and concerned with different people and circumstances, where the differences may bear on outcomes and are both unknown and unknown in their effects: this is casuistry. How can this become non-neutral? What is accepted as science at any given moment can be non-neutral if it is partial (as it always is) and if the partiality is such that the apparent policy consequences of the partial knowledge bear more heavily on one group, or side of a dispute, than another. Avoiding this appearance makes a certain medical sense: medical science shouldn't appear to be discriminatory against women.

'Objective' procedures used in ill-structured (i.e. incomplete) domains are, by definition, partial, and thus open to the possibility of non-neutrality. The procedures need to be stipulated to be 'complete' in order to be the basis of a decision. So, when scientists are asked to form a policy consensus or answer a policy question on the basis of such procedures, they are being asked to proceed on the basis of partial knowledge. The potential for non-neutrality is there even if the policy advice is derived (casuistically!) entirely from accepted scientific truth. There need be no intentional bias. It is simply a matter of this: if we reason analogically from facts that are valid but incomplete, we may come to results different from the results we would get by reasoning from other partial facts, or all the facts.[5] Some environmental disputes clearly have this character, and Beck's criticisms of science trade on it. Beck's point could be restated thus: some partial facts lead by analogical reasoning to 'possibilities' that, if taken seriously, could have serious consequences for decision-making. A practice of reasoning *only* from the best established facts, those accepted as 'science', may be systematically non-neutral because the result would be to minimize threats.

Differentiating the issues of science, objectivity, and neutrality in particular cases does not change the problem of the role of experts. But it locates it far more precisely in the geography of discourse, and shows where the asymmetry between expert and public is an issue. It is not an issue when the problem for which an expert is employed is 'well-structured', that is to say, a technical problem, which the possessor of particular skills and technical knowledge can solve for us. Here the expert is our servant or employee, and although the fact that we do not possess the skill or technical knowledge creates a management or purchasing problem for us as users, it is usually an easily solved one. We can employ other experts to check the work, as we do when we get a second opinion from a physician, or to certify the expert, as we do when we rely on credentials, or employ experts to manage experts. These methods 'work' even when there is a casuistic extension of core expertise, as long as the extension is not into an ill-structured problem, in which the expert's reasoning leads to conclusions in conflict with that of other possessors of specialized knowledge.

Understanding the difference between the core of an expert's expertise (whether it is the objective procedure used to reach certain numerical conclusions or a body of accepted scientific theory) and the casuistical application of the core to actual problems helps clarify what experts do when they make expert pronouncements, and why it can go wrong even if the 'core' is right. But this does not fundamentally change our dependence on experts. Just as with the lawyer or the physician, we are dependent on experts because they have a full understanding of the paradigm cases from which they reason analogically. 'Dialogue' with them does not make us in any useful sense their equals or discursive partners. We are not even in a good position as nonexperts to disagree with the casuistic steps in their reasoning. The construction of analogies is dependent entirely on judgments about what is relevant and what is not that have been acquired by operating from an expert understanding of the paradigm cases. Experts learn what differences are relevant to extending causal reasoning on the basis of, and by, possession of the fullest understanding of the cases. As consumers we may learn that experts have their limitations when they perform these feats, as Wynne points out. And we may learn this very painfully. But this makes us better consumers of expertise rather than equal or symmetric discursive partners of experts.

We become discursive partners of a certain sort when we are in some sense our own experts, and perhaps this is a useful way of thinking about the problem of dialogue and symmetry. We are 'experts' about our own experience and perhaps about a number of other facts about the world that experts are ignorant of and can usefully be made aware of. But the asymmetry is still there. The 'paradigm' model of discourse makes the asymmetry one of the points of view. But common sense is not inaccessible to experts, as expertise is to common sense. The information model is even clearer. We are still in a position of supplying 'information' to the expert, information that the expert can use to resolve problems but that we cannot, since we do not possess the information the experts possess.

There is, in the literature, no theory of dialogue that makes notions like 'balance' into anything more than metaphors. The discussion of well-structured and ill-structured problems is itself only an analogy casuistically applied to the case of expertise controversies. But the analogy, it can be argued, breaks down in the face of differences in worldviews. If experts have different worldviews, then the issue is not reducible to different optimalities, but is a matter of communication. The problem is not disagreement but non-communication – talking past one another, mutual incomprehension, and incommensurability.

Real Communication

In this section I would like to speak informally about the philosophical problem of incommensurability. The core of the problem is that if truth, validity, understanding, meaning, and so forth is understood to be relative to a paradigm or a point of view, then appealing to some common ground outside of any point of view whatsoever is an impossibility and meaningless. Pretending that the expert and the non-expert are in any serious sense ever talking about the same thing, even if they appear to be communicating, is also a mistake: they cannot. 'Dialogue' is an illusion which can only be temporarily sustained.

But what if this all or nothing way of formulating the problem can be improved on, or shown to be a special case of something more general? That is precisely what I will suggest here: the 'paradigm' and 'information' models are not merely insufficient representations of the reasoning relevant to the kinds of discussions that experts contribute to, but that they are rather special cases. The places they fit are forms of rational discussions that are special because they involve training or discipline, such as the training of an observer who is taught how to report something in the form of 'information', and becuase they involve self-limitations on what counts as evidence. These limitations and discipline are characteristic of certain sorts of expert domains, such as science and the law, so the problem is not simply a theoretical one. But they are poor models for rational discourse as a whole.

Consider a very simple concept and a very simple kind of inference. Suppose that I have a common sense concept of life which I extend to plants and animals but not to the biosphere or the world itself. A biologist might say that this common sense notion of life is biologically unsatisfactory, that it is misleading with respect to such things as the beginning and end of life, that the boundaries of the category are not very well defined when it comes to such things as viruses, and also leads to misleading results when applied to something like the biosphere. One might take this to be an example of incommensurability, and argue that biologists don't have a concept that corresponds exactly to the common sense notion of life. Further, it can be argued that they do employ a series of conceptual distinctions that are largely parallel to it, which can properly be extended to such things as the biosphere and viruses, and that sometimes lead to conclusions different from the common sense conception of life. One might further argue that the common sense conception of life is false and needs to be revised, and that ordinary people need to be taught a new conception that allows such things as the Gaia hypothesis to be accepted as legitimate.

Is this a case of incommensurability, or of paradigm relativity, in which the scientist's understanding and the common sense understanding are simply different, meaning that what counts as true with the scientist's concept is just different from what counts as true with the user of the ordinary concepts? Does this mean that the scientist and ordinary person have different conceptions of truth and validity? Do the two occupy different worlds?

One way of answering this question would be to say that the two ways overlap considerably and that one can *partly paraphrase* the claims and terms of the one point of view with the other. From within the more fully developed language of science can be explained the differences between the scientific and nonscientific notions of life. By 'partial paraphrase' I mean a term that has uses, or a statement that has implications, which are partly the same as the implications of the term or sentence being paraphrased. We do 'partial paraphrasing' or 'translation within a language' all the time when we explain technical concepts to non-technical audiences. For example, the notion of a tort in the law, is explained to juries and judges by lawyers as it applies to particular cases in terms of notions of responsibility and intention that are not specifically legal concepts. Indeed this is done in a highly routinized way in jurors' instructions. Epistemic ideas, such as standards of evidence and degrees of belief, similarly, are legal notions that are explained in common sense terms by giving lists of criteria to the people who must apply them to make a particular specified decision on a jury.

The same sort of paraphrasing is applied with science. In both legal and scientific cases we preserve a great deal of the technical meaning. In the legal case, the point is to give the juror the ability to make the inferences and draw conclusions that a person in full possession of the scientific or legal concept would have, so that the jurors can make inferences about guilt or liability – to make decisions about what is legally the case. As suggested, they do so on the basis of restricted information, and judges decide on the restrictions. But the point of this is to force them to see the case in a legal way, and to reason in terms of what is legally relevant. The effect of the restrictions and instructions is to provide a simulacrum of the effect of legal training: to assure that jurors make the factual decisions that objective trained lawyers would have made.

Scientists of course have only the power to make a case to the public and more generally to educate the public about the ways of science and the general principles that scientists reason in accordance with. When they succeed in this sort of public education, they enable non-scientists to *follow their reasoning*. But following the reasoning, in a partial or limited way, is not the same as fully understanding it. Here the paradigm model is right. There is a difference between the scientists' command of these concepts and our own command, if it is based on partial paraphrases that enable us to make some of the inferences that scientists make, but not all of them.

Viewed negatively, the ordinary person can learn to reason like a scientist but in a kind of crippled or partial way, because he or she can make only some of the inferences, or employ some of the reasoning and draw only some of the implications that the scientist can. But scientists and technical experts ordinarily are also limited in the concepts that they fully master. Characteristically, specialists in different domains have only a partial understanding of the reasoning in other domains. They employ what Peter Galison calls trading languages – like a scientific pidgin language (1997). This means that they *can* communicate, and communicate their reasoning, at least some of the time, if the inferences that they make can be made in the impoverished but not entirely empty language that can be explained to others, whether the others are experts of different kinds or non-experts. Similarly, when a physician discusses a medical decision with a patient, ideally the physician explains as much as possible using terms the patient comprehends, and teaches the patient as much as possible about the reasoning and concepts involved so that the patient can participate in and make decisions by reasoning, as the physician does.

The ordinary person, non-expert, or non-biologist is of course at a disadvantage in some respects. In particular, the non-expert is less able to assess the question of the validity of the hypothesis, its value as an explanation relative to other explanations, and the quality of the evidence that supports it. This hypothesis is to the ordinary person, merely plausible – but something to work with if scientists assure us it is true. Truth, validity, and so forth, *are* different for the scientist who has mastered these ideas than they are for us. But it is a difference of degree rather than the totalizing difference of kind assumed by the paradigm concept. Truth, validity, and so forth are different for the scientists because they have mastered more inferential uses, and thus have a wider scope of evidence against which to test and evaluate the idea. However, the advantages of the scientist (or lawyer) who has mastered the inferences in this special domain are advantages that accrue from the special limitations under which discussions operate in these domains. Persuasion is possible because everyone involved in the discussion is trained in the same way, counts more or less the same things as relevant, excludes the same things as irrelevant, and is selected for 'membership' on the basis of their mastery of the rules of the game. It is a separate question whether the results of science are 'truth' or those of legal argument are 'justice.'

There are two main solutions to the issue of the status or validity of these special domain claims. One has already been discussed in Chapter 2: to externalize them and treat them as neutral givens for political discussion. Of course, we cannot simply exclude them from 'government by discussion', as we can exclude religious argument. But we can exclude from discussion the issues that arise in these domains *between* practitioners. This is done every time a political body sends for a legal opinion, or passes a technical question on to staff members for an answer, or establishes a commission to look into the question.

The second solution involves using expert claims, partially paraphrased into their relevant implications, to redefine the choices that are the concern of political discussion. Where does this model of partial paraphrasing leave us with the problem of expert knowledge and expert authority? From the point of view of the person making a decision, the choices are likely to still be very unclear if the decision is ill-structured, meaning that the reasoning that one can apply to the situation involves different definitions of the problem and alternatives that are not wholly comparable or not equally credible. Clearly it is not the case that the expert always knows best in these situations. Different experts may have different opinions, and the 'best' decision may be the one made by the person who understands part of the reasoning of various experts and makes the best judgments of the credibility and relevance of the different expert arguments.

In some 'fundamental' sense it is true that experts and non-experts and experts cannot 'fully' communicate and what they say is not 'fully' intelligible to other experts. However, if a part of the reasoning, if some of the inferences made by experts and some of the grounds for belief, are intelligible either to other experts of a different kind or to ordinary people and policy makers who know things that the experts do not, then something very important becomes possible, something that the paradigm model appears to rule out. It becomes possible for problems to be formulated and solutions to be discussed in terms of these 'incomplete' inferences and forms of reasoning. The reasons can be strung together to form arguments and solutions and policies that no expert, reasoning entirely within a single expert paradigm, could have formulated, or which an expert combining expertise with common sense could formulate. The person who has partially mastered several other relevant domains has an advantage in the face of these problems. The partial master of several domains can arrive at new definitions of the problem itself.

Such re-definitions of issues not only occur, they represent the normal case in the face of complex ill-structured policy problems. Consider the case of the arid lands of the American west. John Wesley Powell proposed a solution that enabled lasting settlement by altering the legal conditions of land ownership to create communities, and consequently interests, organized around the possession of water rights, which were allocated on the basis of geological studies of drainage and water supply, to be regulated and limited to assure that the rights were meaningful. The solution did not prevail. But the proposals certainly advanced the discussion, and what eventually emerged as policy reflected in some respects the arguments he made for the interrelations of the various aspects of the problems.[6] Powell did something crucial by going beyond the casuistical application of geological expertise to produce a genuinely novel, political/legal/geological/agricultural/land policy definition of the problem that enabled an exchange of opinion on a newly defined issue. It is this kind of rational discussion that the 'paradigm plus faith' model of expertise rules out as impossible.

The reason for the failure of the 'paradigm plus faith' and information accounts can now be seen more clearly. There *are* questions of the validity of the particular claims of scientists and other special domain 'experts' and questions about the validity of the domains themselves. A decision can be made to treat astronomy as neutral and valid and astrology as invalid or simply to exclude it from consideration along with religion. And these decisions can be made, indeed must be, on 'political' grounds, meaning not in the language of the specialized domain, but on 'ordinary' grounds: practical expedience, the trustworthiness of science, or constitutional tradition, among many possibilities.

These questions about particular claims would be unjustified, or at least very peculiar, if they were directed at core statements of science such as Maxwell's equations, or core statements of legal precepts such as law school case examples of legal liability. But they are not. They are directed at casuistic applications of the principles or truths established in those special domains. Climatologists select the variables in their models and analogize and simplify a real world which, it is certain, will behave differently than the model, just as the lawyer simplifies a complex situation to select those features which are legally relevant. It is a further decision – a decision to accept a casuistic extension – to accept these simplifications or their implications and to act politically on them.

With this we come to a more important result. The reasoning of experts in these special domains may be 'better' than that of non-experts. Non-experts may even come to incorporate the results, and some of the patterns of reasoning, justifying, and inferring, into 'normal' public reasoning. But problems of applicability and relevance, the problems associated with casuistic analogizing, do not go away. These problems typically cannot be reduced to the problems that can be solved in the limited conceptual range and self-imposed limits of methodology and theory of the special 'expert' domain. Completeness of understanding within the expert domain is not completeness enough for this purpose. So there is a continuing need for discussion that evaluates relevance, plausibility, and applicability, and this discussion can only be carried on outside the limits of the expert domain, and therefore of expertise itself.

This account allows for rational discussions in which problem formulations and solutions that are genuinely novel and genuinely belong to no paradigm or expert domain can emerge and be discussed 'rationally'. The 'rationality' appropriate to this discussion is of course a compound of evaluative reasoning about expert opinion and about the opinions themselves. The weight and credibility of a claim is a matter of degree and the judgments about them are influenced by the credibility of the proposer and the credibility of the grounds for proposing it. Considerations of objectivity, inherent bias in science, neutrality, and perhaps many other things are entirely appropriate parts of the making of these judgments, and the judgments warrant not belief in the paradigm of the proposer but in the partial paraphrases, intelligible to us, that we have distilled from the proposer's claims, or that the proposer has distilled for us.

This account also makes sense of the kinds of discussions and negotiations that occur and can occur within standard-setting bodies, within commissions involving citizens and scientists and interested parties in dealing with such questions as the regulation of biotechnology, genetic engineering, and so forth. These committees are of course political devices, which have no magical 'authority' but which can prove themselves useful if their conclusions are not mere compromises but are intelligent arguments for policies that politicians and citizens can accept, and because such committees can earn legitimacy. By simply bringing together participants who represent a variety of interests a modicum of balance can be achieved, and the meaning of 'balance' can be better understood: as a situation in which no single interest predominates or determines outcomes. Consequently, genuine rational discussion, defined in terms of the openness of *all* parties to persuasion about the truth or justice of some course of action, can have an effect on outcomes by shifting the pre-existing balance of interests.[7]

This effort at establishing conditions of discussion that prevent it from being sham can be aided by excluding, by convention, stipulation, or agreement, those issues on which 'experts' might *legitimately* claim special knowledge in order to prevent them from illegitimately doing so in the course of discussion. But the decision about what is 'legitimate' and 'illegitimate', and where to draw the line, is, as with the question of what constitutes a religion, ultimately a political question- even if, for political reasons, we choose to let experts make it for us by creating a commission that is asked to give an answer.

This approach also enables us to know what is occurring when bodies of expert scientists of different persuasions and backgrounds are asked to deliver opinions of a consensual kind on vexed scientific-civic questions such as global warming: something other than science, but something that is rational. Furthermore, consensus can be reached *by* scientists, not *of* scientists speaking as scientists but rather the consensus of a group selected according to a convention chosen to see what people with these competencies would say. In the next chapter these and other conventions will be discussed in detail.

Notes

1 Cf. Posner (2001: 162), who analyses the courts themselves in these terms.

2 Theodore Porter provides an extensive discussion of the political uses of objective procedures, emphasizing the political motivations for 'objectivity,' notably the attempt to provide publicly accountable depoliticized grounds for decisions rather than reliance on experts (1995: 196).

3 Of course, the existence of an objective procedure itself tends to create a bias toward resolving issues in terms of it. In *Trust in Numbers* (1995) Ted Porter gives a history of this phenomenon. But biases and trust may be rational in any of several senses. Minimally, decisions based on numbers reduce some costs. As the Chinese reformer Lord Shang saw, they can overcome the biases of personal judgment as well (Handelman 1995)

4 Legal training may itself produce gender biases – or so a major school of feminist jurisprudence argues (MacKinnon 1989).

5 An excellent study of the way in which client communities can produce non-neutrality while preserving 'objectivity' is provided by Daniel Breslau, who studied the use of two expert communities as evaluators of the success of job-training programs. The experts offered different 'objective' methods, those of econometrics (performed by prestigious academics) and those of applied psychology (performed by 'beltway bandits'). Job-training programs were mandated to demonstrate their effectiveness. Government bureaucrats wished to justify the programs. The econometricians showed no effects; the psychologists showed some effects. They became the experts of choice for the policy community, despite their lack of 'scientific' prestige and legislative eagerness to abolish the programs. This study beautifully illustrates the complexities of the issues and the organizational embeddedness of expert 'consensus' (Breslau 1998).

6 See Reisner (1986) for a vivid account of the ongoing consequences of the compromises that were built into the policy that ultimately emerged.

7 Schmitt's point in using 'truth and justice' was to distinguish this kind of discourse from the brokering of interests, which doesn't involve persuading anyone to change beliefs.

4

Filling the Gap: The Rise of Knowledge Associations and 'Expertization'

> Once upon a time, it was thought necessary to protect democracy against the machinations of the Dr. Strangeloves of the world who would hide their moral obtuseness or viciousness behind a command of esoteric lore. Now all sides have their scientists. The problem is not only how to choose between rival views based on access to the same body of knowledge but also how to know enough to make sense of the subject. The scientific literature is more specialized than ever, but the controversies now give us, as citizens, a better chance to make up our own minds. (Aaron Wildavsky 1995 :396)

In Chapter 1 I remarked that recent theorists of liberalism had (with a few exceptions) ignored the phenomena of both science and expertise. I left open the question of whether they might have been justified in doing so, but pointed out that a considerable part of present day politics as depicted in the daily press (also, one might add, exhibited in parliamentary and, in the United States, congressional hearings and supreme court cases) has to do with the assessment and utilization of expert opinion. In Chapter 2 I considered the problem this poses for liberal theory, namely that the inequalities of knowledge produced by the phenomenon of expertise may in and of themselves subvert the conditions of liberal democracy, which presume at least some sort of practical equality, at least sufficient for 'discussion', between the various participants in the discussion through which governing is accomplished – including, in the category of 'governing', both decision-making and legitimation. I identified two sets of circumstances – two types of expert – for which there was a problem of 'democratic deficit'.

In essence, approaching the problem of knowledge simply with the raw concept of expertise is insufficient. Some kinds of expertise, including many of the forms of expertise that writers on these subjects have considered to be paradigmatic of expertise itself, such as science in the narrow sense, pose very little 'threat' because there are rarely problems in simply agreeing to delegate to the relevant community (of physicists or herpetologists, or hematologists, as the case may be) the problem of determining what the participants in public discourses should treat as fact. This chapter also showed that there were forms of expertise that could not be taken 'off the table'. These forms of expertise had some characteristic and problematic features. One of these kinds of expertise is concerned, at least in part, with influencing public opinion in order to produce political results.

The example of this I gave was the Social Survey movement. But there are innumerable other cases, many involving scientists speaking to the public or to organizations representing experts whose aim is to influence public opinion. David Guston has called some of these organizations 'boundary organizations' (2000). Since this kind of expertise is not for sale to its intended user, but is given away to the public, it necessarily requires funding, which raises the familiar problem of conflicts of interest. A typical case would be an 'educational' program about global warming funded by a political movement or business group with interests that are affected or potentially affected by political actions that might be taken in response to global warming. The other problematic form of expertise is expertise employed by bureaucrats using discretionary powers, and who, so to speak, belong to a culture or community of persons with similar 'knowledge', and operate in terms of a consensus that is internal to this community and, practically speaking, unchecked by public scrutiny – unchecked because the discretionary decisions of these bureaucrats are themselves, practically speaking, unchecked by public scrutiny.[1]

The two types are not completely distinct. Professional organizations designed to serve the 'informational needs' of experts in bureaucracies often speak to the public as well. In each case they may be self-funded membership organizations, or enjoy some sort of official recognition and status. And in some cases, such as professional certifying associations of lawyers, Bar associations, they may become activist organizations with political agendas, and terms that purport to be neutral, such as 'judicially qualified', have a significance which the legal experts themselves recognize as no longer uncontroversially 'neutral'.

In the following chapter I went on to consider the puzzle of what public scrutiny and more generally rational persuasion could possibly consist of in the face of expert knowledge, if the situation is understood as one in which one co-discussant, the citizen, cannot fully understand another, the expert. I ask whether this situation in and of itself made public discussion into an elaborate sham that did little more than conceal an actuality of largely mindless but necessary subordination to experts. Here again, it proved useful to make some distinctions between the kinds of claims made by experts and to consider what sort of cognitive resources, and what sort of practically feasible means of judging, could be reasonably ascribed to ordinary public discussion. I pointed out that the case of science, again, is misleading as a model, simply because the actual core beliefs certified by the ordinary processes of certification of the scientific community very seldom are problematic for public discussion, if only because it is seldom the case that anything in the core of science is in any way decisive for public issues, and because politicians have an interest in avoiding conflicts with results at the core of science, and for the most part do in fact avoid such conflicts.

Matters are quite different with respect to large and important zones of discussion that employ 'objective' procedures of various kinds, sometimes with, and sometimes without, the addition of significant content from the core of science, to provide predictions or facts that *can* be utilized in public discussion. Judgments about these objective results are often quite difficult because the grounds for the results are often difficult to assess. They are 'objective' because the procedures for getting from the premise to the conclusion are publicly accessible, replicable, and at least comprehensible to persons familiar with the techniques themselves. Some of this knowledge may be very arcane, such as knowledge of the accounting rules used to determine future liabilities for pensions, or the statistical problems of selection that arise in assessing the impact of job training programs, the concern of a recent Nobel laureate, James Heckman (Breslau 1998: 71-72, 83-85).

The difficulty faced by the outsider to the community of those who are adept at these techniques, be they econometricians, accountants, or global warming model-builders, is to distinguish what they should treat as fact and 'objective', on the one hand, and on the other, what they should regard as a matter of questionable and politically relevant assumption and open to non-expert discussion. *Typically* the models used by experts in policy settings require particular assumptions or particular definitions of the problem in order that their objective technical features, their calculations, can operate on the data in order to produce policy relevant conclusions. And because these cannot be obtained either from science or from uncontroversial common sense, they are necessarily mixed creations that require a different and more suspicious consumer response.

There is a sense, however, that the fact of interest-the possibility that any discussant in the public domain is arguing out of self-interest, concealed ideological interest, values or religious motivation, or open motivation of those kinds- is familiar as a central condition of liberal democratic discussion in the first place. The experience of liberalism has shown that at least under many circumstances it is possible to make issues about interest into a relevant part of public discussion without completely de-rationalizing it in the sense of making it impossible to rationally persuade others with respect to the facts or to ends and other beliefs. When a drug manufacturer delivers opinions on patent protection or drug costs, ordinary citizens know that the manufacturer has interests affected by public policies that relate to these subjects. The relevant question in the face of these two novel kinds of expertise is whether the techniques of assessing, discounting for, and interpreting in terms of considerations of interest also work for them. If this and other devices fail in the face of new kinds of claims, then there is a genuine and serious problem regarding the competence of public discussion, of whether citizens and their representatives are capable of reasonable discussion in the face of these claims, that does indeed support the suspicion that this discussion is essentially a sham. However, the very fact that so much discussion, and such lively and contentious discussion, occurs in the public press on such matters suggests that while there is a continuous learning process with respect to these kinds of expert claims, which implies that there is also a capacity to deal with these kinds of questions that can and does increase with experience.

We could, at this point, ask, as Joseph Schumpeter did ([1942] 1950), if the demands of assessing expert knowledge will outrun the capacities of citizens and therefore of the discussion that governing in liberal democracy depends upon to retain its specific character. Or we could express the optimistic hope that an aroused citizenry, attuned to the evils of expert knowledge, will reject it and demand participatory power. Doing so would avoid the interesting question of understanding the new form of liberalism that the omnipresence of expert knowledge claims has begun to produce. We could, in effect, put the problem back in the original categories of liberal democratic theory. But doing so, I have been suggesting, would be a mistake. The problem of the relation between expert knowledge and liberal discussion, especially the joint problem of our dependence on experts and our practical inability to fully understand and hence to judge them, is one that pervades our political institutions and public life. What is needed is to understand the changed way in which politics proceeds and can proceed in the face of this novel situation of pervasive expertise. As a question of political theory that requires us to look at expert knowledge in terms of political forms, both in the formal sense of the actual legal arrangements and the devices that administrations, citizens, and legislatures have devised to deal with them, and in the informal sense of the substance of the underlying relationships that these forms express. But the issue goes significantly beyond looking at novel political devices for the employment of expert knowledge. Many older political forms change their meaning in the face of expertise, so we need also to rethink the significance of many familiar institutions, such as courts and legislatures, and the kinds of voluntary associations that have traditionally been thought of simply as social movements, for today these typically involve expert knowledge.

Behind these questions is a simple political fact. There is a gap between the demand for expert opinions and solutions to problems, and the supply. To some extent this gap is a matter of inappropriate expectations, for example, for science to cure diseases, produce technologies, and make predictions. To some extent the demand is artificial: claims of expertise, and expert claims, produce the demands. To claim that cell phone users have higher than expected brain cancer rates produces a demand for explanations, cures, and prevention. There is a general sense that technology produces new risks that require new expert knowledge: no amount of past medicine or physics will fully answer questions about clusters of cell phone brain cancers; instead new inquiries, and perhaps new objective methods and theories and new forms of expert knowledge are required.

If we de-essentialize these terms – expert, knowledge, science, and so forth – in the manner of the last chapter, we can avoid the problems of determining whether knowledge is 'really' knowledge, demands for expertise are 'really' inappropriate, and whether the gap between demand and supply is 'artificial'. The basic 'political' realities remain: discussions occur in which it is suggested that the issues be delegated to experts, that some particular set of expert claims, or some particular claims to expertise, be acknowledged as valid as a basis for political discussions. By the same token, experts package their claims in ways that make them usable for political discussion, for example by producing fact-surrogates or objects, such as reports or other products, that may be treated as 'fact'. These are not, of course, seamless transactions. That supply and demand do not match up should be no surprise. And this is particularly true with respect to science, where self-denying ordinances necessarily prevent it from answering to all the demands placed on it.

Commissions and 'Knowledge Associations'

Of course, one of the striking features of the fact of expertise *has* been the creation of novel political or quasi-political collective institutions. Advocates of democratic control of science and technological innovation and development implicitly acknowledge the difficulty faced by ordinary citizens in understanding technological issues. Sometimes they have responded to this by scare tactics and simplifications. But other times they have proposed novel institutional devices, such as committees with strong citizen representation, or alternatively, constituency representation structured in such a way that a process of mutual education and persuasion replaces top-down expert pronouncements. The models include councils that might be composed of experts of various kinds as well as representatives of particular interests (such as utility companies or manufacturers whose operations are likely to be subject to regulation) together with 'ordinary' citizens. These are forms of representation. Individuals either are taken in some sense to represent simply the category of the ordinary citizen or sometimes specially defined user categories. (For example, in the case of health care advisory committees, senior citizens or recipients of particular kinds of aid.) Sometimes the appointees are citizen activists who are taken to be representatives of larger movements and are paid or unpaid participants in organizations that have as their agenda particular policy stances, such as opposition to genetically engineered food or the unethical treatment of animals (Sclove 1997).

Focusing on these novel forms, however, produces something of an illusion – the illusion that there is something fundamentally novel here. In fact there is not. Delegating powers to a body that claims to represent, or is constituted to represent, is a familiar governmental device. Indeed it is a form of rule: in Rome, as Carl Schmitt pointed out, the institution of the dictator was a legal form, in which an individual was delegated dictatorial powers for a limited period to deal with a particular crisis. In this case the dictator's commission was a means of preserving the form of state that gave the commission - itself a useful model to keep in mind in what follows. The institutions I will consider here can be understood, loosely, on the model of commissions as well. Three basic types can be distinguished very simply on the basis of their legal status.

Commissions

When bodies are created by governments, they are known historically as commissions, because the state grants a particular portion of its powers for the performance of a particular task. The model of commission has a long history. Commissions became popular in Tudor England, where the practice was not to create commissions as an extension of parliament or the courts but as an extension of the administration. Subsequently, legislatures also created commissions, and the powers devolved to commissions are often judicial in character. As such, a commission is a pre-liberal form that occupies a somewhat mysterious place in the scheme of liberal politics. Commissions have traditionally been associated with expertise in the broadest sense, and if we consider problems that administrations and legislatures have in dealing with matters that are not part of common knowledge, we can see why the commission is such a useful form.

Commissions can be constructed with multiple members selected with the hope of providing balance, and indeed many commissions are specifically designed to be balanced between parties or alternatively between the opposing sides of some question. The nineteenth century Labor Statistics movement in the USA began with fact-finding commissions formed to inquire into problems of unemployment. The legislative support for the commissions came from workingmen's factions, but the appointments to the commission were 'balanced' so that the commission would be credible to both sides. The appointments included well respected figures. The thought is often that persons can be chosen for the commission who possess some sort of personal legitimacy or can serve in an informal sense as representative of a side to a controversy. More importantly, perhaps, the commission may be selected with an eye toward assembling a large proportion of the persons with significant credibility with respect to some issue, such as the causes of variations in adolescent pregnancy rates, in order that discussions that lead to consensus recommendations can be held which then have, if not unanimity, legitimacy that far outweighs that of individual critics or dissenters from the recommendation. And potential dissenters can be co-opted or marginalized.

As I have argued in the last chapter, *within* a commission, depending on how it is constructed, one faces exactly the same problems of rational persuasion, whether between experts with different backgrounds or experts and non-experts, as exist in any representative liberal institution. Nevertheless one may reasonably claim that, in commissions set up to deal with a specific topic, the obstacles to rational persuasion produced by the lack of relevant knowledge and the distractions of other business are eliminated, or much mitigated, making these bodies much more effective in coming to conclusions than ordinary legislative bodies, while preserving the character of liberal persuasion within them.

Non-Governmental Organizations that Function as Collective Knowledge Bodies

The commission form is available for supra-state bodies as well as for state bodies, indeed international commissions such as the Intergovernmental Panel on Climate Change were formed precisely with an eye to eliminating suspicion of national bias. But it is also striking that these bodies can be constructed in more or less the same fashion by non-governmental organizations to represent, for example, particular industries (for example, with respect to standard setting) or particular groups of experts who represent stakeholders in some particular policy domain, thus creating private 'monopolies of expertise' rather than the publicly created monopolies of expertise familiar from the commission model. Such arrangements are expressions of collective power. One might consider such opinion monopolies as themselves amounting to an attempt to usurp the element of discussion in 'government by discussion'. In these cases the attempt is itself usually the subject of discussion and indeed the subject of precisely the kind of discussion, notably the discussions of self-interest and bias, that liberal democracies are practiced at conducting. Thus, like commissions, they preserve the prospect of 'government by discussion' by breaking discussion down into manageable units.

Commissions from Below: Social Movements as Expertise

A third type of organization is, so to speak, a commission from below, such as an NGO (non-governmental organization) that represents or is at least supported by some interested parties, and which makes 'expert' claims or criticizes other expert claims. The rapid evolution of this kind of organization is one of the most dramatic changes in recent politics. The Sierra Club, Greenpeace, PETA (People for the Ethical Treatment of Animals), and the WWF (World Wildlife Fund) are bodies that use expert knowledge to lobby, to litigate, and in the United States play an expert role by providing friend-of-the-court briefs. They represent a cause, but they are also enterprises that require donors. They are thus 'interested' in several senses: interested in keeping the organization going, and in the cause that the organization's subscribers support.

Organizations of this sort are not new. The social reform organizations of the late nineteenth and early twentieth centuries were very similar, and equally effective. They employed similar strategies – promoted a policy agenda and backed it by facts, educational programs, and claims to expert authority or support by experts, and so forth. Contemporary versions of these organizations differ primarily with respect to the way they are financed – through professionals using marketing practices rather than through donations collected at meetings or secured from wealthy 'angels'.

Boundary Organizations

A particularly interesting fourth type of organization can take any of these three legal forms, but is distinguished by a novel feature: the claim to 'represent' in two directions, usually from a body of expert opinion or knowledge to a user community and from the users back to the experts. A recent working group identified and studied five examples: the Health Effects Institute, Agricultural Extension, the Sea Grant program, the International Research Institute for Climate Prediction, and the Subsidiary Body for Scientific and Technological Advice (Guston et al. 2000). These organizations are living forms that do a kind of work similar to some other media of expert-user relations, known as 'boundary objects' or 'standardized packages'. A geological survey is a boundary object. It is usable to non-geologists but is produced by scientists as a research outcome. 'Standardized packages' are forms of expert-user cooperation, such as the doctor-patient relationship, which provide a framework of flexible mutual expectations on which both sides can rely.

A Tocquevillian Politics of Knowledge Organizations?

These political forms are so central to current politics that they are almost unnoticed. Much of what governs our daily life is the product of commissions of various kinds. The labels on the food we eat, the standards for the air we breathe, and much else is the product of collective decision-making by bodies of this sort, and when the standards or practices are contested, they are contested by other bodies. To take a very simple example of the hidden power of these organizations, consider the simple artifact of the child's playground. In the US, the standards for playgrounds were produced by a knowledge movement subsidized by the Russell Sage Foundation during the first part of the twentieth century. The standards it defined were made an issue in Social Surveys of various kinds promoted by reform groups, promoted by playground associations in each city, and taken up by civic betterment associations, and in a short time accepted by cities as normal (Sealander 1997). This led to a certain uniformity of product, and therefore of experience in the daily life of children – the life-world. Yet this movement was in large part a 'Commission from Below'. No powerful governmental agency authorized it. Its political success depended on the acceptance and endorsement of local leaders and community activists, who pressured municipalities to live up to the standards.[2]

There seems to be no reason in principle why a politics that consists, to a very significant extent, indeed perhaps in the end almost exclusively, of discussions of this limited kind could not amount to a workable form of government. We could consider it a kind of liberalism. 'Public opinion' in such a world would for the most part be opinion about the credibility of expert opinion (and user group opinion and stakeholders' opinions), and serve a largely regulative function, stepping in when a 'commission' goes wrong.

Nor would it be contrary to the fundamental idea of government by discussion. Certainly, disagreeing with the actions of particular opinion-producing bodies might be part of this politics, especially in the periods before delegation occurs. Perhaps this is precisely the point. To be an expert in this politics would mean that in the end one would be accountable to the judgment of public bodies. So the expert would still face the problems of credibility and legitimacy of the sort that are characteristic of public accountability in liberal democracies. However, this would *not* be a liberalism of public opinion as a basis of a centralized sovereign legislature with a powerful (and largely self sufficient with respect to knowledge) bureaucracy, a mass society with a faceless bureaucracy. It would be a Tocquevilleian form in which the bulk of 'political' activity, that is to say the bulk of the rational persuasion, is done in intermediate bodies that the central state is compelled to respect and take seriously, because it has no self sufficient alternative source of knowledge, and because these bodies have their own legitimacy as 'expert' or 'knowledgeable'.

Describing such a form of rule as 'liberal' or as 'government by discussion' obviously is a radical extension of these concepts. This is not 'popular sovereignty' except in the most limited formal sense. The fact of proliferation of non-governmental organizations reflecting internal rational consensuses of various kinds is nevertheless important evidence for the existence of an important new political phenomenon. There is an emerging layer of intermediate institutions on the international level. Their existence suggests that the future of a world politics in which issues like global warming, pollution, and agricultural technology are themselves beyond the control of individual states is necessarily going to be a politics in which intermediate bodies of this sort balance state power. The political implication of the increased significance of expertise, if it is expressed through these bodies, might not be a future of international hegemonic bodies governed by experts, on the model of the European Community, which itself relies very heavily on commissions, but a world in which the expertise of these bodies is continuously challenged by international intermediate knowledge associations.

Such a world could be one in which a great many knowledge 'have nots' are left out of these processes. But even in such areas as economic development and humanitarian aid policy one can see the rapid and substantial extension of participatory models as a consequence of policy failures. Failures in the implementation of programs have led donor bureaucracies to either grant stakeholder and participatory status to the indigenous peoples who are the beneficiaries of aid or to actively seek out participants who can serve as representatives who are possessors of relevant indigenous knowledge and relevant knowledge of indigenous ways, on the model of the commissions discussed above (Agrawal 1995). That participation involves a process of mutual education is a given. The bodies only work if the participants, on all sides, meet the minimal model of rational persuasion with which Chapter 3 began. In this sense they embody the liberal idea.

Expertization

A world of intermediate associations that represent a consensus or the collective affirmation and acceptance of something as knowledge is not a utopian vision. To a great extent it has already arrived. One should expect the persistence of conflict with respect to various issues, especially between traditional interest groups or groups whose origins are in traditional ideological or sectarian religious or nationalist movements. However, the tendency of even these kinds of associations to recreate themselves as knowledge associations, whose claim to credibility rests on a claim to expertise, is intriguing. One no longer finds causes – even such causes as those of peasant rebels in remote regions, such as Chiapas, Mexico – without the machinery of knowledge associations: experts, study groups, talking heads, and so on. These now seem to be the minimum requisite for full participation in contests for legitimacy. It is also striking to see groups emerging as or transforming themselves into what are in effect knowledge associations so as to better influence policy. If one goes back fifty years, one would find an association such as the Audubon Society in the US to be a large and successful group consisting of persons who shared the hobby of bird watching and used various services related to these interests that the association provided. Today it is quite clearly a knowledge association of the kind I have described here in which there is, on the one hand, a claim to objectivity with respect to the facts about which birders can claim to know, such as the results of bird censuses and so forth, as well as, on the other, a clear bias in favor of birds, the protection of bird habitats, and the promotion of policies that protect birds.

The tropism toward associations taking this form is in a way a genuine political novelty. The associations Tocqueville had in mind seldom were primarily concerned with problems of knowledge. Now, to be an effective political association it has become necessary to become a knowledge association: to be expertized. In describing the rise of these organizations, I have not particularly emphasized the content of the knowledge they claim, and indeed the organizations that arise largely as protests against globalization, industrialization, pollution, modern economic life, and so forth, are in a sense anti-knowledge movements. Nevertheless what is characteristic of them is that they are highly aware of the knowledge claims of their opponents and are also concerned to contest these claims, frequently from the point of view of, or through making, knowledge claims of their own, for example, knowledge claims based on personal experience or empathy or claims transmitted through the media which they take to refute the knowledge claims of the more authoritative bodies they oppose. By doing this, they too become knowledge organizations.

'Expertization' is a term that can be applied to state bureaucracies, and indeed to private organizations as well. There is a long history of expert bureaucracies, and regulatory agencies need expertise. They have already been 'expertized'. But other organizations or state bureaucracies that are engaged in activities taken up by knowledge associations, such as the

Audubon Society, are compelled to transform themselves into knowledge organizations. A city government, concerned with such mundane matters as providing building permits, may find its actions challenged on environmental grounds. To respond, it must have its own experts, and eventually it too becomes 'expertized' – capable not only of following routines, but of adapting to the changing demands of new expert claims made by the organizations in their environment. Today, any large enterprise must become expertized in this sense.

Self-Denial as the Political Strategy of Experts

In what I have said so far, it might seem that I have irretrievably confused three entirely different political or quasi-political phenomena: voluntary associations, scientific bodies, and commissions, that is to say, agencies that are themselves arms of the state. Of course, the legal status of the three is distinct. But even these distinctions are not clear, and a good many organizations ambiguously fall in two or more of these categories simultaneously. The British term 'quango' was invented to describe quasi-non-governmental organizations, exemplifying the problem of classification.

Classification is a distraction: an attempt to reduce the phenomenon to categories that are no longer definitive. Is the Bar association of an American state a private voluntary organization or effectively an arm of the judicial system? The powers delegated to the Bar association involving disciplinary powers over legal practice – the ability to represent clients before the courts – are state powers. The organization is not. The National Academy of Sciences in the United States is a government constituted advisory body that self-selects its members and is designed to provide independent opinion about matters that governmental bodies may put to it. Is it public or private? Whom does it represent? Many of the commissions that have been established to provide unbiased expert opinion have a similarly ambiguous legal status, and a mismatch between the formal sources of their powers or funding and their representative role.

More important is the fact that these bodies took the form of knowledge associations in response to the same kinds of problems. Many of the policy concerns of voluntary organizations, such as the Sierra Club and the Audubon Society, arose specifically as a response to bureaucratic expertise (or failures of bureaucratic expertise) and as a means of correcting policies based on what was perceived to be political expedience or bureaucratic convenience as well as bad science or badly designed policy misusing science. Commissions, voluntary associations accumulating expertise, and bureaucracies, which among other things are expected to be bound in some fashion by the findings of commissions or legislators acting on the findings of commissions, are all thus related to one another dialectically: the one calls forth the other and others arise in response. A particularly striking example of this is found in the history of cholera epidemics. The inept health commission of the City of New York was countered by a voluntary organization of physicians who criticized proposed policies, and eventually prevailed by action of the state legislature to replace the city body with a different expert body with authority legally rooted in the state's powers (Rosenberg 1962).

It may seem that scientific expertise is in some fashion the exception: it represents no interest. But of course scientists have an interest in their careers, in the support of their own research, and many other things, just as bureaucrats do. The difference between a society of zoologists and the Audubon Society is not so much in their form, though they may have quite different membership requirements and different purposes written into their bylaws, but in the character of the self-denying ordinances by which they operate. The peculiar power of science, especially science operating in its capacity as a collective body, is as a result of the exceptionally stringent character of its self-limitations: nothing is a scientific fact that is not universally accepted by scientists as such and derived by methods universally accepted by them as scientific. Constructivist analysts of science are quite right to insist that these lines are mutable and that the theoretical language with which scientists characterize the science/non-science distinction is mostly misleading about the way in which the distinction is actually drawn in history and over time. Nevertheless, the aim of drawing such a line, which is sometimes conscious and explicit, though rarely fully explicit, is to assure that the questions that arise in science are the kinds of questions that science can answer, which also is to say the kinds of questions that scientific evidence or arguments can rationally persuade other scientists to accept. The reason something is treated by scientists as nonscientific is precisely because scientists cannot envision a means by which the kinds of evidence and arguments they ordinarily deploy could be persuasive to other persons trained in the use of these arguments and knowledgeable about what has already been established through these arguments. This protective use of the science/non-science distinction thus is analogous to the protective withdrawal of the state from matters of religious conscience that we have seen is central to liberalism, and to its perennially precarious achievement of standards of civility, standards which allow into politics only the sorts of questions on which people are willing to be bound by the democratic process.

One can find many analogies to these kinds of boundaries in other specialized discursive domains, including religion itself, in which particular religious groups, in order to avoid schisms, limit what can count as a religious question, subject either to the authority of a congregation or a bishop or the teachers of a religious tradition in order that these subjects make religious consensus impossible. In the case of the law, law schools and law professors make a distinction between questions of policy and questions of law that is artificial and characteristically only vaguely understood by the ordinary citizens who are consumers of the legal process. But the distinction serves to create a subset of the kinds of action which might be brought before a court: a subset of issues that enables legal consensus, in the sense of coherent legal continuity and predictability sufficient for lawyers to be able to more or less successfully predict what courts will do and also for judges to reason in ways that other judges would accept. Clearly if courts regarded themselves as competent to address all the questions that came before them bound only by the threat of reversal by higher courts, both legality and legal knowledge would collapse simultaneously. So the self-denying ordinances characteristic of scientific discourse thus are simply examples of a much more general phenomenon. They are analogous to the basic legislative institutions of political liberalism itself, understood as a scheme for creating a limited space in a representative body in which political persuasion is possible by limiting the powers of the body, either by rule, or custom, or delegation.

The larger phenomenon is this: associations can make stronger knowledge claims than individuals by concentrating opinion, by resolving disagreements internally, and by answering, in one fashion or another, questions about the credibility of their claims. This is done by self-limitation: by rules that the organization applies to select its members, by rules limiting the claims to competence the association makes, by the transparency of its finances, and by other means. The visible voluntary devotion of its followers is itself a kind of proof of the sincerity of its cause.

To be 'apolitical' is a political strategy with political results. Claims to disinterestedness are strategies, strategies for eliminating the suspicion of partisanship or self-interest. But the strategies have a cost. The claims must be lived up to in conduct, typically through the enforcement of boundaries around what is said to represent the bodies and what cannot be said. In many cases the strategy is to openly acknowledge one's interests, as with the Audubon Society. Whatever discounting is done by the people who are addressed or persuaded by the society is limited to the innocuous, such as the perception that the Society's real interest is in protecting birds, a topic on which they are sincere but perhaps a bit overenthusiastic. It is a constant feature of discussion of these kinds of organizations as to whether such a perception about interest is correct. A typical question in liberal discourse is 'who is "behind" an organization?', meaning who might be using the organization for their own concealed ends. There are characteristic ways, such as pursuing its finances, of answering these questions, and similarly, of fending off suspicion. Not only do these strategies have a cost, they also serve as self-selected, self-enforced limitations on the content of the opinions that the knowledge association can establish a consensus on.

What one may visualize here is a huge and deeply fractious discussion in which real collective bodies with real existence as legal and economic entities struggle to survive and to persuade. Politically significant expertise characteristically takes a collective form: expert claims are not simply 'ideas' thrown into the 'marketplace' by individuals, but are more like petitions in the sense that they are persuasive because they purport to represent a *de facto* monopoly of competent opinion, or at least such a substantial proportion of competent opinion that they cannot be dismissed by persons engaged in traditional parliamentary discussion, or by bureaucrats claiming to be using their discretion impartially.

Politicians and the participants in liberal persuasion are adept at understanding the relationship between claims and interests and consequently discount such advocates as the expert physicists who claim that science will be terribly damaged if billions of dollars are not invested in new particle physics facilities, or physicians who insist that medical care will be severely damaged if physicians are not allowed to make more money.

Politicians do their best to avoid colliding with expert opinion when it is genuinely disinterested. And it is relatively easy for them to do so precisely because what disinterested bodies can agree about amounts in one sense to a great deal but in another sense to very little. The associations that enter into politics by purveying knowledge and claiming expertise, and are the vehicles through which knowledge has force, seldom are politically innocent in the sense of being disinterested. There is no expert body that is omnicompetent and even the most powerful scientific collectivities depend on self-restrictions to free themselves of the suspicion that their claims to competence and disinterestedness are ill founded. These bodies have their greatest effect when they can concentrate the greatest quantity of intellectual legitimacy at the smallest point. Thus there cannot be an expert culture that directly faces and competes with liberal democracy, but only a myriad of competing knowledge associations that gain power through monopolizing opinion through narrowing the domain within which the monopoly is held. Even the most august general scientific body is vulnerable to the concentration of collective opinion in one of its subdomains. If a group of scientists in some particular small expert domain was moved to disagree with prevailing opinion, and it did so on the basis of some point over which it could reasonably claim a monopoly of opinion, it is likely that it, rather than the general body would prevail. And this suggests that monopolization of opinion is itself a self-limiting phenomenon, self-limiting in a way that renders it no real or permanent danger to liberal opinion or the phenomenon of government by discussion.

Or does it? One must be wary of an illusion. The great attempt of scientists in the last century to assert themselves politically was the Atomic scientists movement. It was an abject failure with respect to its main aims. It failed to achieve nuclear disarmament, the international control of atomic weaponry, or international comity through the personal exchanges between scientists of warring nations. The movement nevertheless had political impact in the form of propaganda value – for which scientists who supported it won various prizes, from the Lenin to the Nobel Peace prize. One of the grim pleasures of reading old issues of *Science*, particularly from the early sixties, is seeing the record of the insistence of western scientists on the importance of their special access to Soviet scientists, on their ability to settle important policy questions by negotiating directly with them, and so forth. The arguments they gave for their special authority in the arena of nuclear warfare and strategy were expansive, based for the most part on a simple claim: that the basic physical processes involved in making bombs were understood properly by them alone; they ought to decide their uses.

These expansive assertions of political right were largely ignored, though they produced a number of public figures and science celebrities, from P.M.S Blackett to Edward Teller.

Scientists eventually, for the most part at least, withdrew from these claims. There was never the near-unanimity needed to claim that 'science' itself deserved what was demanded. But the episode was also a learning experience. Scientists established organizations, some of which survive, such as the Federation of American Scientists. These are 'boundary organizations', or 'commissions from below' presenting themselves as boundary organizations. They produce standardized objects, such as reports of danger, seek publicity, and collect money.

Why is 'Science Proper' Special?

Self-denying normative structures of the kind found in different forms in many 'knowledge associations' play a particularly prominent role in science, and to understand what makes science distinctive as a knowledge association, and to understand the 'power' of science, requires the application of 'principal-agent' theory. The subject of this theory is trust in the face of asymmetries of knowledge. These are not unique to science. A stockbroker should be aggressive and motivated by money. A stockbroker who is not would be unlikely to do what was required to retain your business. Similarly, a lawyer needs to be aggressive and motivated by money in order to do anything on your behalf. Yet at the same time both lawyer and stockbroker must substitute the client's interest for their own interests. Therefore in each case there are visibly enforced self-denying ordinances. The norms of legal representation and stockbroking are characteristically statements of the absolute subordination of the stockbroker's and lawyer's interests to the client's interests.

Scientists have a large and complex set of institutions that in one fashion or another involve people acting (or speaking) authoritatively on behalf of science. Science is thus 'political' in a mundane sense. Scientists make authoritative *decisions* in the name of others, such as on behalf of organizations or collective bodies, or in the name of science itself, and have such decisions made about them. Many of these are 'gatekeeping' decisions, and indeed the business of gatekeeping is perhaps the primary means of exercising authority in science. The making of evaluative decisions and the exercise of authority or advisory authority is a pervasive fact of scientific life; in directing the work of subordinates, in asking funding bodies for resources, and the like. But this political 'decision-making' character of science is also a largely undiscussed fact – whether by commentators on science, philosophers of science, or sociologists of science.[3]

The reason for this neglect, in part, is that these decisions occur under a particular theory or ideology: the idea that the scientists making the decisions are operating neutrally or meritocratically, and that the public role of science itself is neutral. A scientist who reviews articles or gives out prizes acts on behalf of 'science', just like any other representative exercising discretionary power. But the scientist is not acting 'politically' in an illegitimate sense – precisely because the scientist is conceived to be a perfect and impersonal representative of science. Science is thus mundanely political, but its overtly political features are conceived to be unpolitical. In political terms, we may think of this as the representational myth of science.

When scientists exert discipline, reward, exclude, or accept, they act as 'agents' or representatives; and when it is done on behalf of a journal or professional society, the society itself is the political embodiment of a collectivity. If we ask 'what does a scientist gain by being a citizen of the scientific community, and what does he or she give up in exchange?', the answer must be, roughly, that the scientist gains the power to speak as a scientist, to participate in the certification of knowledge (which I will shortly call 'bonding'), and to be heard by other scientists *as* a scientist. These are significant benefits. But in exchange the scientist must accept the results of other scientists and the standards set by the achievements of them. As these standards are not experienced as dictated to the scientist by an 'authority', there is usually a seamless and unselfconscious acceptance and self-application of these standards to the scientist's own work: the scientist for the most part 'internalizes' the standards, and scientists produce with an eye to being bonded by other scientists acting in their capacity as representatives.

Although the discipline of the scientific community is not experienced as the meeting of 'obligations', where this inner discipline breaks down, the hidden political reality shows itself, and 'political' remedies, such as removing individuals from boards, or exclusion from journals, are employed. There have been various 'political' devices for doing this in the history of science. The traditional difference between the French and British Academies of Science is a difference between means: in the British case, informal means of exclusion were used (hence the Gentlemanly ideal); in France, formal means were employed, and controversial scientific claims were themselves judged in a quasi-juridical way, at least in several important cases (cf. Hahn 1971; Collins and Pinch, 1993).

The appropriate contrast to scientists, who are bound up in a complex system of representative certifying bodies, is 'market' experts of the sort discussed in Chapter 2, such as inventors and uncertified therapists, who are not 'members'. The costs and benefits of membership are apparent in the contrast. Unlike inventors, for example, scientists present themselves and their findings as reliable and certified through the adherence of the scientist to accepted scientific procedures. So they need not, like inventors, rely on the performance of specific inventions, or like therapists on the satisfaction of clients. They can trade on the general utility of science, which they represent and are certified to represent.[4]

The power of 'bonding' by the scientific community or by great scientists acting as representatives is quite extraordinary. Consider the case of military technology. In World War I many proposals were made and rejected by the military – proposals made by inventors whose ideas had to be judged with no 'bonding'. In World War II, Einstein signed a letter to Roosevelt, written by Leo Szilard, mentioned earlier, who did not have the same stature, about the possibility of an atomic weapon. Immense resources were invested on the basis of this 'bonded by science' statement. If it had been handled as the proposal of an inventor – and inventors flooded the military with suggestions, almost all of which were ignored – it is quite inconceivable that the investment would have been made.

The judgment of peers is central to this process of certification. But this is not the end of the story: these judgments themselves require bonding because there are known conflicts of interest that arise in judgments of competitors and judgments of work in the same specialty. Evaluators may be biased in judging the general significance of work in a particular area that resembles theirs, and if they are competing for fame and fortune they have a general interest in seeing work that cites and extends theirs being funded. By the same token, they may have an interest in impeding the research of a competitor. Mere collectivization of opinion is not enough. Science does something more, which makes it especially distinctive: its use of 'representative' or political mechanisms is almost entirely indirect, and these mechanisms, such as peer review of journal articles, are themselves disciplined by market competition, competition between 'bonders'. Publishing an article, or awarding a degree, is an act performed by a body which competes with others, for a reputation for quality.

The reputation makes the degree, or the publication, valuable, or credible. So our confidence in the statements made to us by 'a Harvard Ph.D. in Physics' is a result, largely, of a reasonable inference that the individual with the degree has been certified by an institution eager to remain at the top in competition with other institutions, and thus unlikely to give the degree away to an incompetent. Our faith in the writings of this person as science, published in a prominent science journal, is a result of our reasonable inference that the science journal is motivated by analogous competition. And we also reasonably infer that these mechanisms of control are so pervasive, redundant, and effective that scientists are 'kept honest'.

This unusual structure of indirect methods of rule, bonding decisions, market constraints on bonders, and massive redundancy and decentralization of decision-making power can not be easily extended to other topics. Scientific knowledge is what is accepted as scientific by a consensus of competent opinion, meaning that there is no competent minority that rejects it and it has been given competent scrutiny. What counts as 'scientific' may on occasion be contentious, but competent minority opinion ('competent' in the sense of being certified through this system of redundant and overlapping indirect mechanisms) rejecting it suffices to exclude it. That is the theory, at least, and it is this theory that is invoked when criticisms are made of certain scientific claims, such as those of global warming modelers (for example, Singer 1999: 16).

Powerful or Powerless?

Are scientists powerful, or powerless? One answer to the question is that merely appearing on the editorial pages of major newspapers with a statement about policy is a significant achievement requiring a structure of help, collusion, and inside knowledge. The costs of producing an editorial that appears in a large number of newspapers, or making the evening news, are significant. Asserting one's special intellectual authority, identifying the committees and organization that one represents, and the imprimatur of academic rank, with whatever this implies, are all familiar political acts – interventions in discussions by notables representing voluntary organizations are standard moves in liberal democracy. And, in fact, in the US especially, experts at various levels, particularly Type IV experts, paid with an eye to persuading the public, dominate the editorial pages and talk shows on television.

Yet some writers, such as the American journalist Dan Greenberg decry the powerlessness of science. When they do so, they have in mind a variety of comparisons, and a number of indices of power. These include the lack of a cabinet-level department of science, the low status of the congressional committees that govern science, the relatively low status of science advisory positions in the White House, the inability of scientists to establish themselves in traditional civil service structures, such as the State Department (a miniature version of the problem of science in the British civil service system), and, especially, the absence of science as a big player in the domain of big money politics supporting political campaigns (Greenberg 2001: 254). Greenberg also has in mind the quite different thought that some forms of expertise, notably economics, have a large influence in situations where decisions are made, and that defense spending on dubious weapons systems research is large relative to basic science. He also devotes a long discussion to the fact that few scientists hold elective office in the federal government.

Greenberg associates the weakness of science with the withdrawal of scientists from various weapons related advisory panels in the 1980s as a result of the collapse during the Reagan era of their [the scientists] decades long effort to promote arms control (2001: 331-2). Much could be said about this episode, but it needs to be observed that the scientists who were most aggressively in favor of arms control at the time made predictions that were wildly wrong in the direction of doomsaying – more than wrong enough to lead a reasonable person to doubt their competence to deal with the issues. After this, Greenberg argues, American scientists returned to the 'science ghetto' and concerned themselves with the problem of procuring money for science, which they did primarily by making what he exposes as false claims about impending shortages of scientists, international competitive threats, and shortages of research funds.

At the same time, in context after context, Greenberg concedes that scientists have had 'political' roles. They were leading figures in the environmental movement (2001: 321) and scientists are found throughout the government on advisory boards (2001: 149-50). The fact that there is no department of science does not concern them, since their dispersal through agencies gives them access to a variety of different sources of funding. Greenberg also comments on 'boundary' disputes, cases where scientists were accused of partisanship or informed that the issues they were asserting themselves over were political, not scientific issues, cases that indicate the aggressiveness of scientists in making their case (2001: 287-88). But he also recognizes that science funding has flourished when scientists have abstained from partisan politics (2001: 256).

What is one to make of these apparently contradictory claims? Greenberg is not a political theorist. But these claims presuppose a particular·view of politics. What is real power? Who has it? Those who raise money, the politicians? Those who give money? Greenberg thinks that these are all closely connected questions – little more than restatements of one another. In the next chapter I will deal with presuppositions of this account of politics, and pose the following question: are these questions directed at a form of politics that is passing away?

The argument of this book is thus to a large extent orthogonal to Greenberg's concerns. Greenberg identifies politics with electoral politics; everything else is not political. This leads him to quote the biographer of Leo Szilard (an important figure in the history of the atomic bomb), who writes that in the early 1960s

> Szilard's plight as a freelance thinker and policy proponent is poignantly described by his biographer, William Lanouette, who observes that, by the early 1960s, 'Szilard had begun to realize his limits as a humorist and "outsider" in Washington - a serious and self-important city that squanders laughter and lives by cliques. . . . He was still a professor of biophysics from the University of Chicago. Not a consultant to the Arms Control and Disarmament Agency (ACDA). Not a member of the President's Science Advisory Committee (PSAC). Not a fellow at a local think tank or a consultant to a congressional committee. As he discovered during his first months in the capital, Washington is a city where what you do is often less important than where you do it'. (William Lanouette, with Bela Szilard, 1992: 446, 448 quoted in Greenberg 2001: 246n.2)

The irony, and its relevance to the argument of this book, will become clearer in what follows in Chapters 5 and 6. But it will suffice to say here that if Szilard was excluded from these long lists of commissions, other scientists were not. These bodies were dominated by scientists. And they exercised 'real' power, as Szilard was well aware.

Greenberg also acknowledges that in many if not all of the episodes he decries for their neglect of the opinions of scientists, the opinions of scientists were divided – at least some credible scientists went against positions of 'good science' that Greenberg thinks deserved to be taken more seriously. The point, simply, is that the strategy of concentrating opinion by making it unanimous within a group in the fashion of science, is not, as Max Weber famously said of the principle of causality, like a taxicab that one can alight from at will. It is, rather, the sword that one lives and dies by. The cases he cites are cases in which scientific opinion was neither unanimous nor, by the agreed standards of what is science, 'scientific'. They were opinions of scientists, but not 'science'.

Scientific Consensus and Consensuses of Scientists

The distinction between the corpus of basic scientific knowledge and other kinds of assertions by scientists is not without its problems. Results that at first appear to be part of the corpus, may, as a result of later scientific investigation, cease to appear to be. The difference between the kinds of activities that add to the corpus of scientific knowledge and coming up with what I have been calling 'fact-surrogates' for policy purposes, for example by performing statistical analyses of risks, despite their substantial differences, are not entirely and obviously distinct in practice. From a political point of view these differences are best understood in terms of the difference between the *consensus of scientists* and *scientific consensus*.

Scientists themselves distinguish what is and is not a genuine scientific fact. Speaking *as scientists* they may also attempt to construct a consensus of competent scientific peers, not merely with respect to their opinions about the truth of a model but with respect to their opinions about the sufficiency of the evidence and the adequacy of their explanation. With this we are already in a domain of 'science is required but not sufficient'. The 'meta' judgments about sufficiency of evidence are *unlike* those made within science. And it is those judgments, incidentally, that most closely resemble those involved in the governance of science.

Many problems are also subject to discussions among scientists and attempts are made to establish a scientific consensus with respect to the relevant facts. In attempting to identify a scientific consensus with respect to given problems, the National Institutes of Health regularly hold meetings that include experts of various kinds who are asked to evaluate the existing research, fit it together, iron out and evaluate inconsistencies, and arrive at a policy relevant to scientific conclusions. These are in effect status reports, reports on the state of the evidence with respect to a particular question and of the areas in which the evidence supports some policy-relevant conclusion more or less strongly.

What are these: scientific consensuses or consensuses of scientists? Clearly the latter. The consensus that these reports represent is a forced consensus in that it asks for an assessment of the evidence at a particular point in time and with respect to a particular evidential situation. Judgments about the status of something as an accepted scientific fact are different in intent. They are not understood to be time relevant or evidential situation relevant, though it may well turn out that the evidential situation changes in an anticipated way that undermines the previous consensus. But the two kinds of consensus are illegitimately run together in discussions of science as it relates to policy questions, and indeed the distinction is frequently intentionally ignored or obscured. The IPCC, the Intergovernmental Panel on

Climate Change, a United Nations-sponsored body, claimed 'scientific consensus' on the fact of global warming and that 'the balance of evidence suggests a discernible human influence on global climate' (quoted in Singer 1999: 1). The phrasing is significant: it is not claimed that this is a 'scientific fact'. And the critics are attempting to show that there is competent minority opinion to the effect that it is not a fact at all – a fact of the sort that policy should be made with.

We are not, here, in 'science proper'. But we are in the realm of questions about what is to be treated politically as 'fact' because it is a matter of some sort of consensus among scientists – what I have been calling fact-surrogates. The gap between the 'some sort' and 'scientific consensus proper' is crucial. And to understand it we need to distinguish between two kinds of consensus involving science. Attempts to employ standards appropriate to science, such as peer review, to judgements about policy relevant issues, such as global warming, for example, run together the two kinds of issues, typically without explanation or argument. The fact that claims made about global warming are subjected to 'peer review', for example, does not make them into facts like those of core science, even if the reviewers and the review process are the same. Peer review is a procedure of evaluation, a decision-making device, but it is one that places a (usually low) threshold on what is to be included in the literature for the purposes of scientific communication.

Peer panels can produce many other things as well, and do, especially in the governance of science: decisions regarding the funding of research or the awarding of prizes, fellowships, graduate student support, and so forth. And they can also be used to produce, or simply legitimate, claims about global warming or adolescent pregnancy. These are topics in which methods of modeling are controversial and where there are 'facts' that are accepted as scientific, but where these facts alone are far from sufficient to warrant strong predictions, especially about the effects of policy. They do not concern closed systems, in which all parameters are known and all relevant causes included. They represent good guesses, and typically the topics themselves are such that good casuistic guesses are the best that one can have.

In the case of adolescent pregnancy, to choose a behavioral science example, it will never be true that all variables will be known, or that an isolatable basic process will be identified that is subject to control. But policy requires 'knowledge'. So it is not unreasonable to do what in fact was done: to bring together the main researchers, with their data, for a discussion that was designed to determine what consensus existed, both on the problem and on the state of the evidence.

There may well be perfectly good *political* grounds for adopting such a strategy for obtaining a 'consensus of scientists', and it may be perfectly appropriate to apply them in these cases. Fact-surrogates may serve to advance policy discussion by being acceptable to both sides – stipulations. And there may be good political reasons for making other choices. Standard-setting and regulatory decisions are often made by committees that reflect the representatives of both interested parties, scientists familiar generally with what is known about the causal processes and scientific knowledge about the relevant chemicals or disease processes as well as the relevant technologies.

The political question to ask about such committees, and the discourse that occurs within them, is somewhat different from, but not entirely independent of the epistemic question of what it is that these committees know that justifies their decisions. Granting a committee the right or responsibility to set standards, for example, for the concentration of some particular chemical in drinking water, is a political act. It presumes that a committee of a particular kind is in a sense a better way of making a decision than other available options, and 'better' may mean a great many things. It may simply be more convenient to delegate such decisions when legislatures feel that they are either not competent to make the decisions or if, for more Machiavellian reasons, they consider it useful to shift the blame for decisions onto another body. Or it may simply be that it is more convenient for representative bodies set upon by specialized interest groups to remove from their own consideration decisions that cannot be made in ways that these groups regard as beneficial.

The Power of Expert Bodies

So powerful is this political strategy of producing consensus that it has been copied for a tremendously large array of other activities. Chief among these is of course the regulation of medical practice through the standardization of medical training and the creation of certifying bodies that endorse particular medical practices, training regimes, standards, and so forth. The 'scientific' basis of these practices is often real and substantial, but also often far removed from the actual practices that are being recommended, so that the basis of the practice is in fact a combination of the scientific with the non-scientific, often with elements that are objective, such as studies of drug effects, or studies of efficacy, which are themselves not simply matters of facts of science but rather the results of a mishmash of assumptions, common sense, and statistical results.

More interesting than this, perhaps, is the proliferation of expert bodies in fields where there is organized training or organized knowledge for which there is no scientific basis in a strict sense but nevertheless a great deal of technical and objective knowledge. For example, some years ago, questions were raised by accountants about the accounting evaluation of pension obligations of various companies. To some degree, this was an arcane technical matter, in the sense that any solution to the problem of assessing exactly what it was that a pension system represented in accounting terms as a liability depended on a great many unknowns, such as the value of a cash commitment in the distant future, which depended on such things as assumptions about inflation – obviously that no expert could reliably predict – as well as actuarial assumptions about which reasonably reliable conventions existed, but that obviously would be undone by a significant event such as an epidemic or war, as well as assumptions about the continuity of business practices such as the continued employment of particular classes of workers to retirement age, which could be undone simply by a manager. Nevertheless, the liabilities were real in the sense that some day, some class of persons could claim rights under contracts that the company had entered into and in this sense the value of these unfunded liabilities was as much a problem for assessing the value of a company as the question of the size of its accounts receivable.

Here, in this apparently arcane matter of expert but essentially entirely conventional though objective knowledge, or rather objective knowledge in which the knowledge itself was constituted by accounting conventions, was an issue that had very interesting and consequential implications. The key implication was this. A company that under the then current accounting rules was profitable might in fact be bankrupt, that is to say unable to ever pay off its obligation, and not be aware of it. Since these rules relate to investing, and conventions of financial transparency, enforced by other expert bodies such as the Securities and Exchange Commission, require adherence to certain accounting conventions, the value of the company and the ability of the company therefore to raise money was at stake. In fact, once these liabilities were valued, companies quickly began to eliminate these unfunded liabilities and this produced a revolution in the way in which first in the US, and then increasingly in Europe, retirement pensions were funded.

What is striking about this example is that it is almost an immaterial question as to whether these changes were initiated by a state or initiated by an expert body that sets accounting standards for the accounting profession, that is to say a professional body. The relationships between this kind of expertise, the regulatory expertise of exchange commissions in the US, the accounting practices that this imposes on world markets, on those who wish to avail themselves of American capital by listing themselves on an American stock exchange, and then consequently on governments that in the course of their own efforts at securing economic well-being for their citizens must respond to the concerns of investors, show there is no freedom from the consequences of these expert bodies. And the sheer number of these bodies, the fact that government bodies, particularly regulative bodies, depend on them in many circumstances, does mean that these bodies are a kind of quasi-government and indeed a kind of quasi-government whose powers extend beyond borders if only because regulatory bodies in one country attend to the actions of regulatory bodies in other countries and find themselves advantaged or disadvantaged by the actions that these bodies take.

In France, there was the scandal of the health commissioners who allowed the use of HIV-tainted blood out of a kind of misplaced patriotism (they wished to wait for the availability of a French method for testing blood despite the fact that an American method was available), and found themselves branded as criminals. This is a simple instance of the global character of expertise, and very far from the only one. The decision of Daimler-Benz to sell its stock on the New York Stock Exchange forced them to present results in American accounting terms, which led to the 'discovery' that the company, one of the world's most powerful and respected, had been unprofitable for years, and this led to changes in business strategy and even to changes in industry-state relations in Germany. Yet accounting standards are in a way a paradigm case of the exercise of expert power that is independent of the state yet hand in glove with it.

The fact that so many bodies have emerged that take the form of expert consensual action is testament to the success of such bodies, their value both for the practitioners they certify and for users of the expert knowledge, who may simply be purchasers of the services of the expert, such as the accountants who apply these methods. But a strategy of certifying people as experts or certifying claims such as about global warming as the consensus of experts is politically powerful. Where liberal democracy deals with these claims or these bodies it does so by assessing the interests that they represent, particularly their self-interest, and sorting out those claims that are rejected as self-interested from claims that are accepted as properly matters of expertise. Physicians who characterize health problems collectively in ways that are clearly self-interested are characteristically thus written off as self-interested by politicians and publics. Similarly for lawyers, drug companies, and the like, self-interest is always an issue. Mark Twain's famous saying that every profession is a conspiracy against the public is a bit of liberal wisdom that liberal democracies live by. But this does not mean that they ignore experts, avoid professionals, or that they reject the strategy of delegating to experts. They take their experts with a grain of salt and compel them to go out of their way to establish that their claims are disinterested, rewarding those who can do so and punishing those that cannot. The exemption of science or its exceptionalism is a matter not so much of the distinctive cognitive character of science but of the ability of scientists to free themselves from the suspicion of self-interest, and this is precisely how scientists themselves understand the situation. The great radio astronomer Bernard Lovell was once told by an admirer that all he needed to do to secure the funds necessary for radio astronomy was to report that he had discovered evidence of extra terrestrial intelligence. Lovell said correctly that to do so would have been to destroy the trust on which scientists depended. And scientists police one another with respect to these kinds of claims. In this way they avoid the suspicion of dishonesty even as the public assesses and often dismisses their demands for funding as excessive and self-interested. But in science characteristically the claims and the interests have little to do with one another, at least directly.

Commissions as a Form of Rule

The 'commissions' described in this chapter are surrogates for liberal democracy – delegations of the discussion in government by discussion. The participants in these discussions participate by virtue of their special knowledge, though the knowledge may be that of stakeholders rather than experts. Nevertheless, most of what goes on in these bodies involves some sort of expert knowledge. But it is rarely knowledge in the strict sense of scientific truth or 'objective' knowledge. The 'expert' reasoning that goes on in these bodies is mainly casuistic: an attempt to apply what is clearly known in one domain to a domain that is complex and poorly understood. Frequently there are other experts with a different base from which to apply their knowledge casuistically, to a problem that is ill-structured, so that there is no optimal solution.

Why does the 'commission' form have such an affinity to these problems? The answer is that they fall in a large gap between liberal discussion and expert knowledge in the strict sense. These are problems that cannot be completely removed from political discussion and solved by experts, if only because for these problems there is not a single 'expert' solution. Commissions are *surrogates* for expertise proper, and at the same time surrogates for liberal discussion by non-experts. One could give some kind of rational choice analysis of decisions to delegate discussion to such bodies, to the detailed choice of the particular roles of membership and procedure under which they operate and the costs of delegation. And one could give a similar account of the rationality of strategies to organize expertise by creating an expert consensus to bring about reforms. But the analysis would merely rationalize what is apparent. The inadequacies of representational liberal discussion motivate delegation; the limitations for policy of uncontentious expert knowledge motivate attempts by experts to provide more, to go beyond the 'facts' to fact-surrogates that more directly bear on policy. Organized opinion, 'consensus', is more effective than unorganized opinion. So there is a motive to organize. Commissions are a device to mediate these wants. But it remains to be asked whether these devices are means of extending liberal democracy, or something more – an alternative form of rule.

Notes

1 There is an interesting parallel here in Schmitt's discussion of judicial discretion, in which he argues that the undecideability of legal questions on legal grounds requires a non-legal consensus by judges (cf. Scheuerman 1999)

2 It is perhaps more emblematic of present American uses of expert knowledge than ironic that today in the playground the burden of standards has shifted to the courts. Old style playgrounds still exist, following these old standards. But for new equipment and new types of equipment, the threat of litigation over injuries is the dominant fact, with the result that even simple pieces of manufactured playground equipment come with complex, lawyer-written, warnings. But this is simply another form of the delegation of expert questions to other bodies, in this cases the courts, which then must hear expert witnesses about the risks of given designs, based on objective measures of injury and on research about the product.

3 There is a good but small literature on peer review (cf. Chubin and Hackett 1990) and on ethical issues (La Follette 1992).

4 Occasions when the self-disciplining character of the scientist's political obligations

breaks down are thus useful research sites for the political theorist, for it is here that the 'citizenship' aspect of science, usually undiscussed, is explicitly discussed. In fraud cases, for example, there are often debates about the seriousness of the violation and the way it should be presented to the public. These discussions not only reveal the ways in which the agency relationship is understood by scientists, they reveal tensions that are characteristic of these relationships, and indicate the ways in which they are 'solved' through institutional devices of various kinds.

5

Three Eras of Liberalism

> The ideal of democracy, in short, is government for the good of the people by the people, and in accordance with the wish of the people; the ideal of collectivism is government for the good of the people by experts, or officials who know, or think they know, what is good for the people better than either any non-official person or than the mass of the people themselves. (A. V. Dicey [1905]1962: lxxiii)

One way of interpreting the history of liberalism is to see it as the continual expansion of the circle of civility, of democratic participation in 'government by discussion', so that more and more people participated in the discussion. At each stage in the history of liberal democracy, especially in the nineteenth century, there was an extension of the franchise, or the elimination of obstacles to open discussion in the determination of decisions. In one sense, the state of European and particularly American politics at the end of the twentieth century reflected the fullest realization of a process that Albert Venn Dicey had identified a century earlier, namely the rise of public opinion as the ultimate basis of political power ([1914]1962). At the point at which politicians' every move and every utterance is dictated by strategies that are the product of expert advisors poring over the results of opinion polls and focus groups, we see in some sense the absolute triumph of public opinion.

In another sense it is the absolute reduction of politics to the pursuit of public office. Ultimately this amounts to a very peculiar game in which politicians regard public opinion as an obstacle to be outmaneuvered or outguessed, in order to stay just ahead of it and thus to preserve the appearance of 'leading' – and then to take credit for leadership. Certainly, this represents a kind of control by public opinion. But it is a very peculiar one, in which the relationship between public opinion and the utterances of politicians has collapsed the distance that the earlier notions of representation presupposed, and altered the relationship. J. S. Mill already feared this in the nineteenth century (1861). What ends is the idea of the representative as a kind of teacher or persuader, where the representative is not merely the unthinking spokesperson for opinion, but a party to a moral relationship in which the representative stands in for those who are represented, as a persuader willing to be persuaded and obliged to persuade the represented. In its place we get a relationship in which the representative actively attempts to pursue a path in which utterances are pretested attempts to produce an effect – the effect of increasing support for the politician. This may seem like a distinction without a difference, but it has considerable bearing on the problem of 'discussion'. Electoral politicians became ciphers, more or less transparent vehicles for opinions produced elsewhere.

Habermas' Public Sphere

The sheer influence of Habermas' *The Structural Transformation of the Public Sphere*, with the telling subtitle *An Inquiry into a Category of Bourgeois Society* ([1962]1991), and its appropriation by scholars worldwide, particularly on the Left, makes it necessary to begin with a consideration of this text in order to clarify a number of potential issues. The book is important also because of its intellectual quality and power, quality and power, which impressed many later writers, such as Craig Calhoun (1992) and in particular James Bohman (1996), who have followed it up by posing questions about the nature of the public sphere and deliberative democracy in contemporary circumstances. Habermas was attempting on the one hand to make a very complex argument about the fundamental fraudulence of liberalism, and on the other to claim that the bourgeois category of the public sphere really represents an appropriation of a preexisting form of publicness, a form that he intimates was more fully representative or more meaningfully represented the kind of ideal relationship between ruler and ruled. One of the striking features of the text in retrospect is the extent to which it amounts to a dialogue with Schmitt, and consists of a complex combination of repudiation and appropriation of Schmitt's account of the origins and nature of liberal democracy, and, not incidentally, of the failure of the Weimar Republic and the role of the Left in this failure. The immediate occasion, and indeed the source of the only contemporary empirical material in the text, was the 1957 Bundestag elections, in which Konrad Adenhauer and the Christian Democrats successfully portrayed the Social Democratic Party as an unfit participant in German parliamentary politics and untrustworthy as a governing parliamentary party. Habermas' dialectical purpose was to turn this portrayal on its head and to argue that the bourgeois parties, and the form of liberal democracy itself, represents a usurpation of the public space by the private, a much more serious and profound kind of unfitness and untrustworthiness.

Schmitt is mentioned only twice in the index to *The Structural Transformation of the Public Sphere*. But clearly what is at stake is Schmitt's interpretation of the rise and demise of classical liberalism and also of the character of classical liberalism. In many places in which Schmitt is not mentioned, such as Habermas' discussions of Hobbes and of representation, it is clear that Schmitt is the target. Schmitt in this context amounts to a defender of *classical* liberalism, simply by virtue of the fact that he considered classical liberalism to be a genuine form of representation in which genuine rational persuasion occurred. Needless to say, the destruction of the form of liberalism represented by Weimar democracy that both Schmitt and the Left actively hastened was seen by both of them as the destruction of an empty shell. Where they differ is in their account of the liberalism that pre-ceded this in the eighteenth and nineteenth centuries and the prehistory of these forms of liberalism. Their differences on this topic have implications for their whole construal of the significance of liberal democracy as a polit-ical form.

Habermas' key argument is that the bourgeois public sphere was a form of usurpation. It rests on the claim that the core ideology of classical liber-alism, which for convenience we may call Liberalism 1.0, was a fiction – the fiction of that property owners were identical to 'the people'. Property owners were the only participants in 'public' discourse, and in the formation of 'public' opinion. It was they who reasoned with one another to arrive at basic conclusions about political matters. The state was expected to imple-ment the results of these discussions. One can see the logic of Habermas' point in terms of the discussion of the concentration of opinion in the last chapter. Public reason was in effect a kind of commission from below, that is to say a concentration of opinion rooted in agreements made within a group that had constituted itself as a form and at the same time as a repre-sentative voice. The objection Habermas has to this is that they represent-ed only particular 'objective interest correlations' ([1962]1991: 63). Thus they appear (and depict themselves ideologically) as representatives, but are in fact usurpers in the public sphere. And they do this in the name of rea-son. So the problem is not only a matter of the substantive falsity of the claim to *represent*. It also a matter of the falsity of the claim to represent *public reason*.

Public reason for Habermas is a strongly normative, even utopian, idea. It is not merely a matter of the possibility of persuasion with respect to ends or truth: the Schmittian definition. For the physiocrats, a favorite source for Habermas, (appearing at the end of *Theory and Practice* as well [1973: 281-82]) public opinion or the *public éclairé* represented an ideal achievement, and in this sense a standard against which the mundane persuasion of actu-al politicians could be held and found wanting. He ascribes to the phys-iocrats the view that public opinion in the strict sense was 'an opinion purified through critical discussion in the public sphere' ([1962]1991: 95). The basic structure of the argument thus produces a conclusion that does not depend on historical evidence but is fixed in advance: actual public dis-cussion in the concrete conditions of social life never can reach this stan-dard; thus all claims to achieve public reason will be, by definition, false. But this allows Habermas to engage in a vigorous and persuasive *Ideologiekritik* of liberal justifications for actual regimes of discussion and representation, which is quite astute at picking up these nuances. The apparently egalitar-ian Rousseau, for example, is caught out by remarks such as this: 'The sim-ple people, indeed simpletons, would be merely irritated by the political maneuvers of public discussion; long debates would bring particular inter-ests to the fore' (cited in Habermas [1962]1991: 97).[1] Rousseau also warned against the 'dangerous appeals of silver-toned orators' (quoted in Habermas [1962]1991: 97-8) which led him to his notion of the general will, something which, as Habermas puts it, 'was more a consensus of heart than of arguments' ([1962]1991: 98).

Habermas consistently interprets these considerations in light of the larger thesis of usurpation in the name of public reason, as indications of the interested and consequently sham character of 'public opinion'. Each particular limitation of discussion or participation is taken as evidence of its sham character. Marx emerges as the wholesale demolisher of all of these fictions of public reason: the inequality of economic opportunity meant necessarily that the forms of liberal democracy amounted to the perpetuation of domination in a different guise ([1962]1991: 124). This implies that the extension of the franchise did not overcome the effects of the fundamental reality of inequality of opportunity and consequently the meaninglessness of rational debate. Indeed, the ultimate consequence was the degeneration of sham 'debate' into something quite different but even more bogus. The older 'public' necessarily literate, since the debates needed to be read, which demanded engagement. In contrast, new forms of opinion are barely internalized, and represent just 'talk' influenced by the mass media. Public opinion is now a quasi-public opinion which is institutionally authorized. In this sense today's 'public' is even less of a public than the now vanished communicative network of a public made up of rationally debating private citizens, the world of classical liberalism. In modern politics debate is staged as show for the purpose of manipulation rather than for enlightenment or rational persuasion.

In even this very brief sketch, one can see the debt Habermas owes to Schmitt's analysis, but not the more subtle changes of perspective. Unlike Schmitt, Habermas says almost nothing at all about religion and the model of religious toleration. It is mentioned only once in Habermas, in passing ([1962]1991: 135). This omission reflects a fundamental difference of opinion about the conditions for, and character of, rational discourse in the first place, a difference that has a great deal to do with the problem of expertise. Schmitt believed that the removal of religious questions from politics was an essential condition for the birth of liberalism in the form of rational public opinion. The moralization of politics, the condemnation of one's opponents as sinners or tools of the devil was the end of a rational discussion, and the beginning of religious warfare. This indeed was the experience of Europe in the seventeenth century. Religious warfare – the suppression of religious opinion and its expression – was the basic fact of European experience. According to the traditional liberal account that we will discuss shortly taking the state out of the business of religion and therefore separating religion from politics was a solution that created a space for a kind of civility. The advantage of this traditional account was of course that it made sense of the dramatic, and traumatic, political history of Europe during the seventeenth century and the actual phenomena of war, civil war, the diasporas of Huguenots and others, the rise of religious solidarity across national boundaries, and the terms of the eventual end of religious warfare.

Subsequent Marxist scholarship, notably by figures on the British Left, reinterpreted the English revolutionary period and its struggles in class terms.[2] Class was relevant: in many particular historical settings, the traditional conflict between town and countryside and between the class of merchants and craftsmen and the aristocracy did indeed relate to religious conflict, if only because Protestants and radical Protestants were very often to be found in those settings that were most open to new contacts, especially through books, at a time in which censorship was still routine. And within particular movements, notably of course Cromwell's army, there were significant ideological divisions that more or less corresponded to divisions of class. Yet Habermas' reduction of this complexity is stunningly extreme, and his elimination of the religious question – the matter which, in traditional historiography and in the minds of the combatants, was the defining or central issue, vanishes from view – depriving liberalism and toleration of the greatest claim that it made: that it was a means of establishing and securing domestic peace.

One need only look at the authoritarian solutions proposed by such figures as Hobbes, who considered that the state should regulate all thought, to see how different Europe would have been had not liberalism established itself. The strife that motivated the theorizing of Hobbes disappears in Habermas' account in order to make a place for a story in which the bourgeoisie, in the course of its 'rise', silently usurps the public's space in the name of a 'reason' that is merely that of private persons pursuing private interests. This means that the present stability of liberalism and of government by discussion is projected back to the distant past, and threats to liberalism, particularly the threat of ideological exclusivism and of anti-liberal worldviews demanding exclusive authority, are made to evaporate. Habermas' polemical purpose, however, is clear: to excuse German socialism in the Weimar era, and to justify its working class that marched to the chant: 'A Republic is not so grand, for socialism we take our stand'. Habermas' history is thus an indirect absolution of the Left of its historical responsibility. The 'rising bourgeoisie' are assumed to simply have had their way with history, liberalism was a by-product of deeper forces, and liberalism now needs to be unmasked and overthrown.

By noting this I do not mean to take sides in a long running historical dispute over the fate of the Weimar Republic. It is perhaps more reasonable to see it as an experiment that was already doomed precisely because the traditions of a democratic civility that a liberal constitution required simply had never been established in Germany, and the gift of a liberal constitution was unappreciated by its recipients, who, as Weber famously remarked, had never cut the head off a monarch, and thus earned it. But to say this is to depart completely from Habermas' mechanical account of the bourgeoisie's usurpation of public reason and return the achievement of liberal civility to the efforts of its friends and enemies, that is to say return it to the kind of analysis offered by Schmitt. Schmitt also viewed the problems of modern politics from the perspective of German history. Ironically, he had a less narrowly Germanic and more European view of the problem of liberalism than did the Habermas of *The Structural Transformation of the Public Sphere*. More important, for our purposes, is that Habermas' argument, because it is based on the presumption that past liberal discussion was sham, and that all liberal discussion prior to the classless society is falsely self-conscious of its nature, eliminates the possibility of a sense of the rationality of public discussion that can usefully be applied to history.

Given what I said about representation in Chapter 4, especially about the idea of scientists speaking as representatives of science, and of other experts speaking as representatives of expert opinion, it is striking that Habermas' argument here, which is that the public sphere is usurped by a 'private' form of representation, is directly paralleled by Schmitt. This is what Schmitt characterized as the economic principle:

> Public life is expected to govern itself. It is to be controlled by public opinion, that is to say, by the opinion of private individuals; and public opinion, in its turn, is to be controlled by a press in the hands of private owners. Nothing in this system is representative: everything is a private matter. (Schmitt [1923]1988: 52-3)

For Schmitt, as for Habermas, the contrast is to the pre-liberal phenomenon of 'publicity of representation' as a matter of the 'public' and 'representative' character of the monarchy, the nobility, and (a point Schmitt stresses and Habermas merely mentions) the Roman Catholic Church (Habermas [1962]1991: 83; cf. Schmitt [1923]1988: 53-60).

The ideology behind these earlier forms of representation is captured in the notion of the king's two bodies, the idea that the king's private personal body was distinct from his kingly 'public' personality which 'represented' as the private body did not. Habermas' idea that *this* sort of publicity was 'usurped', however, seems strange. The various forms of 'representation' in the pre-liberal period coexisted and, over time, related to one another in various ways, and continued to do so in changing ways throughout the liberal era, and into the present, in such forms as constitutional monarchy. Schmitt's point in his own essay on representation was precisely that the Church and its principle persisted and the Church found ways to accommodate the other forms of representation, and could even accommodate to Bolshevism. But he regarded the 'economic principle' as the foundation of both Bolshevism, in which 'things govern themselves', and Capitalist industrialism ([1923]1988: 51-2). The principle of representation that the previous chapter pointed toward can be understood as an alternative to these competing principles. The expert's claim to represent specialized knowledge, in short, is a fundamental idea of representation irreducible to any other.

The Bigger Picture

The account given by Habermas, both with respect to its philosophical commitment to the idea of public enlightenment and its historical claims, focused on the aspect of past liberal democracy that undermined either universal participation or the rationality of the contents of persuasion and public opinion. This focus occluded the problem of expert knowledge. As a practical matter, expert knowledge in general (and science in the sense of full technical mastery of complex ideas) is not a part of 'public' enlightenment if only because the capacity, time, background experiences and education necessary for amassing a significant amount of specialized knowledge cannot be universal. But Habermas operates with a conception of rationality in which everything is accessible to rational scrutiny and examination, including what he takes to be the 'presuppositions' of forms of knowledge. This is a comforting model, but there is good reason to believe that it radically misrepresents the character of knowledge. To the extent that the capacity for thinking like a nuclear physicist in research science, for example, depends on what Michael Polanyi called 'personal knowledge', that is, knowledge about which one can say 'we know more than we can say', it is not possible to articulate presuppositions (or, in Habermas' preferred terminology, to 'thematize' presuppositions). The reason for this is that the knowledge in question, tacit knowledge, is not articulatable. This is an issue that I will return to briefly in the final chapter, but the point is an important one. Habermas is not free from the implications of the acceptance of a model of knowledge, Kantian in origin, informed by the ideal of full explicitness on the model of Euclidean geometry. One can, in science and in logic, treat this model as no more than an ideal of clarity which one can use to make sense of the notion of proof. But this, and similar lines of argument, such as that made by Robert Brandom in *Making It Explicit* (1994), are not open to Habermas. For Habermas must call not only 'presuppositional' knowledge potentially thematizable as explicit propositions or truths, it must in principle and in practice be thematizable for the 'public'. Expert knowledge, and scientific knowledge, in particular, have long since proven to be resistant to this kind of reduction, and the problem is a significant blindspot in Habermas' formulation.

These issues may be left aside when we turn to the much less esoteric realm of the discussion and analysis of the successive forms of liberalism. In what follows, I propose, in part because of the discussion of Habermas' engagement with Schmitt, to formulate this more precisely in the light of some contemporary texts, texts dating from different periods of liberalism. For convenience, we may associate the texts with the varying versions of liberalism. What I will call 'Liberalism 1.0' is purposely not labeled liberal *democracy*, for it is a liberalism of notables, a liberalism defended by Cromwell's son-in-law Henry Ireton in the Putney debate. The arguments Ireton gives are arguments that justify a form of political order that we might call the 'rule by notables', following the title of Halevy's classic discussion of the political failure of this class in France in 1848, *The End of the Notables*. This form not only existed in various forms in Europe as a principle of rule but which persists to the present in many settings. In the last chapter, in discussing Tocqueville and knowledge associations, I suggested that this form continues to function as a principle in many settings and that experts not infrequently appear along with the remaining 'notables', also with 'around notables', or as 'notables' in their own right. To understand this claim, however, it is necessary to understand fundamental political principles of 'notabilism' or Liberalism 1.0, and in its original European context.

It is perhaps best to begin a discussion of the notables with a discussion of basic social relations in the era when they were politically important, and especially one social relation: clientelism. Clientelism, the name of the system of relations between patrons and their clients, is taken from the explicit legal form of this system in the Roman Republic. The term covered different relationships, but the most basic was the relation between a patrician and his freed slaves, clients who enjoyed rights only through their continued relationship to their patrons, to whom they had various obligations. But a similar relationship could be created by taking an oath. In later antiquity the relationships had more to do with conflict. To be without a patron of this sort was to be vulnerable. To be a significant member of the senatorial class required one to have many clients. One's clients could be called upon for support, for example, when one's interests were threatened by another notable who had mobilized his clients in the form of a mob, and indeed battles of this sort occurred throughout the period of late antiquity in Rome (see Eisenstadt and Luis Roninger 1984: 52-61).

The form itself, however, is a kind of pre-political surrogate for politics itself, the default form, so to speak, of the organization of relations of protection and obedience, against which juridical politics is necessarily defined. In the Pacific Islands this came to be described as the 'big man complex'. Members of the society were characteristically involved in and dependent on relations with a 'big man' protector. A more refined version of this occurs in settled Hispanic societies in the form of debt relations. The local landowner is a person to whom one could turn to borrow money, but whose relationship with you was personal rather than a market relation and involved loyalty and subservience. The language of clientelism is familiar to any reader of letters from the European past in which such phrases as 'your humble and obedient servant', used by persons who were not literally servants, is characteristic, frequent, and a relic of a relation of clientelism in which a person without such a relationship to appeal to would have found survival difficult. Clientelism in modern Europe was rooted in court relations and also grew out of feudalism itself, as a result of a complex process of decay in which clientelistic forms served increasingly as surrogates for older relations of feudal subordination that had been corrupted by the creation of new kinds of nobles and the sale of titles and the intrusion of capitalism, and in which individuals acquired multiple patrons (cf. Kettering 1986), breaking down the 'man of a man' model of the feudal relationship celebrated by Marc Bloch in his *Feudal Society* (1964). Characteristically, these were relations of indebtedness that in a practical sense provided an alternative structure of power alongside and eventually engulfing and overcoming the older hereditarian relations of dependence, or involved the securing of state offices through personal intervention.

Cromwell's army was an army led and raised by notables, and parliamentary power in the revolutionary parliament was exercised by notables. Typically the leading figures were landowners, and by definition land and power required dependents for production, either persons living on the land and farming it or specialists within a complex division of labor ranging from gamekeepers to scullery maids. This basic economic structure lies behind the Putney debates, in which the radicals of the New Model Army engaged the representatives of this newly empowered order of notables. The Putney debates pose a conflict between radical democracy, or one concept of stakeholding and rights, and a concept that is bound to the existing realities of clientelism and the radical differences between the kinds of stakes that different groups have in society. The arguments were formulated explicitly on the one side in terms of 'right' and 'rights' and on the other in terms of 'interest'. On the side of the Levellers, Colonel Rainsborough speaks in the famous phrase 'that the poorest he that is in England has a life to live as the greatest he' (1647, quoted in Clarke 1891).[3] The realities of modern warfare stand behind the claim to equal right. The theory was that every soldier was, by virtue of the successes of the army, a member of the society it both preserved and created, and consequently is bound in a compact that extends to all.

Ireton understands the compact differently, because he contrasts those who are without a fixed interest in the society with those who are, a contrast that he frames in terms of the mobility and permanence of their interests. Landowners are the paradigm case of those with fixed interests whose conduct is therefore most closely bound up with the well being of society and are thus compelled by interest to act responsibly. Those whose interests are impermanent, the paradigm of which is the traveling peddler or the merchant who owns nothing, are not. Most of the immobile people in such a society, however, also own little or nothing and are dependent for their well being on those who do have permanent and fixed interests, such as landowners, to whom they sell their goods or labor and with whom they have a clientalistic relationship of dependency. Their connection to the permanent fixed interests of the society are through this relationship of dependence. They have little in the way of other permanent fixed interests on their own.

Given the opportunity to vote themselves a stake, to redistribute the land and wealth of the landowner, they would do so, according to Ireton, but this would be a self-destructive act. Granting the vote to those who are not bound by interests to the well being of the society is fundamentally similar to granting a vote to foreigners who would use the vote to expropriate the wealth of the society for their own benefit. Consequently the franchise should be restricted to those who meet property qualifications.

Although this discussion says little about knowledge (much less expertise), one can fill in by indicating some of the implications of this doctrine. The large landowners and those merchants with fixed interests were, implicitly, men of the world, with experiences that enabled them to reason with one another about their mutual interests. To some extent, they were part of the world of truck and barter and thus able to understand the rationality of deal-making, which is a minimal sort of recognition of mutual interest. In this sense they are 'privately' interested. But as they were representatives of larger complexes of economic activities, representatives of a complex division of labor, they were also presumably able to think not merely at the level of haggling but at the level of indirect and complex consequences of decisions not only for themselves but for the others who were dependent upon them; and by virtue of their interest in these relationships were bound to take the interests of their dependents into consideration. They were, in short, patrons as well as businessmen, and therefore not mere exemplifications of the economic principle of representation. For the most part, there was no difference between the kinds of knowledge that one landowning notable possessed and the kinds of knowledge that other landowning notables possessed. They knew intimately about their own circumstances, but the kind of reasoning they did about their circumstances was similar if not identical to reasoning that other landowners and merchants did. Their dependents did not necessarily reason in this way, or share this knowledge, nor could they be presumed to be *able* to do so. So there was a distinction in knowledge that corresponded to the distinction in interest that fundamentally divided this kind of society.

What I have said so far about this society fits more or less with Schmitt's and Habermas' notion of the economic principle, the idea of organizing the state to serve the private interests of the bourgeoisie. But the notion of stakeholding, which is a concrete implication of the idea of permanent interest, points beyond the Habermasian concept of the collusion of individual interest masquerading as public interest to something more subtle. In the first place it points to a notion that stakeholders have a right to rule themselves, a notion that later became central to the American Revolution with its cry of 'no taxation without representation'. This is different from, and more than, merely a case of private usurpation of the space. It also points to a minimal but very stringent notion of the qualifications for participation in public discussion, a notion that is for the most part cited negatively in terms of excluding the mob, but which points toward the heart of the achievement of liberalism in creating conditions for 'government by discussion' or civility in the first place. As the French Revolution demonstrated, declaring the public space open to all as a matter of practicality did not work. The mob ruled. And the mob, that is to say those persons outside the former boundaries of political discussion and political power, continued to be a threat throughout the centuries between the beginning of religious warfare and the revolutions of the nineteenth and earlier twentieth centuries (cf. Dicey [1914]1962: 327).

Rational Discourse Between the Mob and the Court

Where did the new forms of political discussion that eventually led to traditions of public debate come from? What were the models? It is evident that, to some extent at least, Gramsci's notion of proletarian culture developing full term in the bosom of the bourgeois order, ready to emerge with the proletarian revolution as the universal culture, can apply to the case of the emergence of liberal discourse. People had to be able to talk politically before they could have a political transformation which turned discussion into politics and politics into discussion. How did they learn how to discuss? Habermas gives a particular account of the emergence of 'bourgeois' political discourse based on a German source from the 1950s that emphasized such topics as coffeehouses, the rise of newspapers, letters to the editor and so forth, specifically as they occurred within the setting of British, meaning London, politics. Since that time much more has been done in the way of thinking about the puzzle of the emergence of a form of political discourse of considerable complexity and depth in Europe and especially northern Europe, at this time (cf. Goldgar 1995).

In *Interpreting the French Revolution* (1981) François Furêt argued that the task of nurturing traditions of political discussions had been performed in France by secret societies - the Masons - and emerged as the manner of doing *public* business with the revolution and enabled public debate. The English case, not to mention the American case, is doubtless more complex, but there too Free Masonry must have played a significant role. The study of the Latin and Greek classics, certainly, played a significant role as well, as is evident in the endless quotations, allusions, and so forth in the political speech of the eighteenth and nineteenth centuries. This language was itself obviously not that of coffeehouses swarming with shopkeepers and other petty bourgeois 'private citizens'. Nevertheless these petty bourgeois private citizens had other intellectual sources, as indeed did the working class, as E. P. Thompson argued in *The Making of the English Working Class* (1966). Many of these sources, indeed much of the practical political experience of these citizens, did come from religion. The wars of religion, through expulsion, created an international republic of Protestant letters (Goldgar 1995). Revolts against the state churches created self-governing churches and chapels that legislated for their members and in many cases elected their ministers and made collective decisions based on theological discussion about creedal matters. Indeed one could write a history of theological conferences and creedal discussions for this period that would parallel in innumerable ways the political discussions in matters of rights and state forms and constitutions that were occurring at similar times. Even the method of securing collective assent through negotiation and persuasion has striking parallels. The paradigm cases were the communities of yeomen farmers of the western frontier of the eighteenth century in the American colonies which were settled by, among others, tough minded Presbyterians, Congregationalists, and others who imposed tough congregational rules of conduct, and left congregations and created new ones, practicing both the art of political affiliation and of political disaffiliation before they were called upon to employ them in relation to George III and the Continental Congress.

All this is to say that the practices of liberal discussion were well developed, the product of practical experience and testing, and widely, indeed 'democratically', distributed in many places that were far from the coffee houses of London. It is also true that where there were no 'non-political' training grounds for government by discussion, as commentators have repeatedly noticed, the substance of liberal discussion obtained precariously if at all. And this affected the character of the parliamentary institutions that were created in much of Europe, and especially Germany. Where the non-political training grounds of democracy did not exist, the temptation, as Habermas himself describes the German case, was to treat parliament as a place for registering one's position rather than making it the subject of rational discussion and opening up the possibility of persuasion. It is no accident that protest politics of a particular kind have been associated historically with the presence of authoritarian churches, such as state Lutheranism, that characteristically made accommodations for acts of conscience without permitting matters of theology themselves to be decided in public discussion, or through the marketplace of religious sectarianism.

What does any of this have to do with expert discourse and expertise? More perhaps than might first appear. Religious authoritarianism amounted to a claim of religious expertise coupled frequently with a willingness to employ state violence and censorship, and other methods of stifling discussion and eliminating competition. The professions, notably the law, operated to some extent in the fashion of a secret society with their own internal rituals and hierarchies. These forms of association, like freemasonry itself, secured the possibility of a kind of internal freedom of discussion and a willingness to be governed by collective opinion, but at the price of exclusiveness and political neutrality or subservience. This was the case for the various scientific societies founded under Royal patronage, protection, and financial favor, which necessarily operated in the same way, by practicing both religious and political neutrality, and securing for themselves a limited freedom, freedom understood as a privilege granted by the state to a small group of trustworthy gentlemen. It is perhaps not so surprising that Tocqueville, a paradigm case of a notable, considered democracy to be incompatible with science, and if he chose to he could have used the then current evidence of American science at the time of his journeys to substantiate his point. The first great benefactor of American science, Stephen Van Rensselaer, was also the last and richest relic of the Dutch colonial system. In 1838 in the Hudson River Valley he was still collecting his feudal dues in the form of chickens. The democratic patronage of science in the United States, which in Tocqueville's own time was beginning to burgeon, began with geologists hired by state legislatures whose monies initially were expected to perform practical survey work. But this utilitarian approach to science was changing even at the time of Tocqueville's journeys, and it is among Tocqueville's few weaknesses as a commentator to have failed to see that science and public opinion might come to have a relationship other than that rooted in the social forms of clientelism.

Liberalism 2.0

The rule of the notables, the emergence of national literate audiences, the incubation of discussion in the cells of free masonry and in churches with congregational politics, were, together with the emergence of an international republic of letters, all features of the eighteenth century and its peculiar forms of government and political discussion. The tolerance extended to the 'religious' allowed for emancipation from censorship, often very partial and frequently retracted, of a considerable amount of book publishing, including publication of texts that were in a broad sense politically relevant. The story of the emergence of the bourgeois public sphere Habermas retells is the English one. He tells it in terms of the emergence of newspapers, letters to the editor, and so forth. These are institutional forms that still carry a significant part of the burden of the conduct of political discussion, and provide the material on which representation depends. The French version of this story, particularly the emergence of publishing in the shadow of censorship and suppression as well as an anti-democratic anti-liberal monarchy, has now also often been told (Darnton 1984).

The greater problem these new technologies of communication and the subsequent creation of markets for opinions produced, was a vast expansion of the 'discussing' classes beyond and the old 'political' classes. The mismatch between the two groups could be resolved by a shift in the sense of representation, and particularly by creating or reforming political institutions in such a way that public discussion or opinion had a decisive impact on the way in which the state actually conducted itself. In a crude sense, to the extent that the discussing classes were also the same as the classes that sought power and had means of gaining power, the outcome can be told in traditional Marxist terms. The rising bourgeoisie simply imposed an order arranged for its benefit that cloaked its claims in a systematic scheme of misrecognition or ideology in which the idea of public reason was an essential element. This analysis doubtless has an element of truth in it, though once one begins to consider the details, the element that is true diminishes in relation to the larger picture.

The wider story has also often been told and indeed was told in various ways in the nineteenth century – one of the most acute analysts was Albert Venn Dicey, to whom I will soon turn. But perhaps it would be useful to frame the problem more generally. The institutions of early modern society were already institutions in which popular approval played a role. We may distinguish between *legitimacy* and, as Dicey himself put it, the *influence of opinion on law*, and in this manner distinguish between political forms, which, like the monarchy and the Roman emperor, were legitimate, that is, accepted as possessing genuine rights to exercise sovereignty, and regimes that represented in the sense that they were representing the *opinions* of the ruled or some large subset of the ruled with respect to the actual contents of laws and of state decisions and actions. Dicey's question was 'how did it come to pass that public opinion regimes emerged, and the proportions of those whose opinions were taken into account increased?' This question is almost impossible to answer, at least with respect to its details, if we treat the notion of public reason as a cloak for bourgeois power.

The details of the story, which one might, as a matter of preference, regard either as a very large proportion of the story or as merely a complex decoration to the basic Marxian story line, are perhaps best understood in terms of the notion of civility; and the notion of civility is best approached through the practical political matter that occupied the nineteenth century: the problem of the franchise and its extension. This was a question so completely bound up with all of the questions of government reform, political form, and so forth, that the consideration of the franchise as a topic is inevitable even for those who view it merely as a tactical instrument of bourgeois degradation of the proletariat. But even Marx himself considered at one point that the inevitable consequence of the extension of the franchise would be that socialist regimes could simply be voted in. In this respect Marx and Ireton were as one. So we may turn to the problem of the franchise, both the larger problem of it as bound to its visible purposes, of providing a mechanism by which opinion translates into state action, and the immediate practical problem of the expansion of the franchise, which was understood in the nineteenth century as a problem of giving it to all those who were capable of employing it responsibly, or in such a way that the system of government by discussion or the translation of opinion into law would not itself be undermined.

As previously suggested, this problem was no mere fantastic imagining of the bourgeoisie. Failures of civility were fundamental to the collapse of the Weimar Republic, and deeply implicated in the failures of the French to succeed in institutionalizing a stable form of republican government during the nineteenth and, indeed well into the last half of the twentieth century. The problem of the franchise was not simply a problem of class, because the conditions of genuine discussion, thus the conditions for liberal democracy, extend far beyond the considerations of class. Even Habermas' *The Structural Transformation of the Public Sphere* acknowledges this in a backhanded way by the attention it gives to the (at least partly autonomous) facts of the development of coffeehouse discussion, newspapers, and the like.

A more extended discussion than the one attempted here would deal with the many other conditions that have been thought to be essential for the creation of discussion in the many present elements of discussion that have the capability of undermining it, such as the emergence of a moralizing politics within discussion, the destruction of intellectual independence by the emergence of mass society, and of course the emergence of ideological and thus de-rationalizing politics. In the category of 'external' conditions, the list is extraordinarily long and I will only indicate its potential contents here in the briefest of ways. Liberal democracy requires discussion, which requires people who are secure enough to be autonomous near equals in discussion. A regime lacking strong legal protections of rights to speak and petition, in which no one has security of property , or in which security depends on the clientelistic favor of a patron or nobleman, lacks this elementary material base for liberal discussion. This problem of 'sufficient equality' obviously had extensive ramifications in the nineteenth century, and reaches its one paradigmatic form in the notion that stable 'liberty' requires a Jeffersonian society of yeomen farmers.

One set of problems about civility and the franchise carried over from early liberalism, namely the question of whether the existence of a clientelistic social order effectively precluded liberal discussion, was solved by the market, which slowly eliminated clientelism. For the proletariat, new relations of dependence, enforced by the labor market, potentially had similar effects. Questions of church polity raised other questions, eswpecially because of the hostility to liberalism of the Catholic church. Was it really possible for liberal democracy to occur when in the realm of religious life the population was subordinated to a religious regime that was authoritarian and bureaucratic and was defined by a relationship of, as Kant put it, self-imposed tutelage? ([1784]1963: 3). If the leaders of a religious sect chose directly or indirectly to influence opinion, or to command its adherents to vote in a particular way, was it possible to have government by discussion between the adherents and the non-adherents? As populations moved during the nineteenth century another problem emerged, a problem that followed from the religious problem and was in many cases closely bound up with it. Was it possible to have government by discussion in a situation in which communal, ethnic, or tribal solidarity played a significant role? Weber, for one, argued that the characteristic 'fraternal' forms of Western politics that led to modern liberalism were radically distinguished from Eastern traditions precisely because of 'magical' prohibitions on social contact in the East (Weber [1921]1966: 96-8). American theorists of democracy of the nineteenth century were greatly concerned with problems of creating citizens out of immigrants from southern Europe, and saw no point in even considering Orientals as potential citizens. These issues became tangled up with matters of racial ideology and the like, but nevertheless pointed to problems that have proven to be intractable in places such as the Balkans.

In the nineteenth century a good deal of discussion was given in the light of such issues about civility to the question of the cultural traditions necessary for liberal democracy and in particular to the question of whether a certain culture of individualism that was in practice unique to the 'Anglo Saxon' world was an essential condition for liberal democracy (cf. Mayer 1981: 78-9 for the French discussion). I will simply bracket these questions, as they have been bracketed by history itself. A more serious question deriving from the nineteenth century is the problem of mass society, or to put it somewhat differently the problem of the *de facto* plebiscitary character of mass electoral politics, and the more interesting problem, posed by Habermas, of whether modern techniques of opinion manipulation, which aim at producing acceptance and acclamation, have had the same effects as earlier theorists feared mass society would have on the possibility of genuine discussion. These were of course concerns of Tocqueville ([1850]1969) and Weber. Indeed, Weber dismissed the notion of liberal discussion as an irrelevancy, and viewed modern liberal democracy as a combination of interest politics and the politics of acclamation and party discipline, that is to say a kind of de facto scheme of 'plebiscitary leader democracy' (cf. Eliaeson 2000: 135). However, Dicey is, for our purposes, the more subtle and relevant thinker, for, uniquely (at least among the major figures of the nineteenth century), Dicey grasped the conflict between *expertise* and democratic civility. He understood this conflict primarily in terms of the conflict between collectivist currents of opinion and *laissez faire* liberalism as a current of opinion. Like these other thinkers, Dicey thought liberal democracy was not only doomed, but that the form of its doom had been prefigured in the internal developments of liberal democracy in Britain by the 1870s.

Dicey on Discussion

Dicey tells the story from an internal point of view, that is to say as a problem of accounting for the various currents of opinion that led to changes in legislation, and latterly to the constitution of Britain itself, meaning the relations between the people and the state; particularly as a consequence of the extension of the franchise. His account of the ideological element in these discussions is therefore different from Habermas' or Foucault's. On the problem of ideology, Dicey observed that although interest is obviously a major determinant of the political choices that people make, and of the causes they support, he rejects as naive the theory, which he ascribed to Jeremy Bentham, of 'sinister' interests. This theory is at the core of Marxian *Ideologiekritik*: it is the idea that discussion conceals hidden interests, and in its more extreme form, that behind every political discursive intervention is a hidden interest, so that 'discussion' is merely concealed struggle. Dicey suggests a different explanation of the formation of political convictions: that there is a natural form of bias in the formation of beliefs that results from the fact that individuals are limited in their knowledge of the world and are most aware of (and consequently give greatest weight to) those principles that fit best with their own experience and situation, part of which is their own interests. Dicey thought that there is a degree of detachment of principles from interests, and this detachment is one of the guarantees that persuasion with respect to general ideas is possible. He points to the extensive development of what he calls humanitarian feelings, exemplified by movements to reform the criminal law and reduce criminal penalties, and also the movement to abolish slavery, neither of which were matters of interest. He also attacks the idea of ideological uniformity or as we might say *Weltanschauungen*. As he says, most people hold contradictory 'social theories', as he puts it, by which he means that people reason in both 'individualist' and 'collectivist' ways without ever fully reconciling the contradictions.

These contradictory theories within the governing or widely held opinions of the day are particularly important sites of analysis for Dicey. Conflicts intrinsic to widely held ideas were characteristic of the great disputes over legislation in the nineteenth century, and produced the peculiarities of the movements of reform that characterize the nineteenth century. By the end of the century they had led, in Britain, to a situation common to most of Europe: generally 'liberal' parties or Conservative parties were opposed with varying degrees of success by socialist parties. This eventually led – though in Europe itself only after the political experiment of fascism – to a political order in which there was a kind of moving balance, where socialist parties were constrained by public unwillingness to pay the taxes that socialist party programs required, and balanced by parties or conditions that promised to limit taxation. The liberal reforms of the early nineteenth century played a fundamental role in bringing about this situation. Dicey concentrates, accordingly, on the ideas, successes, and transformation of reformism as it was inaugurated and conceived by Bentham, who was the source of many of the relevant ideas, and also whose own thought contained *in nuce* these conflicts of ideas.

Bentham's main concern, the problem of legal reform, as Weber had also observed, had a certain logic of its own. In the English case the system of common law had evolved as a form of judge-made law in which legal fictions were employed to solve legal problems that could not be readily addressed within the limits of legislation as it then existed or solved in a simple way on the basis of precedent. Judges, faced with conflicts in the law that could not otherwise be addressed, would invent pretexts for resolving the conflict that took various forms, notably the well-known 'fictions' of the common law. Once enshrined as precedents within the force of law, these fictions were the basis for further decisions that constituted precedents and consequently furthered judge-made law. The sheer absurdity and illogic of the results of this stepwise creation made the laws into an arcane mystery that required professional lawyers, and this in turn separated the law from popular notions of justice, and also from the commonplace political ideas of the time.

The electoral system had its own absurdities. The scheme of designating the units that members of parliament represented had always been somewhat haphazard. Economic change in the eighteenth and early nineteenth centuries had produced extraordinary anomalies in which the votes of very small numbers in particular 'rotten boroughs' had the same standing as the votes of many thousands in other seats. Municipal governments were not much better. It was believed that Birmingham grew so successfully precisely because it was a collection of legally independent villages with no municipal corporation to be corrupted. Municipal improvements, revealingly, were characteristically implemented by municipal commissions, rather than by municipal governments.

The reform movement was closely connected to the changes in status and wealth of different groups in the country. Dicey makes the interesting Marx-like observation that the great landowners preserved their power when the mills depended on water but lost it to the urban capitalists when the same work could be done by steam. These were conditions rather than determinants, however. The conditions made conflicts of ideas important. In making sense of the changes of the times, of their own interests, and in persuading one another it was necessary to articulate the conflicts. So those who provided solutions to the conflcits in the form of theories justifying reform became important historical agents. Dicey and Foucault both picked Bentham as the thinker whose ideas and their unfolding best provide the structure for their accounts of the nineteenth century, but there is a characteristic difference in the way they see him. When Dicey considers the Panopticon, for example, he situates it in the context of penal reforms motivated by the broader humanitarian movements of the time, such as the anti-slavery movement. But it is Habermas to whom the account given by Dicey is appropriately compared. Bentham was, along with his fellow reformer James Mill, a relentless believer in what Mill called *un peuple éclairé*, an enlightened people. Mill believed that public discussion was the essential feature of a political order, and that the 'moral coercion' of public opinion was the proper substitute for physical coercion. When Dicey quotes a passage of John Stuart Mill's *Autobiography* he also provides us with a direct statement of the ideas of Liberal Democracy 2.0. James Mill had,

> in politics, an almost unbounded confidence in the efficacy of two things: representative government, and complete freedom of discussion. So complete was my father's reliance on the influence of reason over the minds of mankind, whenever it is allowed to reach them, that he felt as if all would be gained if the whole population were taught to read, if all sorts of opinions were allowed to be addressed to them by word and in writing, and if by means of the suffrage they could nominate a legislature to give effect to the opinions they adopted. He thought that when the legislature no longer represented a class interest, it would aim at the general interest, honestly and with adequate wisdom; since the people would be sufficiently under the guidance of educated intelligence, to make in general a good choice of persons to represent them, and having done so, to leave to those whom they had chosen a liberal discretion. Accordingly, aristocratic rule, the government of the Few in any of its shapes, being in his eyes the only thing that stood between mankind and an administration of their affairs by the best wisdom to be found among them, was the object of his sternest disapprobation, and a democratic suffrage the principle article of his political creed, not on the ground of liberty, rights of man, or any of the phrases more or less significant, by which, up to that time, democracy had usually been defended, but as the most essential of 'securities for good government.' In this, too, he held fast only to what he deemed essentials; he was comparatively indifferent to monarchial or republican forms – far more so than Bentham, to whom a king,

in the character of 'corruptor-general', appeared necessarily very noxious.
(Mill, J. S. 1873: 106-107, quoted in Dicey [1914]1962: 161-2)

Bentham was if anything even more relentless on the subject of the
importance of public discussion, freedom of speech, and the ability of individuals to judge their own interest. He also advocated public discussion in
the colonies, as a solution to the problems of imperialism. The basic idea
behind this view of discussion was, as Dicey says, 'democratic' in one sense
of the word. In more recent usage it would even be called 'populist', in the
sense of populism as the belief, as Harvey Mansfield puts it, in the special
virtue and wisdom of the people. The liberal reformers believed that 'what
made people similar was vastly more significant than what made them different' and that in consequence discussion and persuasion between them
were possible. Nevertheless, they faced the practical difficulty that Ireton
before them had faced: that there was at least a risk that the full extension
of the franchise would lead public discussion itself to collapse by bringing
into the discussion people who were not sufficiently alike with respect to
their wealth, opening up the possibility of, among other things, the rich cur-
rying favor with the poor to conspire against the middle classes.

Dicey saw the collectivist potentialities of Benthamism as an unresolved
problem of reformism itself, and when the franchise was extended on the
basis of Benthamite optimism about the course of rational discussion and
the opinions that it would produce, it led more or less directly to the situation described earlier, in which large socialist parties were constrained only
by the resistance to taxation they engendered. The turning point Dicey
locates in 1865, at the end of the American Civil War, with its visible consequence of extending the franchise to the newly freed slaves. This, Dicey
argues, led to the question of why workers in England should be deprived of
the vote if the ex-slaves of America were not; and this argument led eventually to the extension of the franchise to adult males and finally to women.
The expectations of every observer from Ireton to Tocqueville to Marx were
at least partially fulfilled. The workers supported collectivist doctrines and
the expansion of the role of the state, particularly to benefit the poor
through taxation and redistribution of various kinds.

But Dicey added something important to this. He saw that the socialist
idea was implicitly an idea that was antipopulist or at least hostile to the
notion that untutored legislative preferences, that is to say the opinions held
by ordinary people of what laws should be enacted, ought to be paramount,
and thus implicitly hostile to a related idea that government by discussion
ought to be the center of constitutional order. The 'collectivist current' and
socialist doctrine emphasized instead the superior wisdom of the state, and
the consequent necessity of intrusions into freedoms of individuals. The list
Dicey gives of incidents and governmental measures that show the seriousness of this conflict and the difficulties it produces for Bentham's model of
reform is interesting from the point of view of contemporary analysts of risk.
He gives the example of the man who introduced rabbits into Australia as

an example of a legally innocent act that had untold consequences. He might have added to this the story of the Shakespeare lover who, out of a desire to introduce into the new world all of the birds known to Shakespeare plays, imported starlings to the Americas. Such actions, Dicey saw, were in a broad sense in conflict with the implications of science, which he observes tends to show the interdependence of things previously thought to be unconnected ([1914]1962: lv).

Socialism, as a consequence of generally favoring state action for the benefit of the many, is more or less compelled to embrace the idea that experts are necessary to devise the policy that bring about the benefits Thus he *defines* collectivism in terms of expertise:

> The ideal of collectivism is government for the good of the people by experts, or officials who know, or think they know, what is good for the people better either than any non-official person or than the mass of the people themselves. (Dicey [1914]1962: lxxiii)

The people, he observed, often reason badly about these topics, for example resisting public health regimens that would benefit them. He gives the following case:

> That vaccination, if rigidly enforced, would banish small-pox from England is believed by the vast majority of experts competent to form an opinion on such a matter. Yet the Radicals of Leicester, in the name of freedom or of conscience, claim the right and, with the connivance of politicians who are fishing for votes, exercise the power to propagate small-pox. (Dicey [1914]1962: lxxv)

Yet he also saw that rule by experts had its own problems. Experts themselves were characteristically narrowly limited with respect to their expertise and this led them to make characteristic mistakes. And he used the eminent physicians who opposed Lister as an example to show that experts may be wrong (Dicey [1914]1962: lxxvii).

Dicey's analysis is perhaps overly neat. But it was nevertheless prophetic. The emergence of a broadly collectivist current of opinion did in fact lead to an instrumentalized view of the state as a provider of benefits and the instrumental business of providing benefits required a great deal of expertise. On the continent itself, the same conclusion was reached much more directly. The strategy of state-directed economic development as a means of placating the working class pioneered by Bismarck required bureaucratic expertise and the full advantages of the German bureaucratic tradition enabled the instrumental action of the state to be carried through in a particularly dramatic way. The public that had developed elsewhere in the mid nineteenth century barely developed there before it disappeared. Experts, however, flourished. By the time Mill died in 1870, the Prussians had an advanced statistical bureaucracy capable of answering questions of social policy as experts, and by the first decade of the twentieth century economists were sitting on the privy council. This bureaucratic order, as I have already mentioned, is the reality to which Habermas' otherwise arcane references to expert 'steering' refer.

Liberal Democracy 3.0: Conant and the Liberalization of Expertise

When James Conant became president of Harvard in 1933 many of the processes of working out the basic oppositions indicated by Dicey were already far advanced. In the US, the modern regulatory state had emerged, and regulation was a process of administrative law operated by experts rather than by common law. The administration of Franklin Roosevelt saw the importation of academics into administration. By this time the idea of rule by experts had acquired ideologists on the left, in the form of the 'technocracy' movement in the US, and organized around the idea of 'engineering' and 'efficiency', and in the writings of such figures as Karl Pearson in Britain in terms of 'National Efficiency'. In the 1930s a large discussion of the role of the state in fostering science took place, and, especially in Britain, a movement dominated by Communist scientists emerged. The movement advocated both the replacement of capitalism and the replacement of the existing 'unplanned' regime of science with a model of the governance of science in which scientists, acting as a somewhat autonomous trade union within a communist state organized on a syndicalist basis, would overcome the conflict between science (understood, in accordance with the standard Marxist formulas as a developing 'means of production') and capitalism (understood as a scheme of relations of production that failed to utilize it fully). In this structure of theory science was essentially the mental element of technology (See Bernal 1939, McGucken 1984).

No one now imagines trades-unions as a model for organizing science. But these debates are less antiquated than they appear. In Britain the same debates over capitalist under-investment in research and technology continue to this day. And it is testimony to the persistence of bureaucratic and administrative style that the same British civil service system that is commonly thought to have been an organizational failure in the face of expert knowledge in the first half of the century ago failed organizationally again in the face of Bovine Spongiform Encephalopathy (BSE). Indeed it is striking that national differences that were evident in the very early encounters of states with the problem of telephones, the classic natural technological monopoly continued until the recent past, and beyond. In the US, the pattern of patent law, market competition between major players that eventually yielded to monopolism, and integrated relationships with state regulators and governmental regulatory bodies that began with telephones held for other highly technologized industries. The recent Microsoft litigation was preceded fifty years ago by similar litigation against AT&T, with a similarly inconclusive outcome, and a similar challenge to the technical competence of the courts.

In Britain, the necessity for technical experts to deal with the basic questions of decision-making involving telephones and telecommunications disrupted the basic system of civil service selection, training, and discretionary decision making. Membership in an old boys network and an Oxford degree in classics were simply insufficient as qualifications for making these decisions. In Germany, characteristically, telecommunications was dominated by a state cartel which operated very much like a German state bureaucracy itself with all of the benefits in 'rationality' and in a lack of control by markets or the public that this implied. Further, the Soviet Union appeared to many as the perfect embodiment of expert rule. Even after the disappointments of the 1920s, when intellectuals flocked to Russia to contribute to the creation of the first great socialist state, westerners and particularly scientists and reformers such as Sidney and Beatrice Webb made the pilgrimage to Moscow to be educated about sewer systems, urban planning, and so forth, all systems in which state action on a massive scale directed by experts was the norm.

There were two major 'liberal' responses to the complex issues raised by the new role of science-driven technology. Michael Polanyi's is the most famous. He attacked the idea of 'planning' science on the grounds that technology and science were insufficiently demarcated and based on a fundamental misunderstanding not only of the nature of scientific discovery, but of knowledge. Conant's and Polanyi's arguments are roughly parallel, and they understood one another as allies, but they diverged in some crucial ways and their differences are revealing. The key difference points to a revision of liberalism that goes beyond Dicey.

Regarding Conant's conception of science itself, very little need be said, for what he said was repeated by Thomas Kuhn in *The Structure of Scientific Revolutions* ([1962]1996). This text was little more than a systematic summary of the course material Conant had devised to teach about the nature of science to non-science Harvard students. The method used detailed case studies of episodes of radical conceptual change in science: conceptual schemes and their overthrow and supplanting was the theme. Conant's favorite case was Lavoisier and the overthrow of phlogiston theory: it was the case he chose to illustrate that:

> a well established concept may prove a barrier to the acceptance of a new one. If a conceptual scheme is highly satisfactory to those who use it, neither a few old facts which cannot be reconciled nor a few new ones will cause the concept to be abandoned. (1947: 106)

The same case illustrates this:

> A new concept may be revolutionary and after its formulation a host of old facts may be fitted into the new scheme and many new facts discovered. (1947: 106)

Conant did not like the term 'paradigm', and here there is an important difference with Kuhn. Conant had the view that sciences were theoretical or empirical by degree – some science was almost wholly empirical, some almost wholly conceptual. This contrasted with Kuhn's idea that all observation was theory-dependent in a strong sense, not in degree only. For Conant, progress consisted of 'reducing the degree of empiricism'. Yet he thought that 'new techniques of experimentation may be revolutionary', and, in contrast to Kuhn, believed that such new techniques may 'evolve gradually as improvements in apparatus and method' (1947: 108). Instrumentation and low level empirical results typically survived replacements of conceptual schemes – a point stressed by Kuhn's later critics.

Removing the notion of 'degree of empiricism' from Conant's conception produces Kuhn. Each stressed the community character of science, though here Kuhn seems to have taken his lead from Polanyi's linked ideas of community, tacit knowledge, and the 'autonomy' of science; themes stressed in Fuller's study of Kuhn (Fuller 2000). Conant characteristically was more concrete, less sociological, and more political: for him the rise of professional science, a network of scientific societies, journals and, consequently, communication, was the dominant 'social' fact of modern science. The idea of 'community' thus played a different role. The break in the age of Boyle between the backwards universities and the newly formed scientific societies was critical; the Medici-sponsored *Accademia del Cimento* he viewed as 'a genuine cooperative experimental effort' (Conant, 1947: 71). But these institutions were intentional creations. There was not a whiff of mysticism about 'scientific community' in Conant.

Conant's writings were steeped in a suspicion of scientists and distrust of scientific decision-making that is largely absent from Polanyi and Kuhn. Where Polanyi wanted to show the affinities and similarities between science and liberalism, which he understood to subsist in the fact that they were the same type of enterprise, dependent on tradition and 'rational' in a sense that required an endowment of tacit knowledge, Conant tended to see the problem of the organization of science in terms of, and from the point of view of, the businessman operating in a competitive environment in the face of uncertainty. The problem with scientists, in short, was that they could not be trusted, but not because they were untrustworthy: they were untrustworthy because of the limitations of their understanding and knowledge and their tendency to answer questions in terms of what they knew best, and especially because they tended to be enamored with their own ideas, whose significance they tended to overestimate their significance. A proposal for a technology or project from a scientist was not the same as a fact of science or a statement of a scientific consensus. It was something that needed to be treated with scepticism. What scientists *knew* was limited. It varied between individuals, and individuals, and groups of them, had biases, self-regard, and so forth. Conant took for granted that businessmen and administrators simply could not effectively adjudicate the claims of scientists in this situation. Nor could citizens, and Conant's views on science education for citizens, accordingly, were quite different from his predecessors.

Conant's discussion of science education for citizens, the reform of high schools, and what he called 'education for a classless society', contains much of his 'political' thinking. The material out of which Kuhn constructed *The Structure of Scientific Revolutions* was also largely pedagogical, concerned with the education of non-science college students about science. This is a problem that did not even exist in British and Continental universities – they did not do 'general education'. In the nineteenth century Horace Mann once observed that the best way to disperse an angry crowd was to announce a lecture on pedagogy. The rule holds even more strongly today. So it is important to suspend some prejudices and to accept the need to penetrate some American arcana to see the significance of what Conant said. Conant himself was quite clear about what he was doing. Despite the popular style and popular success of his writings on science, the works are high scholarly polemic; the footnotes often contain engagements of Conant with the claims of his predecessors and his contemporaries such as J. D. Bernal.

Conant quotes Karl Pearson's idea that 'I believe more will be achieved by placing instruction in pure science within the reach of all our citizens, than by any number of polytechnics devoting themselves to technical education, which does not rise above the level of manual instruction' (Pearson [1892]1937 quoted in Conant 1947: 112 n1). This was more than a sentiment: generations of great British scientists, including Nobelist Bernard Lovell, taught science in working men's institutes and adult education schemes as a means of implementing this idea. Part of the motivation, shared with John Dewey in the United States, was for the 'method of science' to be used in thinking about all things. As Pearson says,

> the peculiarity of scientific method, [is] that when once it has become a habit of mind, that mind converts all facts whatsoever into science. The field of science is unlimited; its material is endless, every group of natural phenomena, every phase of social life, every stage of past or present development is material for science. (Pearson [1892]1937:16 quoted in Conant 1947: 112 n1)

These were the sentiments of Comte, into whose mysteries Pearson was inducted as an undergraduate at Cambridge (by a librarian).

Conant rejected this model, and with it the idea of scientific method (cf. 1947: 116 n6) and the idea of science as a positive model for democracy. Abandoning these ideas was a decisive break: to treat citizens as junior scientists, capable of applying the methods of science to their own affairs, was to preserve a continuity between citizens and scientists. One is reminded of Henry de Man's acute observation that socialist intellectuals in different countries envisaged a socialism in which all people could resemble themselves: in England, the community-oriented Fabians wanted 'to make the productive machine . . . work thence forward for the communal advantage instead of the private, and . . . gradually transform the state into a community organization' ([1928]1974: 223). German socialism that 'may be called "civil servants"' socialism – the socialism of persons who hold that the working motive of those engaged in production should be akin to those who serve the state in contemporary civil service' ([1928]1974: 224). The model of the citizen-scientist was, in these terms, an expression of the scientists' will to power: a desire for a society in which the basic motives of citizens were the same as theirs. In contrast, Conant had no desire to make every citizen a junior scientist. The understanding of science citizens needed, he thought, was an understanding of how science worked.

What Conant argued *for* can be seen in his writings on education. Conant devoted enormous effort to the restructuring and reform of the American high school, and this reform paralleled that of Pearson: it was designed to enable this most inegalitarian and peculiar of American institutions to produce members of a liberal public. Conant was under no illusion that propaganda for science in the form of 'science literacy' was a surrogate for the kind of education necessary to deal with the competing claims of scientists as fulfilling the role of a businessman, administrator, or political leader. His commitments were clear from his undergraduate reforms. As President of Harvard, responsible for the incubation of the American variant of an elite, Conant was faced with the choice of whether to educate them in a half hearted way in the rudiments of such disciplines as chemistry, a process which even now consists largely of memorization of unconnected formulae and problem solving techniques, or to do something else, more suited to the roles of decision makers. He chose the latter and this was the genesis for the famous system of recording case studies of revolutionary episodes of science that led to the writings of Thomas Kuhn. But it is in his writings on youth and high schools that he comes to terms with the fundamental issues of class struggle and of Right and Left: the choice between, as he puts it, 'potential Bourbons and latent Bolsheviks' (Conant, 1940: 8). The central motif of these writings is the need to reconstruct schools to do more than to provide the universal education that was part of the Jeffersonian ideal, the model of Liberal Democracy 2.0.[4] Their new goal was to be to provide for educational opportunity as a means of assuring the greatest development of different individual capacities. Schools were thus to serve the purpose of producing social mobility, the modern surrogate for the classless society of Jefferson's time. Social mobility requires not universal schooling in the rudiments of science and citizenship, but universal schooling in preparation for specialization. This implicitly points to the question of how to deal with the specialists that are produced.

Conant also spoke repeatedly to the public about the problem of administering and making political decisions about science, and here his underlying rationale is quite clear. As suggested in Chapter 1, Conant believed that scientists had to be compelled to submit to criticisms by peers, even in the face of apparent consensus. He distrusted what I have called the consensus of scientists as distinct from the scientific consensus. Scientific proposals, weapons systems and projects that involve public commitments needed to be subjected to liberal discussion. He knew citizen participation would be inadequate. He proposed instead to formalize a process by which experts would argue their cases for and against in front of an audience not of peers but of citizens or decision-makers representing citizens. Though this tribunal system was never formally implemented, what we have already seen referred to as 'the duelling experts scenario' resembles it.

Why is this apparently innocuous innovation significant? Even Dicey, who understood that experts were often bull-headed and wrong, did not see these traits as characteristic of experts. nor did he see the behavior of experts in groups as instrinsically problematic for liberal democracy. Conant did. Nor did Dicey envision, much less devise, means to reconcile expertise to liberal democracy. Like Schumpeter later on, Dicey was impressed by the problem of citizens failing to recognize genuine expertise. Conant saw the problem in a new way – as a matter of making claims of expertise submit to a kind of scrutiny consistent with the deeper meaning of liberal democracy.

There is a fundamental distinction to be made here. Conant most emphatically did *not* advocate 'democratic control of science'. The tribunals he envisioned weren't juries of ordinary people. The point was to 'liberalize expertise': to force expert claims to be subjected to the discipline of a contentious discussion that would reveal their flaws, and do so by forcing the experts to make arguments to be assessed by people *outside* the corporate body of experts in the field. The method was a check on expert group-think, on the 'consensus of scientists'.

To see the issues here, consider the arguments of scientists like Stephen Schneider, who advocate, in the same tradition as Pearson, the citizen-scientist. Schneider claims to believe that 'every citizen in a democracy is capable of joining in . . . decisions that hinge on scientific expertise' (1997: 1). But he suggests that citizens 'transcend the current dueling experts' scenario' which he characterizes as politically selected extremes rather than the current scientific consensus (1997: 2). The problem, in his view, is that the duelling experts scenario, with experts supported by special interests, confuses people. We can read Schneider as Habermas read Rousseau. Confused people ought not to make decisions; he implicitly concedes that citizens can't make the relevant judgments unaided. Like Conant, he suggests an intermediate court-like institution. But the institution he proposes has a different aim. It is a 'meta-institution' designed to to tell citizens *how probable* various outcomes are, or, in our terms here, to produce authoritative fact-surrogates on the basis of which the public can choose a course of action. Schneider claims that 'the majority of climate change experts view the odds of at least one degree of global warming [in the next century] at something like nine of ten'. These odds are the sorts of 'facts' that this institution would report. When there is disagreement on the odds, 'you've got to go with the best guesses of a majority of the best-respected experts – even recognizing that every once in a while a scientist with a marginal view may turn out to be right' (1997: 4).

If we look at this proposal politically, we get some simple results. Behind it is a political theory of how science should relate to public discussion. It demands that 'respect' be acknowledged, that 'respectable' opinions be treated for political purposes as a surrogate for truth. One need hardly note the sinister 'Ministry of Truth' implications of this reasoning: Schneider himself makes them explicit when he calls for a government institution that polices public debate, one that, as he puts it, 'can call anyone's statement, including statements by the president or the speaker of the house, "scientific nonsense", if that is what is warranted by the best available knowledge' (1997: 4-5). The best available knowledge is that which is endorsed as such by the consensus of scientists. 'Public understanding of science' thus becomes public deference to the consensus of scientists, a consensus not about 'facts of science' or knowledge, as Schneider misleadingly says, but about a particular kind of fact-surrogate. The consensus of scientists becomes a privileged replacement for democratic opinion. For the citizen-scientist, citizenship consists in simply accepting what the scientists tell them, mediated through this commission-like body. The antiliberalism of this proposal is breath-taking, as is its audacity. Not only does this meta-agency claim neutrality for core scientific facts, it extends this claim to cover whatever respectable scientific opinion agrees to on such fraught topics as global warming. Imagine if the same demands for power were made with respect to economic opinions – that the opinions of respectable economists be enforced by a state agency which was empowered to actively denounce politicians who disagreed with them. Schumpeter's problem with the public's inability to grasp economic principles would have been solved – at the expense of the political liberalism he wanted to preserve.

Schneider's 'solution' is itself political. It does not help the public ascertain the probability of the truth of various alternative claims, except by the purely political device of ascertaining respectable opinion about these probablities. It does not constitue any sort of check against majority expert opinion. It adds nothing to science. Disputes about the weight of the evidence that scientists disagreed about in the first place are not be resolved by handing the problem over to a committee to settle. A committee can no more decide the true scientific weight to be assigned to the alternatives than the disagreeing scientists themselves- and even Schneider concedes that scientific mavericks are sometimes right. As a political device it adds little to the 'commissions' discussed in Chapter 4, other than the sinister idea of denouncing as 'scientific nonsense' opinions by elected officials who question the opinions of scientists.

In practice such an institution would of course not be so sinister. There are already many such bodies operating non-officially, with which it would compete. Unless the agency was empowered to actually suppress the claims of other experts, debate would go on, and the agency would be a voice among others. The public, or decision-makers, could decide to do with this new one what they wish. They could simply ignore any attempt to foreclose discussion of the merits of the 'consensus' results. And one could imagine a future in which the meta institution's claims are themselves routinely discounted to a greater or lesser extent, based on the past experiences of dealing with it, the strength of delegitimation efforts against it, and public estimates of the ideological biases and honesty of the scientists. This is precisely what occurred with the institution that Schneider admired, the Office of Technology Assessment, which became identified with partisan interests and was eventually abolished. Liberal democratic discussion would be preserved, but only by turning the body into just another knowledge association seeking to concentrate opinion.

To get a better sense of how these models rearrange the relations between scientists and the public, it is useful to consider another elaborated proposal, by Aaron Wildavsky. Writing explicitly in the tradition of Robert Dahl on citizen competence, Wildavsky argues that

> by following simple rules individuals of ordinary intelligence can learn what they need to know by reading original scientific studies rather than books devoted either to reassurance or alarm. By preparing themselves to interrogate experts – indeed by going back and forth between experts with rival views – citizens can sharpen their understanding of why there are disagreements. And by talking to friends, neighbors, and colleagues citizens can develop their own preferences. (1995, 395-6)

He suggests that 'for the run-of-the-mill environmental problem, usually involving low-level chemical exposure, an expenditure of some 100-200 hours should be sufficient' and that neighbors might form clubs that addressed 'something like five to eight subjects a year' of this kind (1995, 395). It will suffice to say that if this is a reasonable estimate of the cost in time and effort of self-reliance and self-education in the face of expertise, it explains very vividly why it is that there is so much demand for fact-surrogates that would allow citizens to spend their time more productively, or pleasantly. But it does show what it might mean for there to be genuine 'government by discussion' with respect to the topics that experts routinely address.

One thing that Wildavsky thinks citizens will learn if they engage the subject in this way is how to interpret some of the claims made by scientists. In the case of global warming, Wildavsky suggests, 'No one ... would believe those who peddle the line that there is a consensus among scientists about this subject ...[and] the claim of consensus can be seen for what it is, a tactic in the struggle over whose views will be accepted and become the basis of public policy' (1995, 397). And he is strongly sceptical of the value added to discussions by the kinds of activist 'experts' that typically involve themselves in environmental cases. He considers the problem of cancer clusters, many of which occur randomly, and asks what value is added to the discussion of concerned citizens by a cluster by experts 'whose views are at variance with the scientific literature [note: "literature" not "consensus"] on the subject' who tell concerned citizens what they want to hear, namely such things as that birth defects in a cluster are caused by low concentrations of chemicals (1995, 408). Wildavsky asks 'What have these citizens gained? Before, they were ignorant in the face of industrial and government scientists, now they are ignorant in the face of their own scientists'. The lesson he draws is that 'the only sure way to know what we want to know is through the science itself. Citizens who train themselves to read and understand the primary sources, the original scientific studies, can participate meaningfully; those who do not, cannot' (1995, 408). The conclusion he draws is that 'the best guarantee that citizen preferences will shape public policy' is 'a combination of citizen labor and development of citizenship skills to study the scientific and technical literature so as to understand what is known and, with that understanding, to make intelligent use of experts in order to reach informed judgements' (1995, 409).

For Schneider, despite his praise of the citizen who is self-educated in science and asks the right questions, for example to a physician, the real task of the citizen-scientist with respect to science is, to quote Weber from another setting, to 'shut up and obey'. Questioning the validity of the truth surrogates offered by science and making judgements about scientists' biases is not for him the proper business of public discussion. The point of the meta agency is to foreclose such discussion. The question of the validity of the procedures by which these fact-surrogates are produced by science, or by which 'respectable' scientific opinion is produced, are passed over in silence. Problems of the sort pointed to by Morone and Woodhouse with nuclear power science, discussed in Chapter 2, are also ignored. The problem of 'understanding the science' is solved by the scientists' commission prepackaging the results, the truth-surrogates, in a form ready for policy discussion. For Wildavsky, the task of the citizen is to become competent in 'the science itself' at least sufficiently to 'understand what is known'. However, responsibility for understanding and judging rests squarely on the citizen. Experts are resources in public discussion to be used, but judiciously, with the understanding that they too may have agendas and biases. Though the problem of understanding is not passed over in silence, neither is it convincingly resolved. Epidemiological discussions of cancer clusters might be addressed by neighborhood clubs consisting of ordinary citizens studying science for hundreds of hours (though it seems farfetched to think that this would actually happen in the real world), but a great many other technical decisions would nevertheless be inaccessible to the non-scientist.

Conant's model neither requires ultra-competent citizens nor an ultra-powerful meta institution. The issue of understanding that is a problem for Wildavsky is addressed as part of the design: the point of tribunals was to force scientists to justify themselves in the face of a challenge by a competent specialist in a forum that did not consist of other specialists of the same kind. The tribunals are delegated bodies with decision-making responsibilities, whose members can be selected for their competence. They are, however, outsiders to the speciality. This insistence on persuading outsiders addresses the problem posed by Schneider's proposal.

'Respectable opinion' is not enough for Conant, who rejected any sort of celebration of scientific group-think, and indeed saw it as a grave danger. And with this we reach a fundamental contrast between 'democratic control' and 'liberalized expertise'. The point of Conant's design is to force issues into the open, and in a form that enables them to be discussed and judged by outsiders. The role of the scientist is not to say 'shut up and obey', but to defend proposals or fact-surrogates in the face of criticism from insiders, to an audience of outsiders. This preserves the possibility of government by discussion by giving the issues up to discussion in a discussable form, not as fact-surrogates which are meant to be taken as givens of public discussion.

It should be added that 'liberalizing' tribunals were not his only 'liberal' or indirect means for controlling experts, or even the most important. He understood that direct means of bureaucratic power generated their own kind of corporate thinking. As such he relied on a set of other, indirect means to control experts, in accordance with the classical liberal preference for indirect means. With respect to quality and excellence, Conant was a respecter of markets, and he believed that great corporations and great universities with fully developed structures of decision-making, production, and marketing, would produce the best results if they competed with similar companies and universities. This was an ideal that was only partially realized in either the industrial or the academic worlds. The defense contractors, which were the source of his major concerns, did in fact compete with one another. The need to preserve competition led the government to allow the development of a particular kind of subcontracting that had the effect of keeping the losers in competition employed and their productive and technological capacities preserved. These were, in short, artificial systems of competition. Competition between universities themselves was also to a large extent preserved and encouraged by artificial devices of distributing funding for science in a way that countered the natural tendencies of competition between universities to produce extreme hierarchic differentiations and concentration.

Conant's idea was that politicians and businessmen would act as enlightened decision-makers about science. The idea withered, it would be unkind to say, along with the withering of the WASP supremacy. Conant's self-described 'fanatic egalitarianism' (1940) with regard to opportunity played a role in the transformation. Interestingly, the democratic figure who is invoked by Conant is no longer Jefferson, who assumed that universal schooling produced sufficient common knowledge for citizenship, but Andrew Jackson, for his opposition to the National Bank. Suspicion of central institutions, Jackson's legacy, is a precious part of the tradition that Conant wanted preserved; equality of opportunity explicitly replaces the older notion of rough equality of circumstance combined with a minimum of universal education. As I suggested in Chapter 4, what transpired was not an enlightened citizenry, or a system of Conant-like tribunals, but the development of a vast system of means of concentrating opinion. Scientific opinion was a particularly successful form of the concentration of opinion. The state and the public evaded the kind of decision-making that Conant was concerned with, in favor of 'commissions': the state granted limited powers to expert bodies of various kinds and exercised control over these bodies. Many of these nevertheless served the purpose Conant had in mind. The vast expansion of these commission-like forms has, as I observed, gone largely unnoted by conventional liberal political theorists. Like their predecessors on the Left in the era before Foucault they seem to regard them as the largely neutral means that Saint-Simon had in mind when he spoke of the administration of things. Yet neutrality, as suggested in Chapter 3, is not so much a category of thought as a category of political agreement and convention.

Scientists and other experts had their own strategies for establishing their claims to be in this category. Establishing one's neutrality and the neutrality of the opinions one expressed required political activity. Scientists had to impose upon themselves self-denying ordinances that removed suspicion, such as the suspicion that a given scientist was riding a hobby horse and representing his own ideas as those of 'science', or that the scientist had a conflict of interest in the acceptance of these ideas and was no better than a commission salesman. This meant not making scientific claims, for example about global warming, that went beyond the 'scientific' evidence as these terms were understood by scientists themselves in their ordinary scientific activity, which in turn produced characteristic disputes between scientists about what the 'science' established. Science, however, is an unusual instance of a more general type of commission or knowledge association. As discussed in Chapter 4, different commissions fashion themselves in different ways, as movements, like abolitionism and consumer activism, which were movements from below (or from outside of the state itself), or as commissions of stakeholders, or as 'expert' NGOs, as boundary organizations, or as certified experts governed by particular rules, for example rules involving education and conflicts of interest. The complexity of these processes has already been indicated.

What remains, as suggested in Chapter 1, is to determine the significance of these bodies. Do they represent, as the follower of Foucault might argue, merely the emergence of a new order of politics, an order of inevitably non-neutral expert knowledge capable of indefinite self-replication and beyond the possibility of democratic control? Is the 'Tocquevillian' model I alluded to in Chapter 4, in which competing and contesting intermediate bodies that are knowledge associations keep one another honest, a viable surrogate for liberal discussion? Or is the proliferation of these novel forms of opinion concentration an extension of liberalism by fundamentally liberal means, in which what James Mill called the moral coercion of opinion, in this case 'expert' opinion, is now extended to every nook and cranny of discretionary power? Or is this form the kernel of a third way with respect to the conflict between expertise and liberal democracy? Is there some alternative form of rule hidden in the great mass of political developments of the last half of the twentieth century which has significance that neither the extension of the cohesion of opinion to the far reaches of discretion nor the deneutralization species successfully reach? Is the idea of expert knowledge itself exposed as a sham, as merely politics pursued by different players in an order of decision making in which the old model of liberal discussion has no application, as writers like Bent Flyvbjerg (1998) have recently argued?

Notes

1 The problem of citizen competence, suffice it to say, was not invented by Robert Dahl, but is coeval with liberalism itself. This is not to say, as Habermas rather inconsistently implies, that it is a kind of pseudo-problem that addressing, as Rousseau does, amounts to a kind of special pleading inconsistent with liberalism itself - an acceptance of free discussion only if it comes to a preferred result, or an admission of the impossibility of genuine government by discussion. A utopian 'liberal' doctrine of participation could be formulated for which this would be a problem. But the criticism itself, like Foucault's similar insistence on the significance of the underside of exclusion in actual liberal regimes, applies only if such a doctrine is presupposed.

2 See Harvey Kaye 1984.

3 Col Rainsborough: 'I desired that those that had engaged in it [should speak] for really I think that the poorest he that is in England has a life to live as the greatest he; and therefore truly, Sir, I think it's clear, that every man that is to live under a Government ought first by his own consent to put himself under that Governement; and I do think that the poorest man in England is not at all bound in a strict sense to that Governement that he has not had a voice to put himself under; and I am confident that when I have heard the reasons against it, something will be said to answer those reasons, insoemuch that I should doubt whether he was an Englishman or no that should doubt of these things.' Clarke (1891) 299-307, 311-12, 315-17 and 325-7. *The Putney Debates 1647* http://history.hanover.edu/courses/excerpts/212put.html.

4 Conant provides his own version of this periodization when he remarks on the contrast between the British and American experiences:

To contrast the social history of the United States and that of even so closely related a country as Great Britain is illuminating. If we examine, for example, the recent history by G. D. H. Cole entitled *The British Common People, 1746-1938*, we shall see portrayed the evolution of one type of political democracy within a highly stratified caste system. Compare this picture with the history of the growth of this republic by expansion through the frontier in the last one hundred years- a history in which social castes can be ignored, a history where, by and large, opportunity awaited the able and daring youths of each new generation (1940).

6

The Withering Away of Civil Society?

> What is here already very plainly expressed is the idea of the future conversion of political rule over men into an administration of things. (Frederick Engels writing on Saint-Simon [1894]1947: 307)

At the beginning of this book, I considered the puzzle of the relationship between the increased importance of expertise and domains of expert knowledge and the emergence of liberal democracy as a standard political form. In the course of the book I have argued that the apparent underlying conflict between the necessity of political recognition of expertise and 'government by discussion' was a real conflict. Liberal democracies have used, and used successfully, a large number of devices to 'solve' this problem, but new forms of expertise and new domains of expert knowledge continue to produce expertise requiring new solutions. It would be a form of indulgence and prophecy to conclude with a grand prediction about the long term outcomes of this effort, and particularly about whether liberal democracy in the long run is a viable political form in the face of the demands placed on it by the fact of expert knowledge. We have, indeed, been in this territory before, for example with Schumpeter. And there the predictions were wrong, as were Schmitt's predictions, based on his experience of the Weimar-era democracy, of the final demise of representative 'government by discussion' in the face of totalizing ideologies on the Left and Right, and his prediction, rooted in similar considerations, that democracy and liberalism were incompatible.

Schumpeter was a liberal, Schmitt a conservative, and one might, from the Left, dismiss them as backward-looking. But the record of prediction on the Left has been, if anything, worse. Twentieth century thought on the Left was predominately concerned with giving reasons for the failure of the proletariat to assume the revolutionary role Marx assigned it. This was the point behind the elevation of the notion of false consciousness to the status of permanent impediment to revolution in the writings of Max Horkheimer and Theodor Adorno. Habermas' *The Structural Transformation of the Public Sphere* is part of this genre. So are writings like those of Theda Skocpol, for whom the agency of the state was loosened from the limits given to it by Marx and enabled to act in revolution stopping ways (Skocpol 1979).

But if we leave this 'literature of excuse' aside, there is another literature, from Karl Pearson to J. D. Bernal and from Veblen's technocratic *The Engineers and the Price System* ([1921]1963) to James Burnham's *The*

Managerial Revolution (1941). These books did predict – badly, to be sure – but in a way that is closely related to the problem of expertise. They forecast an inevitable centrality of expertise in advanced societies, and interpreted expertise as making liberal democracy, and along with it the traditional bourgeoisie and the system of capitalism, outdated.

Burnham's *The Managerial Revolution* (1941), with such chapter titles as 'The managers shift the locus of sovereignty', serves as a reminder of how easily even the most sophisticated theoretical argument – and at the time Burnham was deservedly in the top rank of Marxist thinkers – can go wrong by being largely right. The basic argument of the book was that managers were the new ruling class, supplanting the bourgeoisie. Burnham also makes these observations in his book: 'sovereignty has been slipping away from parliaments' (1941: 143); '"Laws" today in the United States, in fact most laws, are not being made any longer by Congress, but by the NLRB, SEC, ICE, AAA, TVA, FTC, FCC, the Office of Production Management (what a revealing title), and all the other leading "executive agencies"' (1941: 147). This is a Schmittian point: the agencies make law, and decide, using their discretionary powers. Burnham's account of this is secondary to his thesis that managers have become the ruling class in waiting. The shift in 'locus of sovereignty' to administrative bureaus serves their interests, as parliament served the capitalist class.

The 'managers' still have not had their turn at the helm of history, nor will they. However, in many respects Burnham was right. The federal agencies Burnham listed continue to make law – though not the Office of Production Management (tellingly, given his thesis) – and new ones, notably the EPA, have emerged to make new laws. To the list of agencies today we might add the agencies that approve drugs, fund science, plan space exploration, deal with social problems. These agencies employ 'experts' who both exercise discretionary power (powers Burnham understood well under the heading of the 'localization of sovereignty') and are beholden to communities of similar experts. If they are not representations of a class, what are they? If images like the image of a class seizing the helm of history, inherited from Marxism, are to be retired, what can be said about the larger significance of power for expertise? If 'class' is the wrong viewpoint, can something perhaps be said about the changing and already changed significance of the traditional forms of liberal democracy?

The Fading Away of Popular Sovereignty

Popular sovereignty is one of the central notions, indeed the key precondition, of the traditional idea of liberal democracy. The 'people', politically embodied in a nation exercising power through representative institutions that engaged in discussions, possessed sovereign political authority: final or ultimate within the borders of the nation itself. The challenges to this notion of sovereignty in practice are many and need hardly be rehashed here. The necessity for international cooperation in matters of security, the dependence of most nations on a significant amount of international trade, the legal difficulties that arise when the legal consequences of actions do not correspond to national boundaries and where the means of action, such as trade, involve virtual facts, such as electronic data transmitted between computers, rather than physical objects that must be literally transported across borders and exist only in one place at a time, are all challenges to elements of the key terms of the traditional conception of sovereignty. 'Popular' is also problematic. Enough has been said about the problematic character of 'discussion' in the face of expert knowledge. But expert knowledge is, like information, and unlike gold bullion or physical persons, not restricted to national domains. Although different things count as knowledge under different regulatory regimes, and different religious values and historical experiences may lead to different decisions in the face of the same expert claims,[1] in practice regulators imitate one another and rely on one another's judgments. An 'expert' claim about safety or danger in one country is typically transmitted to other countries, where it becomes the basis for a political demand for state action. Indeed, legal actions may be instigated against a corporation engaged in international trade in whichever jurisdictions recognize their actions as being in breach of the law, so that sovereignty is in fact not even a means of protecting a nation's businesses.

Regulatory regimes are potentially significant impediments to trade and consequently to national well being, and it is striking to consider the extent to which sovereignty over these matters has increasingly been given up to international organizations. The infamous regulations of the European Community are one example of this. It was recognized that the widely divergent and in some cases hyper aggressive regulatory regimes of some European nations effectively served to harm not only trade but the economic and social standing of the nations that pursued them. This was one significant impetus for the European Community's increasing role. Economic regulation more generally has been displaced, through treaties or customs and monetary unions, onto international bodies that are expected to, and indeed bound to, rely on experts.

This obviously represents a significant transfer of practical sovereignty not unlike the strategy of the early modern state in the face of religious conflict. Rather than tying its own hands by removing itself from the regulation of religion, or by establishing a state church and defining a specific limited legal relationship to it, the twentieth century state more closely resembles an alcoholic who voluntarily gives up his car keys. By giving control over monetary matters first to an independent national bank run by experts, who are at least partially immune from political pressure, the next step is taken: monetary policy and even the currency are removed from national political control entirely. These are quite straightforwardly grants of elements of national sovereignty to other bodies, frequently bodies that are 'independent', from democratic control, yet governed by experts. A good deal of the phenomena of globalization is the replacement of national democratic control with control by experts. While some of this is resisted on various grounds, the reality is that even the resistance relies on internationalized expert knowledge, the pronouncements of international expert bodies, such as the IPCC (International Panel for Climate Control), therefore contributing to the same process of the expertization of politics and the dissolution of the significance of the traditional national liberal democratic political order.

The expansion of civility, or rather the creation of liberal democracies based on civil societies, as suggested in the last chapter, faced enormous obstacles. It is a matter of dispute as to whether it ever extended very far, in substance rather than merely in form, beyond the Anglo-American world. Conant, when he was the first American ambassador to the Federal Republic of Germany, clashed with Konrad Adenauer over such matters as Conant's eagerness to meet with the leaders of the opposition Social Democratic Party (SPD). Conant believed, no doubt correctly, that Adenauer did not understand liberal democracy. Adenauer, a veteran of Weimar democracy, no doubt believed that Conant did not understand his opposition. Adenauer's understanding formed the basis of the campaign against the SPD that is the real subject of Habermas' argument in *The Structural Transformation of the Public Sphere* that the public sphere was an illusion cloaking bourgeois power. In a sense the three agree: in Germany there was no public sphere of the sort discussed by Jefferson and Dicey. They also disagreed on the reasons, and consequently on the prospects for liberal democracy.

If we side with the sceptics and agree that for Germany, and perhaps for much of the world transformed by the imposition of Napoleonic bureaucratic forms, popular sovereignty was partly an illusion, and government by discussion always somewhat spectral, we can see some larger continuities. Sweden, touched by the Napoleonic brush due to its Royal family, presents an interesting case in point. Sweden possesses a robust parliamentary tradition and political ideals of popular sovereignty reaching back to the time before Charlemagne. There are parties similar to those of other European countries, and historically, in the case of the Socialists, connected to them. But what is electoral politics about in Sweden? Once, upon arriving there during a campaign, I asked a Swedish friend what the election was about. He found this banal question to be sufficiently intriguing to write a newspaper story on it. Why? Because, not only was there no great issue in the election, the phenomenon of elections based on large issues was un-Swedish, and the question itself misguided. The reasons for this are many, and they include a particular tradition of compromise politics. But some of them point beyond Sweden. Like Germany and much of the rest of Europe, there was no protracted period like that in Britain in the mid-nineteenth century, during which a liberal bourgeoisie ruled through discussion. Liberal Democracy 2.0 was a phase that was partly a matter of form, a superficial phenomenon that barely touched the continued power of state bureaucracies. This is part of the answer to the question of how one could have an issue-less politics.

The other part of the answer involves the political form of the commission, because it relied, to an unprecedented extent, on the substitution of commissions for politics in the liberal democratic mode. Consider the saying 'everything in Sweden that is not nailed down is a subject for a Royal Commission' (Austin 1968: 48, my translation). In these, commissions 'every conceivable public body and interested association is consulted' (1968: 48). Similarly, when something goes wrong, after 'a glare of angry publicity. . . . All the experts in the country are mobilized overnight' and organized as an '*utredning* – a commission-to-inquire-into-something – most Swedish of institutions!' (1968: 29).

If one has followed my argument here, the pattern, and the point, should be recognizable. This *is* a form of politics: a surrogate for liberal democracy. Publicity has its role, but only in a drama of legitimation. The public does not decide. As Austin says, 'in all things Swedish the expert rules'. He gives the following example: 'In 1957 a plebiscite was held to enquire whether Swedes wished to be like other Europeans and drive on the right-hand side of the road, instead of the left. The vote went strongly against. Ten years later the change is made, even so. Public opinion, having evidently made a fool of itself, is not again consulted' (1968: 37). And another, where a newspaper reports a protest against a selection of a work of public art and also the response of the State Art Council:

> The Council has authority to force through its wishes in the choice and placing of works of art in public buildings owned by the State. Usually this can be done in complete agreement with local personnel; even in those very rare cases where the protests have been violent and categorical, people have quickly got used to our decisions. Our choice of works of art takes a long-term view, and therefore cannot concern itself with the tastes and caprices (*tycken*) of such personnel as happen to be employed there at the moment. (1968: 37)

This is the pure voice of expert bureaucratic power. The pretense of representing *vox populi* is absent; the test is legitimacy, not opinion – the fact that people stop protesting eventually is enough. Protest is a cost to be borne. Yet the form of government is in every aspect 'liberal' and 'democratic', the delegation of power completely legal.

With this we arrive at the solution to the conflict between expertise and liberal democracy: Liberal Democracy 3.0. It will suffice to say that the transformation to Liberal Democracy 3.0 is a matter of politics increasingly approximating the ideal-type of relying on rule by commission (implemented, typically, through bureacratic power). The closer it is approximated, the less it leans on traditional 'bases' of authority, such as the Royal stamp. It becomes a politics in which expert opinion establishing fact-surrogates alone suffices, and the legal distinctions (and particularly the public-private distinction) between commissions, movements, and boundary organizations cease to have significance.

In stating the point in this way, I have left aside the question of why, or to put it in a form that Burnham would have preferred, what is the 'basis', and therefore the historical trajectory of this transformation. I have hinted at an answer to this question. In concluding with the answer, I will tie together some loose ends and place the argument in a specific relation to both science studies and the questions of 'classical social theory'. Nineteenth century social theory was firmly rooted in the problem of interests, and therefore in the question of class. Science studies has been closely associated with the concept of practices and thus with the collapse of 'making' into 'knowing', and 'knowing' into 'making'. The effect of this collapse is the demise of the nineteenth century model of a division of labor, and along with it, the relevance of the theories designed to explain it, notably Marxism. The new division is a 'division of knowledge', which brings with it a problem of mutual comprehension. The problems of the division of knowledge cannot be solved, as the division of labor might have been, by a rearrangement of authority, precisely because of this. But to understand this, we need to consider the 'practices' at the basis of knowledge.

Science as Practice

The concept of practices in science studies has a complex intellectual genealogy that leads back, in one direction, not to Marxism but to a liberal response to the Marxist analysis of natural science pioneered by Boris Hessen (Hessen 1931, Olwell 1996, Graham 1985) and elaborated by J. D. Bernal (Olwell 1996). Soviet analyses of science in the 1930s emphasized the role of rising social classes in producing and demanding particular forms of technical development, which were given an ideological superstructure that conformed to the ideological demands of the rising bourgeoisie. Thus Newton was simultaneously the inventor of technical means for the bourgeois revolution and the creator of a worldview for the understanding of physical reality that coheres with the bourgeois view of the nature of social life. The base/superstructure model is preserved in the argument. For Hessen and Bernal, of course, this analysis implied that the full use of the means of production in *late* capitalism required the transformation of social relations of science in such a way that new social demands could be placed on science to bring it into the position of better serving the needs of mankind than was possible under the capitalist order.

The great Liberal critic of this point of view, Michael Polanyi, argued that science had to be understood (especially with respect to the process of discovery) as a strongly traditional body of practice resting on tacit knowledge and irreducible to mere technology. Liberal societies, rooted in the idea of public reason and 'government by discussion', respect the seeking of truth, and for this reason have a kind of ideological affinity to science. The willingness to not interfere in the market economy has an affinity to noninterference in science as a truth-seeking autonomous enterprise. Polanyi's point was that the state could never 'plan' scientific discovery nor could science be fully rationalized according to some sort of external authoritarian scheme. This was in conflict with the open-ended practical nature of science as a practice. Here the feature of irreducibility was turned against the possibility of planning and thus against one of the fundamental ideas of progress on the left which was the elimination of politics in favor of the administration of things, the phrase which has echoed throughout this book. Science, it appeared, was irreducibly free and 'unadministerable'. It was part of the world of free adherents to tradition, not the world of 'things'.

As discussed in Chapter 5, the tacit knowledge part of this argument reappeared, as did the idea of the autonomy of science, in the work of Thomas Kuhn, who avoided the political aspects of Polanyi's argument. Practice figured as one of the meanings of the term paradigm. Sociologists of science, such as Harry Collins, studied empirically the practices of scientists, and especially the tacit knowledge involved in science (1992[1985]). The studies were primarily designed to show that the practices that serve to constitute objects, to establish the truth of scientific facts, are 'social', required tacit knowledge, and were irreducible to such things as methodological principles in science. These uses of the concepts practice and tacit knowledge were easily stigmatized, as Polanyi's own argument for tacit knowledge had been, as a kind of irrationalism; and in one respect this was justified. They focused on the irrationalizable aspects of the production of knowledge that was taken to be rational or true, the elements that could not themselves be rationalized, such as skills. ''Making', 'construction' was an essential element – the skills element, of knowing. This was a strategy that lent itself to other applications of the idea of the 'social construction of reality' outside of science, such as the social construction of categories such as the category of 'disabled', child abuse, and so forth, which were now seen as social achievements rather than simple matters of truth. The form of constructionist arguments was to show the taken-for-granted structure of practical achievement behind the production of 'facts' and 'truths', and in this way was both inspired by (and cohered with) the tradition of ethnomethodology (which could now itself be reinterpreted in terms of the concept of practice).

The increased importance of specialized knowledge of this kind, however, is itself a social phenomenon. Indeed it is the product of a massive social transformation. The proper point of departure of the transformation in classical social theory is perhaps the discussion of professional morality and its role in the production of organic solidarity in Durkheim's *Division of Labor in Society* ([1902]1933). In retrospect we can now see something curious about Durkheim's characterization of the right kind of division of labor. He envisioned the appropriate, or non-pathological division of labor in modern society (which he of course did not believe had been achieved), in a way that is somewhat suggestive of Syndicalist fascism ([1902]1933: 23-8), but also of some of the ideas we have touched on in discussing expertise, notably Bernal's model of scientific trade unions or the version of technocracy advocated by Veblen – a Soviet of technicians. Durkheim's model of a non-pathological division of labor is a form in which the various professions would be governed, independently, by distinctive professional moralities, in such a way that they contributed to organic solidarity and the good of the whole.

This basic idea, that professional *morality* was the link between specialized knowledge domains and society, was later taken up not only by Talcott Parsons, who elaborated it in terms of the problem of the doctor/patient role-set and its governing morality, but also in the study of the phenomenon of professionalization, which was pursued by the Chicago School of Sociology, whose approach to professions reflected its origins in the study of urban occupations. The problem of professions was thus kept squarely within the nineteenth century paradigm of 'interests'. To be sure, Veblen's 'technicians' and Bernal's 'scientists' were believed by them to have 'modern' habits of mind that would carry over to the social and political realm. This was a different thought, and not part of sociological literature. But even for these two thinkers, the importance of these habits of mind was that they freed their possessors from their attachment to retrograde interests, produced efficiency, and thus served to produce progress. They did not divide people from one another, or if they did, it was a benign division.

Consequently, the human relations of professionals and the peculiar forms of the roles that professionals assumed were much discussed during the twentieth century. But until the rise of science studies very little was said 'sociologically' about the nature of the craft work of the professions, or of the knowledge of specialized workers. The standard discussions of physicians, for example, proceeded without any particular treatment of the specificity of the craft knowledge of surgeons or the skills that could not be articulated that went into such activities as diagnosis and care. The analysis of the social character of the professions, in other words, was limited to an analysis of the *social interactions* of professions and their value orientations. The *knowledge* possessed by professionals was not seen as a topic for social analysis (cf. Parsons 1964: 34-68, 55).

The issue of tacit knowledge came to the fore in science studies in part as a result of something that had little to do with social theory, social formations, or social movements. The application of computer technology to professions led to attempts to provide computerizable forms of expertise on which physicians or lawyers could either rely or which could substitute for them: 'knowledge engineering' as it came to be called. This required the codification of tacit knowledge, or at least a simulation of what was assumed to be tacit. The problem of 'knowledge' in this sense – the problem of modelling the processes of knowing and applying knowledge – can be seen in retrospect as essentially ignored by earlier sociologists. At the least it was not seen as intellectually problematic. A statement by Karl Mannheim exempted scientific, or at least, more vaguely, true scientific knowledge from 'sociological' explanation, leaving only error as a topic of social explanation (Bloor 1976: 8).

The 'Strong Program in the Sociology of Scientific Knowledge' rejected this exemption. Moreover, once the professions were established and became expensive and powerful, questions about the true nature of the craft knowledge in question became more pressing, particularly with respect to such topics as the cost of the 'craft' of health care and whether the expense of 'professional knowledge' was justified.[2] At the same time, the significance and ubiquity of skill and tacit knowledge was increasing recognized, and that recognition extended to other specialized forms of knowledge.

Science studies tended to reduce *all* of the 'social' to 'knowledge understood socially'. What had traditionally been understood as social relationships, matters of morality and power, were neglected as a topic, and to such an extent that the analysis scarcely resembled traditional sociological studies of occupations at all. In this roundabout way, the Durkheimian problem of *specialized occupational moralities* in the face of an advanced division of labor was replaced by a problem of *specialized knowledges* in an advanced, and moreover continuously changing, division of labor. The change is justified: there has been a change in the place of knowledge in the current division of labor. The Durkheimian idea of professional morality seems in relation to many occupations or skills to be largely irrelevant, assuming as it does a kind of 'cold' situation in which professional knowledges and professional culture are fixed, or at least unproblematic for long periods of time. The point made by science studies has been that these forms of craft skill are typically local and also short lived. The knowledge contained in them is very often black-boxed or built into a new technology that makes the skill itself unnecessary. But this disappearing knowledge is quickly replaced at the leading edge of science and technology by new activities requiring new specialized skills.

So what does constructionism have to do with the division of labor? A little consideration of Taylorism, or Scientific Management, which is ruled by experts of a particular kind – a kind that Lenin approved of (1918: 375) – shows that Taylorism is the extreme form of the separation of knowledge and labor. The efficient stop-watch driven workers of Taylorism know almost nothing about what they are doing, and are induced to forget what they do know. Productivity comes from adherence to procedures that are designed by others – experts – for maximum efficiency. Taylor thought of this as a solution to social conflict. Increased productivity allowed higher payments to workers, and thus social harmony.

Constructionism, the collapse of the categories of skills and knowing into one another, undermines this model, and with it the 'division of labor', by undermining the separation of 'labor' and 'knowledge'. The class system that follows from the division of labor is transformed into a non-system of fractionalized knowledge in which mutual cooperation cannot be reduced to instruction-giving, as in Taylorism. When the computer technician arrives, one is, truly, in the Saint-Simonian phrase, an 'associate' and one with whom communication is a serious problem. Authority means little if one cannot understand what one is authorizing or whether one's requests can be fulfilled. Nor is the idea of 'division' of labor very useful. I have my skills and you have yours. They do not come in stadardized 'occupational' or 'professional' packages that are fixed for decades or generations. But maker-knowers can organize, can concentrate opinion, and be actors on the political stage, just as classes used to be. Their creations, however, include such facts as global warming, child abuse, and other 'problems'; that is to say, our problems and the objects of our politics.

This change obviously reflects a very wide-reaching change in the conditions of work in the face of rapidly changing technology. Whereas, in the nineteenth century, and even well into the twentieth century, a physician would receive as a medical student a full set of medical instruments and a medical bag that could be expected to last for many years, modern medical equipment is disposable, constantly redesigned, and skills in its use need to be acquired quickly. Many of the skills that one might acquire are expected to be made obsolete by improvement in technology. Medicine is, in this respect, itself somewhat antiquated and traditional compared to the writing of computer programs and the employment of new complex software technology, which involves skills that are to a very large extent not generalizable skills, and moreover are quickly made obsolete by changes in the technology itself. In these cases there is highly specialized knowledge that amounts to very refined practical skills in operating, fixing, and exploiting a given technology. The 'technologies' themselves are no longer the large, fixed machines or industrial processes to which the worker adapts by acquiring a specific set of skills that, like the processes themselves, last a lifetime. The paradigm case of the old division of labor is that of the steel mills, whose blast furnaces never shut down for a century, and where the operating skills remained the same.

Put simply, the new kind of knowledge is far more usefully understood in terms of notions of practice and practical knowledge than in terms of the notion of a profession or occupation. Professions, with their lifetime certification and their long processes of formal training, seem indeed to be an obsolescent social form. It is for these reasons that theorists like Nico Stehr (1992) have begun to apply the term 'knowledge society' as a characterization of the newest forms of the division of labor, which are dominated by the fact of the division of labor with respect to knowledge. This characterization identifies the reason, namely the transformed role of changing knowledge, for the vast expansion of the notion of practice at the expense of more traditional 'colder' conceptions, such as ideology and professional morality.

In the face of this transformation, traditional nineteenth century usages such as professional morality and ideology are largely useless, except as a language for depicting survivals from past times. The idea of specialized knowledge that is not reducible to formula and cannot be deskilled without relying on new kinds of skills – the idea, that is, of a permanent frontier of highly skilled specialized knowledge – thus has a deep 'social' significance.

Civil Society and Practices

The idea of practices as the distinctive ground of social grouping in the knowledge society is not merely a successor to the older concept of 'occupation' in a division of labor but poses significantly new theoretical problems. Thinkers like Durkheim had in mind the older model of the guild, and, as I have noted, in some of the early Marxist writings on the role of science in society, Bernal's *The Social Function of Science* (1939) for example, the same model was employed. It was extended to provide a model for a post-liberal civil society. Bernal's idea was that the place of scientific knowledge in civil society could be managed in a civil society organized on socialist lines if scientists were organized like a trade union with a collective structure and leadership that was oriented toward collective social purposes. The thought was that this form of organization would maximize the input of science by planning science in such a way that the planners were themselves scientists but also were committed to, and able to serve as expert contributors to, a society organized around collective goal seeking. All that was needed was to realign the interests and resources of scientists toward the collective good. Needless to say this is a theoretical model only. Veblen's own pessimistic appraisal of the prospects of a 'Soviet of Technicians', explains why it would remain so: the modernization of industrial processes by technicians was enough to prevent a revolution of want, and thus to preserve capitalism (1921). Yet the problem Bernal poses – how to organize the use of expert knowledge in society – is more central than ever.

Theorists like Jürgen Habermas assume that expanding the 'public's' share, and assuring 'full recognition' for all participants including those whose formal rights in liberal democracy are undermined by their social position of subordination in the private sphere maximizes the potential of civil society. Theorists like Roberto Mangabeira Unger seem willing to eliminate any constraint or discussion that protects its rationality – for him the goal is to fully democratize discussion. Traditional liberal ideas about civility and the rationality of discourse are for him merely forms of exclusion and oppression (Unger 1998). The 'science studies' problem of knowledge-producing practices, and the recognition that knowledge in the full sense is extremely closely dependent on the full participation in very specific 'expert' bodies of practice, conflicts very dramatically with these ideas. Experts in a market situation must sell their expertise and their 'power' depends on their abilities to persuade others to buy it. However, in the public sphere, operating under the principles of equal participation in public discourse, the expert becomes merely another speaker whose credibility is formally the same as the non-expert who must be persuaded.

The difficulty is that the non-expert must be persuaded not on the grounds that experts persuade others, because this necessarily requires initiation into the expert practice itself, but on other grounds. If this implies that, say, astrologers and global warming experts may each find that there are people who are persuaded by them, it seems clear that the goal of the older Left of maximizing the contribution of science to society is significantly undermined and compromised by democratizing discourse. Democratizing means dumbing down. Habermas argued that the maximization of discursive rationality requires the elimination of communicative barriers and authority, but he does not explain how it is possible, for example, for scientists concerned with such phenomena as global warming to justify their claims to nonscientists who cannot, because they have not been educated in the practices of this particular branch of science, fully or even minimally comprehend the rational justification. Indeed this is precisely the implication of the notion of practices – that at the ground level of rational justification one finds 'practices'. Specialized practices cannot be further justified, nor can they be rationally scrutinized with respect to considerations of any sort of universalistic rationality. We can of course assess experts by evaluating their achievement, by assessing the social mechanisms of accountability, such as the awards and degrees that scientists have, and so forth, in order to make judgments about the genuineness of their expertise. But these are not means that bring scientists into rational dialogue, but rather means that treat scientists as instrumental things to be administered.

Looked at in terms of basic social formations, then, we can now see the present as a time in which there is a fundamental conflict or a fundamental puzzle about the relationship between two of its most important social formations, namely representative democracy engaging in persuasive liberal discourse, or government by discussion, on the one hand, and on the other hand a balkanized knowledge society consisting of practices within which rational justification and argument is possible but which are not universalizable, not universally understandable, and not transformable into proper subject matter for liberal discussion itself. Nor is this problem ever going to be fully resolved institutionally. Although there are many solutions to the problem of expert power on the institutional level, such as the creation of national academies of science, international panels on global warming, and so forth, these bodies cannot escape the basic dilemmas that result from the fact that expert knowlege is, as a practical matter, incompletely communicable and therefore incompletely intelligible to non-experts.

One can think of the conflict here as analogous to the Marxian conflict between the means of production and the system of capitalism, because it is, like the conflict Marx supposed to exist between the market and new forms of technology, a conflict between a potential, namely the potential good that derives from expert knowledge based on bodies of knowledge, specialized bodies of knowledge practice and the limitations of liberal political discourse as a means of assimilating and employing this knowledge. The nineteenth century problem was the division of labor. All major social theorists addressed this problem, and in a sense it defined politics in that century as a matter of class conflict and agrarian reform. The twentieth century was an era in which two alternatives to the market, fascism and communism were tried, and market regulation expanded. In the case of the division of labor the conflict was between opponents who understood each other – the conflicts were over interests, and to the extent that they were over outlooks and worldviews, the outlooks were reflections of the interests.

Knowledge specialists with skills in producing and understanding knowledge of particular kinds have interests, and form part of a division of labor.

But the older model of the division of labor was, in theory at least, compatible with democracy. Reform, regulation, even the transition to Communism itself could be accomplished through public discussion and persuasion – and if it could not, the obstacles, such as false consciousness, the culture machine, and so forth, were not products of the division of labor itself. The new 'division of knowledge labor', understood in terms of practices, differs. Democratic discussion with respect to the products of specialized knowledge skills is inherently impossible. Only makeshift solutions are possible, and in this respect the parallel to the nineteenth century problem of the division of labor is precise. Utopian schemes were tried but failed. Neither the market nor the command economy were ever fully implemented. The closer they came to full implementation, the more serious the problems became. Democratization of discourse and rule by experts are, similarly, utopias, as is Ulrich Beck's idea of the combination of the two in a kind of higher democratic and reflexive expertise (1998). But these are utopias that are motivated by the basic problem of the conflict between the social fact of the diversity of practices and democracy. The prominence of practices as an analytic concept is deserved. The concept points to the defining new social formation of the age, and a defining tension: between democratic civility and expertise.

Coda

The book began with a question about a future historian. I noted the joint arrival on center stage of science and liberal democracy in the latter half of the twentieth century. But I also pointed out that at the beginning of the century the world was still dominated by monarchies and noblemen, at least in form. The qualification 'at least in form' may be taken a step further. The fact that Europe today has many of the monarchies it had at the beginning of the century should open our eyes to the possibility that liberal democracy and its forms (parliamentary government, parties, elections, and the rest) might persist for a long time while losing substance, just as the monarchies themselves did. 'Constitutional monarchies' are of course not monarchies in a 'political' sense. Politics has moved on from the court. Privy councils no longer exert much power. But royal courts still have politics, even in the 'bicycle monarchies' of northern Europe. Today one could not easily mistake this politics for what is important, as people at the turn of the last century did about the court politics of their time. But is the politics of liberal democracy today 'what is important?' Or is 'liberal democracy' increasingly a constitutional fiction of the same sort as the monarchies themselves became?

Revolutions in basic constitutional structures do not require turbaned Mullahs, constrained only by their corporate group, issuing fatwas. They can come in the form of bureaucrats or experts issuing regulations or studies, constrained only by their own corporate group. That the powers of the state summoned or exercised here are, in a formal sense, done so by liberal democracies, and thus do not threaten their basic structures, is less reassuring if one considers that the monarchs too delegated their powers, and did so to preserve the forms of monarchy.

The use of 'civil society' as a normative ideal today is backward- looking. Recognition, the bringing together of many voices, the rejection of exclusions – all this is Liberal Democracy 2.0, carried to new heights and extended in new directions. But the nineteenth century, in which these ideals had the greatest force, was a world in which the mob had given way to an educable and largely literate public, whose political consciousness was forged by common experiences, such as war and military service, and for whom a rough equality of politically relevant knowledge could be assumed. This public learned from its political experiences, and became politically competent. And its political experiences were serious. The American Civil War was an extension of legislative controversy by other means, and taught a sobering lesson that a politics of moralizing intolerance had a price in blood. The English civil war had taught the same lesson. In the nineteenth century, and the first part of the twentieth, the demands of empire made 'stakeholders' of those who voted, and it both sobered and hardened them. This 'political education' was the tough core of liberal democracy in the English-speaking world.

What does civil society mean apart from a political education of this kind? And what sort of political education does the 'public' get in a world of expert claims? Liberal Democracy 3.0 preserves 'government by discussion' by delegating much of the discussing and much of the governing. The motives for doing this are permanent rather than transitory, at least as permanent as such things get. The transformation of knowledge means that expertise is distributed to small 'communities' of skilled persons, none of which can have a monopoly on any more than a small fraction of the known. As I have argued, liberal democracies have been inventive in creating means for delegating. But a civil society in which everything of importance is delegated is not a civil society in any familiar sense.

In a recent lecture, Toomas Hendrik Ilves, the Estonian Minister of Foreign Affairs, observes that at the root of anxiety about the European Community there is

> the feeling that fundamental decisions previously made in a transparent and legally understandable way at the level of the democratic post-Westphalian nation-state, are being transferred to a higher body. A body where decision-making is not always clear and transparent or understandable from the standard of parliamentary procedure; where the Montesquieuan division of powers are muddled, and where the connection between the individual citizen's opinion and his opportunities to make his opinion clear through established means such [as] through his party or through calls to his parliamentary representative is no longer clear. Or to use the famous words of Saint-Simon (or was it Engels?) in another context, the citizen senses Europe is 'replacing the government of persons with the administration of things'. It is, I believe, the administration of things, that causes unease among European citizens, as does the fear that government of persons is less and less relevant. The democratic nation-state that developed in most of Europe after the Enlightenment and the French Revolution has as its core assumption that the citizen has his say in what happens in his country. It is the absence of this feeling that dis-

tinguishes undemocratic countries from democratic ones, it was the failure to allow the citizen his say that led ultimately to the fall of the Wall. (Ilves 2001)

Politics is made by people looking in the rear-view mirror. Ilves is able to see what is receding behind him. The 'Europe' that is replacing the government of persons with the administration of things is a European Community that governs, in large part, by commissions composed of experts. Form is not fate. But if 'civil society' in the sense of Liberal Democracy 2.0 is no longer an alternative, we are faced instead with the possibilities presented by Liberalism 3.0: liberalized expertise after the fashion of Conant, or 'democratic control' expressed through commissions and executed by expertized bureaucracies.

Notes

1 Differences in the regulation of stem-cell research in Germany and Israel, for example, reflect differences in both religion and historical experience and have produced opposite regulatory results: the Germans opted for control, the Israelis for experiment.

2 The literature on scientific discovery seemed to provide a 'practice' answer to those questions. This literature suggested that the production of scientific facts could *sometimes* be reduced to routines or even replaced by machines (black-boxed, in a phrase of Bruno Latour that recalls 'the administration of things': 'A black box contains that which no longer needs to be considered, those things whose contents have become a matter of indifference' (Callon and Latour1981: 285)).

References

Agrawal, A. (1995) 'Dismantling the Divide between Indigenous and Scientific Knowledge', *Development and Change*, 26: 3, pp. 413-39.

Aristotle ([1921] 1972) *The Works of Aristotle: Volume X: Political*. Tr. B. Jowett. J. A. Smith and W. D. Ross (eds). London: Oxford University Press.

Austin, Paul Britten (1968) *On Being Swedish: Reflections towards a Better Understanding of the Swedish Character*. Coral Gables, FL: University of Miami Press.

Beck, Ulrich (1992) *The Risk Society: Towards a New Modernity*. London; Newbury Park, CA: Sage.

Beck, Ulrich (1994). 'The Reinvention of Politics: Towards a Theory of Reflexive Modernization', in Ulrich Beck, Anthony Giddens, and Scott Lash (eds), *Reflexive Modernization*. Stanford, CA: Stanford University Press, pp.1-55.

Beck, Ulrich (1995). *Ecological Enlightenment: Essays on the Politics of the Risk Society*. Tr. M. Ritter. Atlantic Highlands, NJ: Humanities Press International, Inc.

Bernal, J. D. (1939) *The Social Function of Science*. London: Routledge & Sons Ltd.

Bernal, J. D. (1979) *Science in History. Vol. 4, The Social Sciences: Conclusion*. Cambridge, MA: The M.I.T. Press. (1st edn, 1954.)

Bliss, William D. P. (ed.) (1908) *The New Encyclopedia of Social Reform*. New York; London: Funk & Wagnalls Company.

Bloch, Marc (1964) *Feudal Society*. Vol. 1 & 2. Tr. L. A. Manyon. Chicago: University of Chicago Press.

Bloor, David (1976) *Knowledge and Social Imagery*. London: Routledge.

Bohman, James (1996) *Public Deliberation: Pluralism, Complexity, and Democracy*. Cambridge, MA: MIT Press.

Brandom, Robert (1994) *Making It Explicit: Reasoning, Representing, and Discursive Commitment*. Cambridge, MA: Harvard University Press.

Beck, Ulrich (1998) *Democracy Without Enemies*. Cambridge: Polity Press.

Breslau, Daniel (1998) *In Search of the Unequivocal: The Political Economy of Measurement in U.S. Labor Market Policy*. Westport, CT: Praeger.

Brown, E. Richard (1979) *Rockefeller Medicine Men: Medicine and Capitalism in America*. Berkeley, CA: University of California Press.

Burnham, James (1941) *The Managerial Revolution*. New York: John Day Company.

Burtt, Edwin A. (1927) *The Metaphysical Foundations of Modern Physical Science; A Historical and Critical Essay*. London: K. Paul, Trench, Trubner & Co., Ltd.; New York: Harcourt, Brace & Company, Inc.

Buxton, William and Stephen Turner (1992) 'From Education to Expertise: Sociology as a "Profession"', in Terence C. Halliday and Morris Janowitz (eds), *Sociology and its Publics*.Chicago: University of Chicago Press. pp. 373-407.

Calhoun, Craig (1992) *Habermas and the Public Sphere*. Cambridge, MA: MIT Press.

Callon, Michel and Bruno Latour (1981) 'Unscrewing the Big Leviathan: How Actors Macro-Structure Reality and How Sociologists Help Them Do It', in K. Knorr-Cetina and A. Cicourel (eds), *Advances in Social Theory and Methodology: Towards An Integration of Micro- and Macro-Sociologies*. London: Routledge and Keegan Paul, pp. 277-303.

Chambers, Clarke (1971) *Paul U. Kellogg and the Survey; Voices for Social Welfare and Social Justice*. Minneapolis, MN: University of Minnesota Press.

Christie, Richard and Marie Jahoda (1954) *Studies in the Scope and Method of 'The Authoritarian Personality'*. Glencoe, IL: The Free Press.

Chubin, Daryl and Ellen W. Chu (eds) (1989) *Science off the Pedestal: Social Perspectives on*

Science and Technology. Belmont, CA: Wadsworth.

Chubin, Daryl and Edward Hackett (1990) *Peerless Science*. Albany, NY: SUNY Press.

Clarke, William (1891) *The Clarke Papers*. Vol I, C. H. Firth, (ed). London; Royal Historical Society. The Putney Debates 1647.

Collins, Harry M. (1992[1985]) *Changing Order: Replication and Induction in Scientific Practice*. 2nd edn. Chicago: The University of Chicago Press.

Collins, Harry and Trevor Pinch (1993) *The Golem: What Everyone Should Know About Science*. Cambridge; New York: Cambridge University Press.

Conant, James B. (1940) Charter Day Address delivered at the University of California on March28,1940.

The Atlantic Monthly. http://www.theatlantic.com/issues/95sep/ets/edcla.htm

Conant, James B. (1947) *On Understanding Science*. New York: New American Library.

Conant, James B. (1951) *Science and Common Sense*. New Haven, CT: Yale University Press.

Conant, James B. (1952) *Modern Science and Modern Man*. Garden City, NY: Doubleday & Co.

Dahl, Robert (1989) *Democracy and Its Critics*. New Haven, CT: Yale University Press.

Dahl, Robert A. (1993) 'Finding Competent Citizens: Improving Democracy', *Current* Vol. 351, pp. 23-30.

Darnton, Robert (1984) *The Great Cat Massacre and Other Episodes in French Cultural History*. New York : Basic Books.

Davidson, Donald (1973-74) 'On the Very Idea of a Conceptual Scheme. Proceedings of the American Philosophical Association' Vol. 47. Reprinted in Davidson (1984) *Inquiries into Truth and Interpretation*. Oxford: Clarendon Press, pp.183-98.

de Man, Henry ([1928] 1974) *The Psychology of Socialism*. Tr. Eden and Cedar Paul. New York: Arno Press.

Dewey, John (1922) *Human Nature and Conduct: An Introduction to Social Psychology*. New York: Henry Holt and Co.

Dicey, Albert Venn ([1905]1962) *Lectures on the Relations between Law & Public Opinion in England During the Nineteenth Century*. London: MacMillan & Co. Ltd. (1st edn, 1905.)

Dicey, A. V. (1962[1914]) *Law and Public Opinion in England during the Nineteenth Century*. 2nd edn. London: MacMillan & Co. (1st edition1905)

Durkheim, Émile ([1902]1933) *The Division of Labor in Society*. Tr. George Simpson. New York: Free Press. (First published as *De la division du travail social*, 1902).

Durkheim, Émile (1984[1902]) 'Some Remarks on Professional Groups', Preface to the Second Edition, *The Division of Labor in Society*. 2nd edn. Tr. W. D. Halls. New York: Macmillan. (1st edn. *De la division du travail social*, 1893).

Eisenstadt, S. N. and Luis Roninger (1984) *Patrons, Clients and Friends: Interpersonal Relations and the Structure of Trust in Society*. Cambridge: Oxford University Press.

Eliaeson, Sven (2000) 'Constitutional Caesarism: Weber's Politics in Their German Context', in *The Cambridge Companion to Weber*. Stephen P. Turner (ed.). Cambridge: Cambridge University Press, pp. 131-50.

Engels, Frederick ([1894]1947) *Anti-Düring: Herr Eugen Düring's Revolution in Science*. Moscow: Progress Publishers. Translated from the 3rd German edition (1894).

Feyerabend, Paul(1978) *Science in a Free Society*. London: NLB.

Fish, Stanley (1994) *There's No Such Thing as Free Speech and It's a Good Thing, Too*. New York: Oxford University Press.

Flyvbjerg, Bent (1998) *Rationality and Power: Democracy in Practice*. Tr. by Steven Sampson. Chicago: The University of Chicago Press.

Fosdick, Raymond (1952) *The Story of the Rockefeller Foundation*. New Brunswick, NJ: Transaction Publishers.

Friedman, Michael (1999) *Reconsidering Logical Positivism*. New York: Cambridge University Press.

Fuller, Steve (1999) *The Governance of Science: Ideology and the Future of the Open Society*. Buckingham, UK; Philadelphia, PA: Open University Press.

Fuller, Steve (2000) *Thomas Kuhn: A Philosophical History for Our Times*. Chicago: The

University of Chicago Press.

Furêt, François (1981) *Interpreting the French Revolution*. Tr. Elborg Forster. New York: Cambridge University Press.

Galison, Peter (1997) *Image and Logic: A Material Culture of Microphysics*. Chicago: The University of Chicago Press.

Gieryn, Thomas F. (1994) 'Boundaries of Science', in Sheila Jasanoff, Gerald Markle, Trevor Pinch and James Peterson (eds.), *Handbook on Science, Technology and Society*. Newbury Park, CA: Sage, pp.393-443.

Gieryn, Thomas F. and Anne Figert (1986) 'Scientists Protect Their Cognitive Authority: The Status Degradation Ceremony of Sir Cyril Burt', in G. Boehm and N. Stehr (eds.) *The Knowledge Society*. Dordrecht: Reidel, pp.67-86.

Goetzmann, William H. (1966) *Exploration and Empire: The Explorer and the Scientist in the Winning of the American West*. New York: Norton.

Goldgar, Anne (1995) *Impolite Learning: Conduct and Community in the Republic of Letters, 1680-1750*. New Haven, CT: Yale University Press.

Graham, Loren (1985) 'The Socio-Political Roots of Boris Hessen: Soviet Marxism and the History of Science', *Social Studies of Science*, Vol.15, pp. 705-22.

Greenberg, Daniel S. (2001) *Science, Money, and Politics: Political Triumph and Ethical Erosion*. Chicago: The University of Chicago Press.

Greenwald, Maurine and Margo Anderson (eds) (1996) *Pittsburgh Surveyed: Social Science and Social reform in the Early Twentieth Century*. Pittsburgh, PA: University of Pittsburgh Press.

Guston, David H., William Clark, Terry Keating, David Cash, Susanne Moser, Clark Miller, Charles Powers (2000) *Report of the Workshop on Boundary Organizations in Environmental Policy and Science*. Environmental and Occupational Health Sciences Institute, Rutgers University, New Brunswick, NJ.

Guston, David H. (2000) *Between Politics and Science: Assuring the Integrity and Productivity of Research*. Cambridge. New York : Cambridge University Press.

Habermas, Jürgen ([1962]1991) *The Structural Transformation of the Public Sphere: An Inquiry into a Category of Bourgeois Society*. Tr. Thomas Burger. Cambridge, MA: The MIT Press.

Habermas, Jürgen (1970) 'Technology and Science as Ideology', in *Toward a Rational Society: Student Protest, Science, and Politics*. Tr. Jeremy J. Shapiro. Boston: Beacon Press, pp. 81-122.

Habermas, Jürgen (1973) *Theory and Practice*. Tr. John Viertel. Boston, MA: Beacon Press.

Habermas, Jürgen ([1981]1984). *The Theory of Communicative Action*. Vol. 1. Tr. Thomas McCarthy. Boston, MA: Beacon.

Habermas, Jürgen ([1985]1987). *The Theory of Communicative Action*. Vol. 2. Tr. Thomas McCarthy. Boston, MA: Beacon.

Hahn, Roger (1971) *The Anatomy of a Scientific Institution: The Paris Academy of Sciences, 1666-1803*. Berkeley: The University of California Press.

Halévy, Daniel (1974) *The End of the Notables*. Tr. Alain Silvera and June Guicharnaud, Alain Silvera (ed.). Middletown, CT: Wesleyan University Press.

Handelman, Don (1995) 'Cultural Taxonomy and Bureaucracy in Ancient China: The Book of Lord Shang', *International Journal of Politics, Culture and Society*, Vol. 9, pp. 263-93.

Haraway, Donna (1984-85) 'Teddy Bear Patriarchy: Taxidermy in the Garden of Eden, New York City, 1908-1936', *Social Text*, Vol. 11, pp. 20-64. Reprinted in Donna Haraway (1989) *Primate Visions: Gender, Race, and Nature in the World of Modern Science*. New York: Routledge, pp.26-59.

Hayek, Friedrich A. von (1937) 'Economics and Knowledge', *Economica*, NS 4, pp. 33-54.

Hessen, Boris (1931) 'The Social and Economic Roots of Newton's Principia', in N. I. Bucharin et al., *Science at the Crossroads, Papers from the 2nd International Congress of the History of Science and Technology*. London: Kniga. (2nd ed. 1971, London: Frank Cass and Co. Ltd.)

Hinde, Julia. (1997) 'Wales Gets Genes Jury', *Times Higher Education Supplement*, January 6, p. 17.

Hobbes, Thomas ([1651]1839) *De Cive: Philosophical Rudiments Concerning Government and Society*. London: R. Royston. Sir W. Molesworth's edition of the complete works, 11 vol.,

1839-268-9. http://www.marxists.org/reference/subject/philosophy/works/en/decive.htm;

Ilves, Toomas Hendrik (2001)' Constructing a New Europe', Lecture by Toomas Hendrik Ilves Minister of Foreign Affairs, Estonia at Humboldt University, Berlin 5 February 2001.

Jaffe, Naomi (1994) 'A Hard Look at a Controversial New Book on Race, Class and Success', Letter to the Editor regarding IQ (October 24, 1994, pp. 53-62). *Newsweek*, Nov.21, p. 26.

Jasanoff, Sheila (1995) *Science at the Bar: Law, Science, and Technology in America*. Cambridge, MA; London: Harvard University Press.

Johnson, Guy and Guion Johnson (1980) *Research in Service to Society: the First Fifty Years of the Institute for Research in Social Science at the University of North Carolina*. Chapel Hill: University of North Carolina Press.

Jonsen, Albert R. and Toulmin, Stephen (1988). *The Abuse of Casuistry: A History of Moral Reasoning*. Berkeley: University of California Press.

Kant, Immanuel ([1784]1963) 'What is Enlightenment?', in *On History*. Tr. Lewis White Beck, Robert E. Anchor and Emil L. Fackenheim, Lewis White Beck (ed.). Indianapolis, IN: Bobbs-Merrill.

Kautsky, John H. (1971) *The Political Consequences of Modernization*. New York: Wiley.

Kaye, Harvey J. (1984) *The British Marxist Historians: An Introductory Analysis*. New York: Polity Press.

Kellogg, Paul U. (1912) 'The Spread of the Survey Idea. The Social Survey', in *Papers*, by Paul Kellogg, Shelby M. Harrison and George T. Palmer. New York: Russell Sage Foundation. 2nd edn. Reprinted from *The Proceedings of the Academy of Political Science*. Vol. II, no. 4, July 1912.

Kettering, Sharon (1986) *Patrons, Brokers, and Clients in Seventeenth Century France*. New York: Oxford University Press.

Kevles, Daniel J. (1977) *The Physicists: The History of a Scientific Community in Modern America*. New York: Knopf.

Kuhn, Thomas S. ([1962] 1996). *The Structure of Scientific Revolutions*. 3rd edn. Chicago: Chicago University Press.

La Follette, Marcel C. (1992) *Stealing into Print: Fraud, Plagiarism and Misconduct in Scientific Publishing*. Berkeley, CA: University of California Press.

Lagemann, Ellen Condliffe (1989) *The Politics of Knowledge: The Carnegie Corporation, Philanthropy and Public Policy*. Chicago: The University of Chicago Press.

Lanouette, Willliam, with Bela Szilard (1992) *Genius in the Shadows: A Biography of Leo Szilard, the Man Behind the Bomb*. New York: Charles Scribner's Sons.

Lasswell, Harold (1936) *Politics: Who Gets What, When, How*. New York: McGraw-Hill Book Company, Inc.

Latour, Bruno (1987) *Science in Action: How to Follow Scientists and Engineers through Society*. Cambridge, MA: Harvard University Press.

Lenin, Nikolai (1918) 'Lenin on the "Taylor Society", abstract in the form of quotations from the principal parts of an article by Nikolai Lenin entitled "The Urgent Problems of the Soviet Rule", translated from *Pravda* of April 28, 1918, in Donald Del Mar and Rodger D. Collons (eds.) *Classics in Scientific Management: A Book of Readings*. University, AL: The University of Alabama Press, pp. 375-79.

MacKinnon, Catherine (1989). *Toward a Feminist Theory of the State*. Cambridge, MA: Harvard University Press.

McGucken, William (1984) *Scientists, Society, and State. The Social Relations of Science Movement in Great Britain 1931-1947*. Columbus, OH: Ohio State University Press.

Marcuse, Herbert (1968) 'Industrialization and Capitalism in the Work of Max Weber', in *Negations: Essays in Critical Theory*. Tr. Jeremy J. Shapiro. Boston: Beacon Press, pp. 201-26.

Mayer, Arno J. (1981) *The Persistence of the Old Regime : Europe to the Great War*. New York: Pantheon Books.

Mayer, Jacob P. (1974) 'Reflections on Equality', in Kolakowski, Leszek and Stuart Hampshire (eds), *The Socialist Idea: A Reappraisal*. New York: Basic Books, pp. 59-73.

Medvedev, Zhores A. (1971) *The Rise and Fall of T. D. Lysenko*. Tr. I. Michael Lerner. Ed. Lucy G. Lawrence. New York: Doubleday

Merton, Robert K. (1976) *Sociological Ambivalence and Other Essays*. New York: Free Press.

Mill, J. S. (1861) *Representative Government*. London: Parker, Son, and Bourn, West Strand.

Mill, J. S. ([1873]1990) *Autobiography*, ed. John Robson. New York: Penguin. http://www.knuten.liu.se/~bjoch509/philosophers/intros/mill/youth.html

Morgenthau, Hans J. (1946) *Scientific Man vs Power Politics*. Chicago: University of Chicago Press.

Morgenthau, Hans J. (1972) *Science: Servant or Master?* New York: The New American Library, Inc.

Morone, Joseph G. and Edward J. Woodhouse (1989) *The Demise of Nuclear Energy: Lessons for Democratic Control of Technology*. New Haven, CT: Yale University Press.

Myrdal, Gunnar (1944) *An American Dilemma: The Negro Problem and Modern Democracy*. With the assistance of Richard Sterner and Arnold Rose. New York, London: Harper & Brothers.

National Committee of Confederated Supply Associations (1916) 'The American Plan for Public Comfort Stations Approved by the Public Comfort Station Bureau of the National Committee of Confederated Supply Associations'. New York.

Oakeshott, Michael (1962) *Rationalism in Politics and Other Essays*. London: Methuen.

Oakeshott, Michael (1975) *On Human Conduct*. Oxford: Clarendon Press.

Olwell R. (1996) 'Condemned to Footnotes: Marxist Scholarship in the History of Science', *Science & Society*. Vol. 60, no. 1, pp. 7-26.

Parsons, Talcott (1964) *Essays in Sociological Theory*. New York: Free Press of Glencoe. (1st edn.1954.)

Pearson, Karl ([1892]1937) *The Grammar of Science*. Everyman ed. London: J. M. Dent and Sons Ltd.

Pearson, Karl (1919) *The Function of Science in the Modern State*. Cambridge: Cambridge University Press.

Peirce, Charles Sanders (1901) 'Review of Pearson's Grammar of Science', *Popular Science Monthly* Vol. 58 (January 1901), pp.296-306. Reprinted in Charles Hartshorne, Paul Weiss & Arthur W Burks (eds) (1931-58) *Charles Sanders Peirce, Collected Writings* (8 Vols.), Cambridge, MA: Harvard University Press, vol. 8, pp. 132-52.

Polanyi, Michael (1946) *Science, Faith and Society: A Searching Examination of the Meaning and Nature of Scientific Inquiry*. Chicago: The University of Chicago Press.

Polanyi, Michael (1951) *The Logic of Liberty: Reflections and Rejoinders*. Chicago: University of Chicago Press.

Polanyi, Michael (1962) 'The Republic of Science: Its Political and Economic Theory'. *Minerva* Vol. 1, no. 1, pp. 54-73.

Porter, Theodore (1986) *The Rise of Statistical Thinking 1820-1900*. Princeton, NJ: Princeton University Press.

Porter, Theodore (1995) *Trust in Numbers: The Pursuit of Objectivity in Science and Public Life*. Princeton, NJ: Princeton University Press.

Posner, Richard (2001) *Breaking the Deadlock: The 2000 Election, the Constitution, and the Courts*. Princeton, NJ: Princeton University Press.

Price, Don (1965) *The Scientific Estate*. Cambridge, MA: Harvard University Press.

Rawls, John (1971) *A Theory of Justice*. Cambridge, MA: Belknap Press of Harvard University Press.

Rawls, John (1996) *Political Liberalism*. New York: Columbia University Press.

Reisner, Marc (1986) *Cadillac Desert*. New York: Viking.

Richards, Evelleen (1988) 'The Politics of Therapeutic Evaluation: The Vitamin C and Cancer Controversy', *Social Studies of Science*, Vol.18, no. 4, pp. 653-701.

Rosenberg, Charles (1962) *The Cholera Years, The United States in 1832, 1849, and 1866*. Chicago: University of Chicago Press.

Saint-Simon, Henri de (1952) *Social Organization, the Science of Man and Other Writings*. Ed.

and Tr. Felix Markham. New York: Harper & Row. Selected and translated from *Oeuvres Complètes de Saint-Simon et Enfantin*, Paris 1865-76.

Saint-Simon, Henri de (1972) *The Doctrine of Saint-Simon: An Exposition, First Year, 1828-1829*, Tr. Georg G. Iggers. New York: Schocken Books. (1st edn. 1958).

Salter, L. (1988). *Mandated Science: Science and Scientists in the Making of Standards*. Dordrecht, Boston, London: Kluwer Academic Publishers.

Sandel, Michael (1996) *Democracy's Discontent: America in Search of a Public Philosophy*. Cambridge, MA: Harvard University Press.

Scheuerman, William E. (1999) *Carl Schmitt: The End of Law*. Lanham, MD: Rowman & Littlefield.

Schmitt, Carl ([1925]1986). *Political Romanticism*. Tr. Guy Oakes. Cambridge, MA and London: MIT Press.

Schmitt, Carl ([1926]1985). *The Crisis of Parliamentary Democracy*. Tr. E. Kennedy. Cambridge, MA and London: MIT Press.

Schmitt, Carl ([1934]1985). *Political Theology: Four Chapters on the Concept of Sovereignty*. Tr. G. Schwab. Cambridge, MA and London: MIT Press.

Schmitt, Carl ([1923]1988) *The Idea of Representation 1st Rev. Edition*, trans. E. M. Codd. Washington, DC: Plutarch Press. First published as *Römischer Katholizismus und Politische Form*, Hellerau, Germany: Jakob Hegner.

Schneider, Stephen H. (1997) 'Three Questions to Make a Citizen-Scientist'. Paper presented at the American Association for the Advancement of Science Annual Meeting, Seattle, Washington.

Schudson, Michael (1997) 'Cultural Studies and the Social Construction of "Social Construction": Notes on "Teddy Bear Patriarchy"', in Elizabeth Long (ed.) *From Sociology to Cultural Studies*. New Perspectives. Oxford: Blackwell. pp. 379-99.

Schumpeter, Joseph ([1942]1950) *Capitalism, Socialism and Democracy*. New York: Harper and Row.

Sclove, Richard (1997). Loka Alert 4:1, February 14.

Sealander, Judith (1997) *Private Wealth & Public Life: Foundation Philanthropy and the Reshaping of American Social Policy from the Progressive Era to the New Deal*. Baltimore: Johns Hopkins University Press.

Shils, Edward (1956) *The Torment of Secrecy: The Background and Consequences of American Security Policies*. Glencoe, IL: Free Press.

Shils, Edward (1972) 'The Scientific Community: Thoughts after Hamburg', in *The Intellectuals and the Powers and Other Essays*. Chicago: University of Chicago Press.

Simon, Herbert A. (1977). *Models of Discovery and Other Topics in the Method of Science*. Dordrecht, Netherlands: Reidel.

Singer, S. Fred (1999) *Hot Talk, Cold Science: Global Warming's Unfinished Debate*. Oakland, CA: The Independent Institute.

Skocpol, Theda (1979) *States and Social Revolutions: A Comparative Analysis of France, Russia, and China*. Cambridge; New York: Cambridge University Press.

Small, Albion (1909) *The Cameralists: The Pioneers of German Social Polity*. Chicago: The University of Chicago Press.

Smith, Alice Kimball (1971) *A Peril and a Hope: The Scientists' Movement in America 1945-47*. Cambridge, MA: The MIT Press. (1st edn. 1965).

Stehr, Nico (1992) *Practical Knowledge: Applying the Social Sciences*. London, Newbury Park, CA: Sage Publications.

Sullivan, Winifred Fallers (1994) *Paying the Words Extra: Religious Discourse in the Supreme Court of the United States*. Cambridge, MA: Harvard University Press.

Thomas , W. I. (1923) *The Unadjusted Girl*. Boston: Little, Brown, and Co.

Thompson, E. P. (1966) *The Making of the English Working Class*. New York: Vintage Books.

Tocqueville, Alexis de ([1850]1969) *Democracy in America*. Tr. George Lawrence, J. P. Mayer (ed.). Garden City, NY: Doubleday & Company.

Turner, Stephen P. and Regis Factor (1994) *Max Weber: The Lawyer as Social Thinker*. London: Routledge.

Turner, Stephen P. (1979). 'Translating Ritual Beliefs', *Philosophy of the Social Sciences* Vol. 9, pp. 401-23.

Turner, Stephen P. (1987). 'The Survey of Nineteenth-Century American Geology: The evolution of a Form of Patronage', *Minerva*, Vol. 25, no. 3, pp. 282-330.

Turner, Stephen (1989) 'Truth and Decision', in Daryl Chubin and Ellen W. Chu (eds.), *Science off the Pedestal: Social Perspectives on Science and Technology*. Belmont, CA: Wadsworth, pp.175-88.

Turner, Stephen (1990) 'Forms of Patronage', in Susan Cozzens and Thomas F. Gieryn (eds) *Theories of Science in Society*. Bloomington: Indiana University Press, pp. 185-211.

Turner, Stephen P. (1994). 'Relativism Hot and Cold', *History of the Human Sciences*, Vol. 7, pp.109-15.

Turner, Stephen P. (1996) 'Religious Pluralism, Toleration, and Liberal Democracy: Past, Present, and Future', in Jacob Neusner (ed.), *Religion and the Political Order: Politics in Classical and Contemporary Christianity, Islam, and Judaism*. Atlanta, GA: Scholars Press, pp. 275-99.

Turner, Stephen P. (1999) 'The Significance of Shils', *Sociological Theory*, Vol. 17 no. 2, pp. 125-45.

Turner, Stephen P. (2001) 'What is the Problem with Experts?' *Social Studies of Science*, Vol. 31, no.1, pp. 123-49.

Turner, Stephen P. (2002a) 'Scientists as Agents', in Philip Mirowski and Miriam Sent (eds), *Science Bought and Sold*. Chicago: The University of Chicago Press, pp. 362-84.

Turner, Stephen P. (2002b) *Brains/Practices/Relativism: Social Theory after Cognitive Science*. Chicago: The University of Chicago Press.

Unger, Roberto Mangabeira (1998) *Democracy Realized: The Progressive Alternative*. London: Verso.

Veblen, Thorstein ([1921]1963) *The Engineers and the Price System*. New York: Harcourt, Brace and World.

Weber, Max ([1919]1978) 'Politics as a Vocation', Tr. Eric Matthews, in W. G. Runciman (ed.), *Weber: Selections in Translation*. Cambridge: Cambridge University Press, pp. 212-25.

Weber, Max ([1921]1966) *The City*. Tr. and ed. Don Martindale and Gertrud Neuwirth. New York: Free Press.

Weber, Max (1976) *The Agrarian Sociology of Ancient Civilizations*. Tr. R. I. Frank. London: New Left Books; Atlantic Highlands, NJ: Humanities Press.

Wildavsky, Aaron B. (1995) *But Is It True?: A Citizen's Guide to Environmental Health and Safety Issues*. Cambridge, MA : Harvard University Press.

Wynne, Brian (1996) 'May the Sheep Safely Graze?: A Reflexive View of the Expert-Lay Knowledge Divide', in S. Lash, B. Szersynski, and B. Wynne (eds), *Risk, Environment, and Modernity: Towards a New Ecology*. London, Thousand Oaks, New Delhi: Sage Publications, pp. 44-83.

Index